Frank Drown, a man of indomitable spirit and an icon of modern day missions, writes the intriguing account of experiences as a pioneer missionary in the jungles of Ecuador. Frank and Marie's story is one of God-given vision and undaunted perseverance. It is an incredible story of how God used this midwest American couple who had simply responded to His call. As a result, an unreached people has been transformed for His glory.

*Dr. Jean Barsness*
*Missions Consultant and Educator*

The book is straightforward and beautifully written. It's a page-turner. I was staggered and rebuked, helped and cheered by the steadfast faithfulness of this humble (I'm sure they would say merely ordinary) couple. Read it!

*Elisabeth Elliot*

We don't often discover a book which is at the same time interesting, instructive and inspiring. This updated version of Mission to the Headhunters includes all these elements. I've witnessed Frank and Marie Drown in action for more than forty years, having served as a missionary contemporary in the same country, Ecuador. They tell a very true and glorious story of God working through them and their co-workers to bless and lift a needy people. All of us may profit from reading this missionary epic.

*Dr Abraham C VanDerPuy*
Former President of HCJB/WorldRadio
Quito, Ecuador

Fifty-five years ago Frank and Marie Drown began their mission to the headhunters of eastern Ecuador. They endured the hardships of jungle living. They overcame the hostilities of a primitive people. They raised a family to serve God.

What an incredible story of the Lord building His church . .
. Their work continues today! Don't miss reading about this
challenge of the century!

*Dr. Carl McMindes*
President, Gospel Missionary Union
Kansas City, Missouri

Few people know missions from the inside out the way Frank
and Marie Drown do. After all, they've lived a great deal of
missionary history, and in the process, had a significant
impact for Christ. Mission to the Headhunters captures their
commitment and passion for reaching a lost world with the
Gospel. The message of this book is greatly needed by today's
generation.

*Dr. Don Hawkins*
Back to the Bible Broadcast
President of Southeastern Bible College
Birmingham, Alabama

As a young child, I saw jungle headhunters changed into true
disciples of Christ before my very eyes. This wonderful book
tells the story. The events recorded here were used by the
same Christ to change my own life – forever.

*Ross Drown*
Son of Frank and Marie Drown
Former Missionary Pilot with
Mission Aviation Fellowship in Central America

# MISSION TO THE
# HEADHUNTERS

**HOW GOD'S FORGIVENESS TRANSFORMED TRIBAL ENEMIES**

# FRANK + MARIE DROWN

CHRISTIAN FOCUS PUBLICATIONS

Front cover photo
*'After returning from burying 5 missionary companions
Frank Drown remains to determined continue is work
evangelizing the jungle shuar.'*

ISBN 1 85792 721 4

Published in 2002 and reprinted in summer 2002 by
Christian Focus Publications, Geanies House
Fearn, Ross-shire, IV20 1TW, Scotland

www.christianfocus.com

Cover design by Alister MacInnes

Printed and bound by
Cox & Wyman, Cardiff Road, Berkshire

# CONTENTS

# ACKNOWLEDGEMENTS

We could never have created Mission to the Headhunters without the continual help from others. First, we express our gratitude to our son-in-law and daughter, Stan and Irene Derksen. They have lived much of their lives with us and the jungle Indians. Their excitement about producing this book was infectious. They gave themselves to editing, scanning, computerizing, typing, collating, and seemingly endless hours of detail work. For their loving attentions, we express our thankfulness.

We also want to thank Evelyn Stenbock-Ditty, published author and friend, for not only the expert, professional final editing she completed, but also for her enthusiasm and positive vision of the value of our story. "It is very relevant and motivating for this generation. You have a great story and are doing a great job," she would often declare. We learned from her shared skills and were strengthened by her reassurance.

Behind the scenes since July 1945, and into the present millennium, members of our chosen mission organization, Gospel Missionary Union, have worked with us in countless supportive roles. Without their services of administration, instruction, accounting, facilitating international travel, expert handling of financial and legal matters, and assistance in public relations, we could not have fulfilled our call to missionary life. We are grateful for their commitment to excellence and personal faithfulness to us, and to all of their missionaries. It is our prayer that many more of God's people join them in the task of "reaching the world with the Word."

Frank and Marie Drown
April 2001

# DEDICATION

We dedicate this book to our fellow missionaries who served with us during the 37 years we spent in Ecuador, South America, some of whom have moved to other fields or died and some who steadfastly continue serving the Shuar and the Atshuar jungle Indians.

With Gospel Missionary Union, Ernest and Jean Johnson, Michael and Ella Ficke, *Dorothy Walker, Keith and Doris Austin, Ralph and Marian Stuck, Roger and Barbara Youderian, John Stuck and Ed and Joyce (Stuck) Grable, William and Gladis Gibson, *James and Norma Hedlund, Don and Maxine Caswell, Eldon and Phyllis Yoder, Nettie Buhler, Arlowe and Emma Becker, Billy Ogg and Irene (Ogg) Wiens, Steve Ditzler, Stanley and Irene Derksen, *Robert and *Janice Stuck, *Dwain and *Lois Holmes, *James and *Debby Shoberg. Ecuadorian Fellow-workers, Marco and Maruja Diaz

With Mission Aviation Fellowship, Nate Saint and Marjorie (Saint) VanDerPuy, Johnny and Ruth Keenan, Herbert and Olivia Lowrance, Dave and Carol Osterhus and successive MAF missionary personnel.

With Wycliffe Bible Translators, *Dr. Glen and Jean Turner

With Missionary Tech Team, Ken and Irene Edgar

These all have served closely with us and have made major contributions toward establishing the Church of Jesus Christ among the Shuar and Atshuar. We love and highly esteem them. Our heartfelt prayers are with those still sharing their lives with these Indians.

*Frank and Marie Drown*
*April, 2001*

*Those serving the Shuar and Atshuar at this writing.

# FOREWORD
# ELISABETH ELLIOT

As a newly arrived missionary in the eastern jungle of Ecuador, I soon heard the names of Frank and Marie Drown. They were working with a tribe of Indians known as Shuara, at a great distance from the Quichuas with whom I was to work. Now and then I would hear their voices on the jungle radio network, but it was not until January of 1956 that our lives became personally intertwined. I heard on the radio that Frank Drown was suddenly desperately needed. Five missionaries, one of whom was my husband Jim, were reported missing in what was called Auca territory. The very name *Auca* struck terror to other tribal peoples. Who might be willing to investigate what had happened?

It was Frank, a man greatly respected by all who knew him, who consented to form a search party consisting of missionary men, Ecuadorian soldiers, and Quichua guides. Upon arrival on the beach where the five had camped, it was clear that not one had escaped the Auca spears.

Now, more than forty years later, I have read – for the first time, I confess – *Mission to the Headhunters*. My work with the Quichuas enabled me to identify with some of the Drowns' experiences – the agonies of learning unwritten languages, watching a child die in its mother's arms, waiting with baited breath as a jungle pilot made the first landing on a newly prepared airstrip, slogging on many a squishy trail. As I read, I held my breath with Marie as she and her children waited for days for her husband's return from treks to people who had never heard the Good News. Would the people receive him or would they get rid of him?

I have thrilled to read the story of an Indian chief gazing fixedly at a little wordless book, listening to Frank's simple explanation, and then asking if he might have it. He took the book tenderly in his big, dirty hands. Page by page, he told the meaning of the colors – 'accurately and in much better Atshuara than I could have done,' said Frank. An old woman told him of a magic stone that could make gardens grow. 'We thought it would help; we knew no better. If I had known the true God before, I would have prayed to Him. But how were we to find out about Him if you hadn't come?'

A girl named Mamatu had become *Tikishmamtaicawaru* (one who has bowed the knee). 'She kneels and prays by herself every day,' they told Frank. 'The rest of us would like to do it but we don't know how.'

The book is straightforward and beautifully written. It's a page-turner. I was staggered and rebuked, helped and cheered by the steadfast faithfulness of this humble (I'm sure they would say merely *ordinary*) couple.

Read it – it's full of cliffhangers. Read the grisly account of the practice of *tsantsa*, the shrinking of the head of an enemy that becomes a talisman of power and strength to the possessor.

Ponder, then, conditions of discipleship which Jesus laid down:

1. If anyone would come after me, he must *deny himself,* and,

2. *take up his cross,* and,

3. *follow.*

# PREFACE

In 1959 Marie and I were encouraged to write our story. The publishers of "Through Gates of Splendor" by Elisabeth Elliot said, "We want an account of regular missionary life. You know what it is like to live as missionaries among a savage tribe of uncivilized Indians. The books about the recent deaths of five missionaries by the spears of Waodani (Auca) Indians are in great demand. We are sure that a book about your lives among a similar tribe would be well received also." Thus our book, "Mission to the Headhunters" by Frank and Marie Drown, was first published in 1961.

At that time we had been in Ecuador only 15 years. It seemed to us that our life commitment to establish Christian churches among the revenge-killing tribes of the Shuar and Atshuar Indians had just begun. Although there were a few small churches among the Shuar with believers who refused to carry on the traditional enmities, there were no Christian churches among the Atshuar. We kept trusting God to use us and our fellow missionaries to do whatever it cost to bring the revenge warfare to an end before these tribes would be further decimated.

Now, after forty years, we are offering the true story of how God replaced the long, sad history of suspicion, hatred, and killing with forgiveness and peaceful living in the jungle. To those who found forgiveness of sin and new life through faith in Christ's death and resurrection, God also gave assurance of being with Him forever.

Our story includes glimpses into the individual lives of many of our Indian friends. All are true accounts as seen through our eyes and understanding. In order to avoid confusion caused by two persons having the same name or to protect the privacy of others, we have changed some of their real names.

The Indian people have taught us much about God's abundant grace. If we were in our twenties we would go again to live among them. There is still much Bible teaching and church leadership training to do in this new millennium generation. May our book inspire many to commit their lives to obey Christ's command to "make disciples of all nations, baptizing them in the name of the Father and of the Son and of the Holy Spirit and teaching them to obey everything I have commanded you" (Matthew 28: 19, 20).

Frank and Marie Drown<br>
April 2001

# CHAPTER ONE
# PREPARATION FOR A MISSION

And repentance and forgiveness of sins will be preached in his name *to all nations* (Luke 24:47).

As the plane droned over the jungle of the Oriente in eastern Ecuador, taking me back to rejoin Marie in the coastal city of Guayaquil, my mind was a tumbling kaleidoscope of vivid new impressions.

I had just had my first glimpse of the lonely, insect-infested outpost where Marie and I would soon be stationed to carry on missionary work. In a few days' visit, I had sampled the life that would be ours.

I had seen for myself how hard was the daily existence of the missionary couple now living there, how much it took out of them just to survive, to feed themselves, to fight against ill health, to communicate with a strange tribe that had no written language.

I had learned something of the primeval customs that held

the Shuara Indians in their spell – of the dark ways of witchcraft, of the murderous and constant warfare, of the grisly practice of hunting and shrinking heads.

Looking down, I was awed by the vastness of that great ocean of trees. The rivers cut so clearly through the beautiful map below. But I knew that the smooth carpet of leaves was only a camouflage that hid the tangled and turning trails beneath, the steep ascents and descents, the swamps and seas of mud. It also hid the forces of evil at work in the hearts of the Shuara. Would we ever be able to prevail against the long-entrenched power of the devil?

I tried to get it all into perspective. I thought of the ant and what he has to overcome to crawl half a mile with his load of leaves. The big log he climbs must seem like a mountain. He climbs, he falls, he climbs again. But he never gives up.

Then I thought of the hummingbird and how he sees both the obstacles and strugglers from high up, in proper proportion. The plane ride gave me the chance to see the problems that lay ahead of us from the viewpoint of the hummingbird.

I was on my way to tell Marie that in spite of the hindrances and the hardships ahead, this was the place to which God had called us, the place where we would find happiness and satisfaction in serving Him. I had no doubt that she shared my faith.

It was only four months ago that we received the final indication that God wanted us to serve Him in the jungle of Ecuador. It came on a snowy November morning in the year 1945, back in Kansas City. Marie and I, not long married, had been spending several months as young candidates at 1841 East 7th Street, the headquarters of the Gospel Missionary Union. We had no funds of our own – only the promise from the Berkley Community Church in Berkley, Michigan, that if we were accepted as missionaries the church would pay our minimum monthly support. This was an encouragement to us; but there still remained one question: How was the plane fare of five hundred and ninety-eight dollars to be paid? Time was running out. An older, experienced missionary was returning to Ecuador in December and we hoped to travel with her. But only God knew how the plane fare would be supplied.

Marie and I stood in the hallway with several other missionary appointees watching the mailman unload his pack. We were hoping for letters from our families, but looked in vain for the familiar handwriting. Only one businesslike, impersonal envelope was handed to us. We took it to our room, feeling neglected and forgotten. Sitting on the edge of our bed, we opened it without much interest, expecting some bit of advertising. Imagine our surprise and delight when out dropped a check for six hundred dollars! With it was a note from a casual acquaintance who knew of our situation, instructing us to use the money for our plane fare to Ecuador. We knelt to pray and gave praise to the Lord.

We could see then that through all our lives God had been preparing us for missionary service.

I was a country boy, born and raised on a small farm just outside Curlew, Iowa. Next to the youngest in a large family, I learned from growing up with my two brothers and four sisters to live in love and respect with my fellows.

My father, Jay R. Drown, though of sound Christian principles, was no great one to preach or even to talk about God. Not until I was older did I hear him pray aloud in the family circle. But he lived by the standards of the Bible, which he instilled in us by the force of his example, and on occasion, his big right hand. He believed that children should respect their elders and that hard work and sweat were necessary to life. We were never allowed to make fun of anyone less fortunate than us. If any of us broke this rule, his heavy hand came down quickly. To this day I am thankful to my father for also teaching us, by not giving us much spending money, what a nickel was worth.

From early childhood, we all had to do our part to earn a

living from our eighty-acre farm. But Father saw to it that we had our good times, too. He loved to take us hunting or fishing. Before I was old enough to hold a pole, I'd dig myself a few worms and go out with my brothers to the old dredge ditch along the road. We usually came home with a few bony bullheads which we'd throw into the livestock tank to watch them swim around. I can still hear my father's deep voice when he took us hunting, reminding us always to be careful, take no chances, obey the game laws, and consider the rights of others.

Mother was a devout Christian who knew the Lord as her personal friend and Savior. She taught us all to love Him and His Word. It was she who instilled in me the urge to preach. She led us in prayer, and in the singing of hymns. In snow or rain, Mother took all seven of us half a mile down the road to every service that opened the doors of the little white Baptist Church. Through sermons heard there and my mother's teachings and prayers, we were all converted before we were twenty-one. Today all of my brothers and sisters are active in their churches.

From boyhood, I had developed a love for Iowa's rich black soil and for the work it took to make it produce the best in corn, hay, and oats. I would have been perfectly happy to spend the rest of my life on the farm. But God's call to preach had first claim on my life and before I was eighteen I was practicing sermons out loud, while guiding the plow down the straight rows of the cornfield. I started going to neighboring towns to take part in street meetings with other young folks. This strengthened my faith, and also my desire to take the good news about Jesus dying for humanity to others. Before long, I was given an occasional opportunity to preach in a nearby church which was too small to support a regular pastor.

Each of my older brothers and sisters had gone on to Bible school after high school and I knew the Lord would want me to go too. But all I had was the conviction. I had almost no money when I landed up north at Minneapolis to attend Northwestern

Bible School (now Northwestern College). Minneapolis seemed like a huge city to me. I was homesick; I was lost. But I didn't have much time to brood about it. I had to get busy and find something to do to pay for my board and room and school expenses.

I took all kinds of jobs during my three-year course. I washed dishes in a big hotel; I cleaned rugs in the middle of the night. It took a lot of my energy. But I'm not sorry for it. I learned many lessons in practical Christian relationships with my many employers.

In spite of my broken schedule, I concentrated on the Bible, taking as many courses as were offered. I studied its doctrines, its arrangement, its history, its application to daily living. I also learned homiletics – the way in which Bible truths should be preached. But I was often thankful for those preparatory lessons I had received sitting in the front row at the Curlew Baptist Church.

All through school I had planned to preach. Then, in my senior year, in January 1944, a zealous young missionary named Paul Fleming came to Northwestern. He was one of many special visitors who addressed us, but through him the Lord spoke directly to me. I no longer remember Mr. Fleming's words. But I do remember that, sitting alone at the back of the church, I heard God commanding me, 'I want you to go.' For the first time I stood up and went forward. I felt great joy. From that moment on I never questioned God's call to me. I promised I would go anywhere in the world to serve Him. After that I would judge my every decision in terms of preparing myself to be a missionary.

I began making plans. The lands to the southward had always appealed to me. Although there were not many Spanish-speaking people in Minneapolis, a fellow student and I found a little Mexican mission where we started taking Spanish lessons. I got up early every morning to attend a 7:00 a.m. student prayer meeting for missionaries.

Now that my direction was clear, I thought of finding a wife to share my calling. I'd had a number of girl friends already. But now I needed much more than a friend. There was no rule that missionaries should marry; but I felt the need of a partner.

Several girls in my class were going to be missionaries, but only one attracted me. Marie Page was a pretty, lively girl from a small town in Michigan. I watched her with keen interest for many months. But I was too bashful to approach her, partly because I had the idea she liked somebody else, partly because I felt she was far beyond the reach of a country boy like me.

With the unexpected help of our roommates and in answer to prayer, wonderful things began to happen.

In March, after a heavy late winter's snowstorm, the senior class got up a sleigh ride. I always enjoyed a good time. But I didn't have the nerve to ask Marie and I didn't want to ask any other girl. I told my roommate all about it. Teasing and encouraging, he kept at me until I called Marie on the phone. She wasn't in her room. I was ready to give up – but not my roommate. He dashed out, calling, 'I'll find her for you!' He checked both girls' dormitories until he learned where she was. Then he wrote an invitation, signed my name to it, and gave it to one of the girls to take to Marie. Soon there came back a reply with Marie's name signed to it. She would love to go with me. Oh joy! Oh delight!

A long time later Marie told me her side of the story. After a day of wearying work and study she was definitely not planning to go on the sleigh ride that cold and snowy night, particularly since she had no suitable outfit. But her roommate made up her mind for her. After insisting on loaning Marie her own snow suit, she wrote out an acceptance note, and signed Marie's name to it. In spite of ourselves we were brought together by the determined plotting of roommates.

Lumbering along under the frosty stars, sometimes singing with the group, sometimes rolling in a snowdrift and running again to catch the sleigh, I soon found that my fears that Marie would prove remote and unfriendly were without foundation. From the first moment, we felt as though we had known each other all our lives. That night when I left Marie at her dormitory I found it easy and natural to ask her for another date. I invited her to go with me to a missionary meeting our class was sponsoring at the YWCA. But even when she said 'Yes' I still wasn't sure whether she had accepted because she enjoyed my company, or whether she just wanted to encourage my interest in missionary work.

That meeting brought me my first real understanding of what a missionary's life would be. The speaker was a veteran from the China Inland Mission, the Reverend George Kraft. As he told us of his work and answered our questions, what impressed me most was the sheer happiness which he radiated. He did not talk about the snakes or the hardships; he just told us how much he enjoyed serving the Lord as a missionary.

As the meeting broke up and I bent to help Marie with her boots, to my surprise I heard myself blurt out in a clumsy, half-joking way, 'There's nothing I wouldn't do for you – even zip up your snow boots.' As soon as the words were out, I knew that was how I really felt.

The rest of the year went by in a happy hurry. Marie and I were together often and I was beginning to hope that I might one day win her. The great night of the senior banquet came and of course I asked Marie to go with me. As we led the line of our classmates into the dining hall, I could hardly take my eyes off her. I had always thought she was nice-looking. But tonight I saw that she was beautiful.

In the past months I had come to know and appreciate her character and personality. I knew now she would be an ideal missionary wife. She had been converted at thirteen. Since that time she had always looked forward to going to Bible school. Back in Berkley, Marie had been one of a small group who did not take part in the school dances and parties. Her own life was full enough as it was. Marie was a girl of good humor, spirit, and energy. She played the flute both in the high school orchestra and the high school band. After school she worked behind the counter in a nearby drugstore. Her evenings she devoted to church activities.

Bible school gave her all she had hoped for. She loved, as I did, to listen to speakers from the foreign field. She was an avid reader of missionary biographies. As the year came to an end, she understood that nothing less than a lifetime spent in God's service would be satisfying to her.

I was very much in love. But I refrained from making my feelings known because I wanted to be sure. She, too, seemed fearful of mistaking our attraction for each other for more than God wanted it to be.

June came, and graduation. Marie was to spend the summer in the pine country of northern Minnesota, near Park Rapids, teaching in the same Daily Vacation Bible Schools for children as the summer before. I, too, was going to northern Minnesota to do evangelistic work. We discovered we would be only thirty miles apart. But there was no direct highway between the two towns and strict gas rationing was in force, so we had little chance of seeing each other. We said goodbye with only the promise to answer any letters each might receive from the other.

In spite of a busy schedule, I couldn't let a day go by without writing. And what was even more surprising, she answered every one of my letters.

By the last of July Marie's Bible Schools were over and she was going home to Michigan. I could not let her leave without seeing her once more, so I arranged for her to come and visit me in the camp where I was working.

On the night she arrived we went for a walk along the lake. I knew that the moment had come. I asked Marie if she would be my wife and go with me to South America. What joy when she accepted! I was now as certain that this sweet girl was the right one to be my partner as I was that God had called me to the mission field. Our love was truly from the Lord.

Once again we parted as Marie boarded a bus for her home in Michigan and I went back to Iowa. It looked now as if we might be separated for some time. Marie had already arranged to go to a missionary training center in Chicago. I had made my plans to return for another year of seminary at Northwestern. All we could do was hope and pray that the Lord would bring us together somewhere.

In August I made a hurried trip to Michigan to get better acquainted with her family. On my way home I decided to stop in Chicago and visit the training center to learn more about it. As a result I realized that God wanted me to go there too. It was a happy decision. I could profit from the training course and also be near Marie. Now that we were to be together, we saw no reason for not planning a fall wedding.

Wise friends urged us not to marry until we had been in the mission field for at least two years. They pointed out that this would give Marie a chance to get her basic language study before taking up the responsibilities of married life. But after talking it over we decided that we would rather share all our experiences – getting ready, going to the field, and learning the language. Also, we both felt we needed the stability that marriage would give to our lives. And so, on 11 November, 1944, with our dear friends and roommates from Northwestern joining in the wedding party, we became man and wife. Within a few days we returned to Chicago to finish the first part of the missionary course.

The focus of the training period was on what a missionary's main task should be. This was more than learning a strange language and holding Bible classes, more than winning people to Christ. A missionary's chief goal should be to establish churches – indigenous churches that would be self-governing, self-supporting, and self-propagating. 'If your work as a missionary does not result in strong native churches that can carry on without you,' our leader pointed out, 'you will have failed as a missionary.' This had been the Apostle Paul's method, we realized, and with God's help, it would be ours.

The following January we went to northern California to complete the second half of this missionary training course at 'boot camp.' Here we learned the practical side of missionary work – everything from the principles of linguistics to basic medicine, carpentry, butchering, bread-baking, barbering, and other skills which would be useful in helping a primitive jungle people. My own life would one day be saved by what Marie learned at the boot camp about treating tropical diseases.

What a wonderful six months that was: an education, a challenge, and a delayed honeymoon all rolled into one. We relished it all, the overnight hikes, sleeping out-of-doors, the hymn-singing, the lessons, the fellowship.

Then it was over and we had no plans. We had no affiliation with any mission board and were no closer to getting to the field.

But we did not pass the summer in idleness. Responding to an invitation from friends, we returned to northern Minnesota. This was another link in the chain of events leading us to Ecuador.

One evening the guest speaker at a special missionary service was Rev. G. Christian Weiss, then president of the Gospel Missionary Union. He was a short, jolly man with graying hair and dark expressive eyes. Although we had heard him speak before in Minneapolis, we had never met him personally. But knowing he had served as a young missionary in Morocco, we felt he would understand and direct our ambitions.

After the service we introduced ourselves. We talked with him at length about our desire to go to a needy field. In our innocence we asked if he knew of any tribe of Indians that was without knowledge of the Savior. To our delight he began telling us at once of the Shuara, a wild and reputedly ferocious tribe, who lived in southeastern Ecuador and the jungle flatlands of northern Peru. This was the first time we had heard the name of those primitive people among whom so much of our future work was to be carried on. Then Mr. Weiss, his dark eyes mirroring our own enthusiasm, drew from his pocket some application forms and handed them to us. Even though we were still not sure anything would come of it, we were excited, for this was our first definite indication of any future prospect.

The summer evangelism opportunities ended. We were broke. I had to earn some money right away. The threshing season was at hand. I knew that threshing paid well and it was something I could do, so I took Marie to my family's farm in Curlew, Iowa. By then I knew our own family would soon number three and I had to take seriously the responsibilities of coming parenthood.

The outlook for Marie and myself was not exactly bright. We had no home, not a stick of household furniture, no money, and no steady job. All of these lacks should have given us great concern. But they didn't. Our hearts' wish to get to work in the mission field was further intensified by our desire to get there before the baby was born. The idea of establishing a State-side home to wait for the birth of our little one seemed only a hindrance to our missionary calling. We were missionary parents; he – or she – would be a missionary baby, born on the foreign field.

One night after a hard day's threshing, I sat with Marie at the dining room table and we began to fill out the applications Mr. Weiss had given us for the Gospel Missionary Union. But we were in a hurry. Because Marie was pregnant the board might not want to send us for another year. We decided to go in person to the GMU headquarters. Halfway through the forms Marie went to the telephone, called the Curlew depot, and inquired about train connections to Kansas City.

We spent the weeks that followed in getting acquainted with the organization's sound biblical policies and godly leadership, and in learning about the Shuara and the country where we hoped to live. We searched the atlas to find out where Ecuador was, looked at many pictures of the Indians among whom we would be living, and listened by the hour to the stories by returned missionaries. In response to our questioning they told us of the dangers and discomforts, the heat, the heavy rains, the poisonous snakes, the vampire bats, the stinging gnats, and the strange diseases. Only through experience would we learn what grace and patience the Lord would give us to put up with all of this!

The stories of the Shuara themselves were enough to daunt the most daring adventure seekers. We wondered if we would be able to make friends with, and live among, such Indians as these. Though outsiders called them 'Jívaros', we read that they called themselves 'Shuara,' a term meaning 'the people.' They must have been among the most primitive and savage tribes left on earth. They must have been among the last, too, to follow the practice of headhunting and head-shrinking. The blackened, shrunken head of an enemy, hung inside the door of the conqueror, was a valued talisman called a *tsantsa*. We tried to picture how it would be to live with Indians who had taken part in shrinking an enemy's head.

We discovered that the Shuara in Ecuador had once lived mostly on the eastern slopes of the Andes called the Cutucú Mountains. But as Ecuadorean colonists entered their territory, many of the Indians pressed steadily farther eastward and southward toward the jungle flatlands. Here they encountered their most hated enemies, the Atshuara. Although Shuara are subdivided into many hostile groups, the two principal tribes called themselves the Mura Shuara (hill people) and the Atshuara (lowland people), a contraction of Atshu Shuara, so-called because the *atshu* palm grew in the jungles where they lived.

For generations the Mura Shuara and the Atshuara had been destroying each other with their ceaseless feuds. As the Mura Shuara moved eastward and southward from the Cutucú Mountains, armed with muzzle-loaders obtained from colonists, they drove the spear-carrying Atshuara ahead of them. But as the Atshuara made contact with Peruvian traders, they also came into possession of guns – big repeating Winchester .44's. With such deadly weapons, they resumed the conflict on more equal terms. Warfare increased until there grew between the two tribes a kind of jungle no-man's-land in which members of neither group dared settle for fear of being murdered by the other. Within the larger tribes there were also smaller factions which hated and killed one another. Each killing brought in its wake many more. According to their code, every death was attributed to an enemy's curse, and had to be avenged. This was true even of death from natural causes.

We shuddered to realize that their revenge killings, witchcraft, and related customs were leading to the extinction of the tribe. Unless their basic attitudes could be changed, unless they could become born-again people of God, they would not long exist and would be eternally separated from God.

The Indians' whole way of life was dictated by the tribe's unwritten laws which they called *Shuartica*. They regarded *Shuartica* as immutable and so were very resistant to changing any of their ways. Not that they were all bad. We saw many of their customs as good, that is as contributing to the wellbeing of everyone. They felt obligated by *Shuartica* to help family members and friends build homes and plant gardens. They taught their young ones to skillfully choose and use jungle materials for roofs and walls according to the age-old traditions. *Shuartica* also required that they generously share what they had with visiting relatives and friendly travelers.

But *Shuartica* also led them to seek the supernatural powers of demons and the devil himself in times of suffering, sickness, and revenge warfare. Because of the practices of polygamy and the taking of child brides, family unity and marital happiness were eroded by quarreling, fighting, and harming each other. There was no natural trust. Divorce, infanticide, and suicide were increasing. The Shuara were unable to change any of their ways by themselves. The belief that *Shuartica* does not change was too strong. *Shuartica* admits of no element of progress. Its strength and pride lie in its immutability. We thought again of our goal to plant Christian churches in the jungles – churches whose ministers, evangelists, and supporters would be jungle Shuara. How could illiterate, revengeful, demon-controlled Indians ever become propagators of the gospel of Jesus Christ unless the evil destructive customs of *Shuartica* would change?

One custom in particular of the savage Shuara haunted us. When an Indian goes to avenge a death he never goes alone. Using the words of an age-old ceremony, he challenges another. These two in turn may challenge two others. The object is to whip up a large raiding party to attack the enemy. Marching toward each other and then back, they repeat the words of the staccato chant, sometimes antiphonally and sometimes in unison. The emphatic syllables of the challenge are synchronized with the first of the forward and the first of the backward steps, while the guns in their hands are thrust upward on the same beat. For a full half-hour the ceremony may continue. Although the exact words of the challenge are in an archaic form of the language, no longer fully understood by either challengers or listeners, the chant, with its accompanying dance, has the power to carry the performers to a peak of malevolent hypnotism. When their frenzy has reached its height they start out after the enemy. We trusted God to lead them to replace such customs with forgiveness and friendship for even their enemies.

None of these things which we heard dampened our ardor. These people, too, were loved of God. Who, on this earth, could benefit more from learning to know Christ and His forgiveness and power to overcome hatred, revenge killing, and eternal death?

The work of the Gospel Missionary Union missionaries among the Shuara already had a very long and lonely history, dating back to 1903. At that time, a solitary couple, Mr. and Mrs. L. Freeland, began to live among the Mura Shuara in a frontier jungle settlement called Macas. In time they were joined by Charles Olson. Not long thereafter Mr. Freeland died, Mrs. Freeland returned to the States, and Mr. Olson carried on alone.

Then in 1919, Charles Olson married the widowed Mary Freeland. Together they established the still existing mission station at Sucúa, a day's hike south of Macas in a valley in the eastern slopes of the Cutucú, at that time deep in Mura Shuara territory. For years they served alone until, in 1936, a single missionary, Ernest Johnson, joined them. In the meantime, Mr. and Mrs. George Moffat, working under the Christian and Missionary Alliance, had set up a station two days' walk to the south of Sucúa. But throughout the years right up until 1945, these were the only two places where the gospel was being preached regularly to the Shuara in their own language.

Mr. Olson had since died, but Mary Olson was with us in Kansas City. Fellowship with her was one of the highlights of our candidacy. She was an inspiration. She had been widowed twice, had undergone every imaginable hardship and ordeal. Yet there she was, with her wrinkled, dimply smile and her bright eyes, lively as a cricket, radiating joy and love, a living testimonial to the satisfaction of a life spent in the service of the Lord.

Hour after hour she held us spellbound with her tales of riding over the Andes on horseback, traveling on foot along jungle trails, or crossing swift rivers on rope bridges or in dugout canoes.

Every weekday morning she would begin the day with an hour's instruction in Spanish grammar and the customs of Ecuador.

'You know,' she said to encourage us when we faltered, 'I was thirty-three years old when I first went to Ecuador. And yet, with the Lord's help, I learned not only Spanish, but Shuara. Why, you young people ought to pick up a language or two a whole lot easier than I did and learn to speak it much better.' We agreed all too readily, without any idea of how difficult it would be to learn an unwritten Indian tongue.

Then came welcome news. Every evening at the dinner table, letters from missionaries on the fields were read aloud. One of them had special meaning for us. It was from Mr. and Mrs. Ernest Johnson who were trying to get a mission station started among the Shuara along the Makuma River. They very much wanted a young couple to come and help them. Daring to hope we might be that couple, we set our sights on arriving in Ecuador by the first of the year.

The one remaining problem, how we were going to pay for our transportation, was solved by the arrival of the letter with the six-hundred-dollar check.

Things then began to happen fast. We applied for passports and visas, took health examinations, received our shots, and started packing our belongings. These didn't amount to much, for we had never kept house. We had blankets and sheets, books, a few tools, and a highly prized aluminum double boiler which some friends had sent as a wedding present from Canada. This was wartime and aluminum was unobtainable.

In high spirits we left the mission headquarters for last brief visits with our families and friends in Michigan and Iowa.

But we did not accomplish our goodbyes without some tears and sadness. Our parents felt the sharpest pangs at our parting. We were young and had our minds on the intriguing jungle. They understood far better than we what our first term of five years or more of separation would mean.

It was six days before Christmas and our last evening in Kansas City. Seven of us were about to leave these homey and familiar walls for foreign lands. The Gospel Missionary Union held a farewell service for us in the chapel room. There were hymns and messages of special comfort.

The words of Mr. Weiss, the president, on the subject of 'The Complete Man of God,' were so full of wisdom and sound counsel that we were to recall them long after:

As each of you goes out to the mission field, four men must go with you: the spiritual man, the intellectual man, the social man, and the physical man. You dare not forget any of them on pain of failing as a missionary. You must have robust physical health; consecrated practical intelligence; the ability to make genuine friendships out of casual social contacts; you must build a strong spiritual life maintained by regular and consistent prayer and Bible study habits. The latter is of the most importance, for we are waging a spiritual battle against spiritual powers with spiritual weapons.

The next day we left Kansas City for New Orleans where we would board the plane for Guayaquil, Ecuador. We were glad that everything was ready in time for us to go with the returning missionary, Mrs. Julia Woodward. She knew a great deal about Ecuador, having spent forty-five years of her life there, twenty-five of them without returning to the U.S. She was going back to live among the Quichua Indians of the Andes, for what was to be her last term of missionary experience.

Seventy-eight-year-old Mrs. Olson not only went to the train with us, but insisted on carrying Mrs. Woodward's suitcase because our arms were loaded. There in our seats, between laughter and tears, we said goodbye. Mrs. Olson's parting words were to tell us how happy it made her that we were going out to work among her beloved Shuara and to assure us that she would be praying for us.

The first lap of our long journey had begun. We were on our way.

# CHAPTER TWO
# SCORPIONS + VAMPIRE BATS

*The Lord is ... not wanting anyone to perish, but everyone to come to repentance (2 Peter 3:9).*

Shortly after noon on Sunday, 23 December, 1945, our plane touched down at Guayaquil, Ecuador. Our hearts sank as we stepped into the smothering heat and saw no one on hand to meet us. Evidently our attempt to get word to the local missionaries who were expecting to hear from us had failed.

All around us quick, smartly dressed Latins greeted one another in rapid Spanish. How glad we were that Mrs. Woodward was familiar with the confusing routine in this airport. We followed her about in the noisy, crowded office while she calmly addressed the uniformed officials in Spanish, helped us clear our passports, pursued our baggage through customs, and guided us to a waiting taxi. She easily directed the driver to the home of our hosts, Mr. and Mrs. Cornelius Klaassen, the leaders of our Ecuador mission.

With keen interest we looked out the windows at this foreign city. The first streets through which we passed were lined with lovely Spanish villas, their gardens bright with hibiscus and roses, surrounded by bougainvillea-covered walls.

When we reached the poorer districts where low ramshackle buildings crowded against the sidewalk and burros and barefooted cart pushers nearly filled the narrow streets, we felt even more strange and far from home. People in dark doorways stopped their jabbering to stare and point at us as we went by.

We saw little to remind us that this was only two days before Christmas. There were no snow-covered streets, gaily decorated store windows, carols, or tinkling bells such as we had left behind in Kansas City. Here, it was hot – as hot as the Fourth of July – and just as noisy. Raucous music blared loudly from sidewalk cafés and firecrackers burst in our ears. A wave of homesickness swept over us.

Our taxi drew up at a two-story frame building protected from the street by a whitewashed mud-and-stone wall. The only entrance was a locked wooden double door. We stood on the sidewalk feeling lost as the taxi went off down the street. Mrs. Woodward gave three sharp raps. We could hear the sound of footsteps scurrying about on the cement inside. Then the doors opened and everything changed. We were engulfed by warm embraces. The Klaassens had been awaiting our arrival and expressed their delight that we had come to share in spreading the gospel.

Unfamiliar sounds, sights, and smells surrounded us in those first days.

Early in the morning we were awakened by the sound of running, shuffling footsteps of those who sold the daily papers. The resident of Guayaquil had only to reach out his window to get his breakfast from passing vendors who loudly advertised their commodities, and, in the process, taught us not a little useful Spanish.

The man who sold butter in little three-cent paper-wrapped

pats proclaimed his product in a high-pitched wail, *'Mantequi-i-i-i-illa! Mantequi-i-i-i-illa!'* Hot rolls came by in baskets balanced on the heads of boy runners; oranges in two-wheeled carts pushed by barefoot men; milk in metal containers swung over the sides of braying donkeys.

Life in Guayaquil was one long succession of loud noises. A roaring motor, squealing brakes, the dispatcher's whistle, constant cries of *'Vamos!'* ('Let's go!') announced the passing of the always overcrowded bus. Blaring of taxi horns, grinding and grating trolley wheels, added to the din.

The commanding *'Basura!'* of the street sweeper made us drop whatever we were doing to dump our day's trash and garbage into his cart. Then there was the broom man shouting *'Escobas y escobas'*, brooms of every description, from ten-foot ones for sweeping cobwebs and scorpions from the ceiling down to kitchen brushes, making him look like a walking corner of a United States hardware store. And there was the deep baritone, *'A uno cincuenta los vasos,'* telling us that drinking glasses could be bought for six cents each. *'Hay que soldar'* proclaimed the coming of a stooped, soot-covered fellow with his soldering iron and bucket of glowing embers, ready to mend any pot in need of fixing. Fruits and vegetables in season, tables and chairs, undergarments, charcoal in gunny sacks, pencils, shoestrings, tinware, glasses of fruitades or Coca Cola – these were some of the items that could be bought from vendors who passed our house in unending stream.

All the life of the neighborhood spilled out onto the street, as people escaped from their suffocating dark rooms to the slightly cooler air outside. Children played with their hoops, kites, or marbles, or practiced soccer; lovers strolled hand-in-hand; office workers and teachers peddled by on bicycles; whole families spent hours in non-stop animated conversation.

And the smells! The air of this port city was not so fresh as its ocean breeze promised. A nearby coffee factory produced its own strong burnt odor. The smells of onion and garlic from our neighbors' soup kettles were constant and overpowering.

But we had our quiet pleasures. One was walking along the Malecon or river drive.

Downtown we saw the formal side of Guayaquil. There was no such thing as casual streetwear. The men wore suit coats and neckties in spite of the heat, the women, the highest heels and latest fashions. Introductions, salutations, and farewells, though businesslike, were courteous, complete, and friendly, and took a great deal of time.

Guayaquil was to be our home for nearly a year while we studied Spanish under the tutelage of senior missionaries and helpful nationals. Having the intricacies of the grammar drilled into us every day turned out to be tedious work.

Those who have never struggled to master a foreign tongue do not know what it is to open one's mouth, hopeful of relieving the pressures of thought and feeling, only to bring forth a few feeble stammerings. But we took it as a challenge and learned to express ourselves little by little. Spanish is such a beautiful language that we wished we had more time to give it deeper study.

We had been in Guayaquil about six weeks when our friend Mr. Weiss arrived from the States. He had invited me to accompany him on an inspection tour of the jungle mission stations of Sucúa and Makuma. With the enthusiasm of youth – I was then twenty-three years old – I could hardly wait to get started. It seemed a long time that I had been looking forward to seeing these stations – out among the jungle Shuara.

Early one morning I reluctantly kissed Marie goodbye – this was our first separation since we had been married – and left Guayaquil with Mr. Weiss by train. All day we jolted over the coastal flats, then through the twists and turns of the mountain gorges, up, up, up. By evening we reached the mountain town of Cuenca where we spent the night with missionary friends. The next morning we continued our journey by bus until the road ended high up in the cold, barren, windswept Andes. There we switched to horseback, jogged up and over the divide, and started down the eastern slope.

Then the fun began. I had been leading a sedentary life studying Spanish and my muscles were soft. It was about a four-day trip to Sucúa through mountain wilderness. We were on the trail all day, the only resting places the so-called hostels along the route which were nothing more than open, chilly, lice-infested shacks.

The eastern slopes of the Andes, rocky above, green with jungle below, are like the folds of a skirt. Rushing torrents cut deep ravines in the steep mountain sides. The trail criss-crosses back and forth, now going down in a descent so sheer we had to clutch at branches to keep from falling, now climbing back up. In some places the trail was so faint we had to trust the instinct of the horses. And there were torrential rivers to be forded. Some of them we waded, up to our armpits. Others we went over on shaky bridges or fallen logs, dismounting while the horse driver went ahead with the animals. Just when we thought we were making progress down the mountainside, the trail led back up again. We were never quite sure where we were.

It was a relief to hit the warm jungle air and tropical foliage. But the trail was still up and down: more hills to climb, more rivers to cross, and the added deterrant of mud.

Back in Kansas City when Mrs. Olson had tried to describe such trails to me, I could hardly believe her. Now I knew she had understated them. Yet, the missionaries stationed in Sucúa and Makuma had traveled this way with their babies. Maybe I was soft.

When Mr. Weiss disclosed his plans to set up a missionary aviation program that would make such an ordeal unnecessary, I was heartily enthusiastic.

That night, trying to get to sleep in one of the damp, chilly hostels, I could not help praying, 'O Lord, don't ever let Marie have to go through this. Please bring a missionary plane before the time comes for Marie and our baby to go into the jungle.'

On the last day on the horse trail, I came down with dysentery and had to spend a week in bed at Sucúa. For the first time, I met Michael Ficke, a big, warm-hearted ex-woodsman, and Ella, his generous wife, who were running this mission station. During the time I spent with them I had a chance to reflect on what we had learned about the pioneer missionary effort which had its springboard in this valley town.

When the Olsons first came to the Oriente, Macas was the last settlement along the horse trail. After living there several years Mr. Olson bought land from the Indians at Sucúa and eventually moved his family there. At that time the country around Sucúa was mostly jungle, inhabited by Indians. For over thirty years Mr. and Mrs. Olson had worked to gain a few converts. The difficulties of maintaining their health and food supplies, of reaching the roving, sparse population of Mura Shuara hidden over thousands of miles of jungle, of learning the complicated Shuara language, of traveling the trail, sapped their strength and vitality until they had little left for direct evangelism. They had established no Christian Shuara churches. But their faithful work had laid the foundation for those who succeeded them.

Through the years, colonists followed the Olsons along the road to Sucúa. By the time I first saw Sucúa, much of the jungle had been cut down and the land taken from the Indians. The town itself was a Spanish-speaking white settlement of about a hundred inhabitants with a courthouse, a jail, a slaughterhouse, and a Catholic mission. Many of the Mura Shuara who had lived around here were moving eastward.

That was why Ernest Johnson, who had lived at Sucúa for several years, first as a single missionary and then with his bride Jean, was establishing a new station deeper in the jungle along the Makuma River.

Even though I was weak and shaky, the moment came to take to the road again, and this time on foot. I was glad to hear from Mike Ficke that he was going with us and was bringing some of his Indians. There were four more wearying days on the trail. Then, at the end, as darkness was closing in and I did not see how I could walk another step, I saw a clearing ahead. We had reached the mission station where Ernest and Jean Johnson lived.

The cleared space wasn't very big. In the middle of it was a low thatch-roofed hut with palm-pole walls. But to me it spelled shelter, warmth, and friendship. After our nights in the hostels or sleeping on the damp ground, no palace could have looked more inviting.

While shaking our hands and pounding our backs in enthusiastic welcome, the lean blue-eyed missionary and his slender dark-haired wife took us right into the kitchen, helped us get off our mud-caked shoes, and brought us warm water in tin pails to wash up. When dinner time came we all sat down to the best they had to offer – roasted green plantains and smoked monkey meat.

Dinner was a festive occasion. We all talked at once. The Johnsons were starved for news of other missionaries and of the outside world. We compared experiences on the jungle trails. Looking back, we could all laugh at our close calls and discomforts.

But being tired, we didn't talk long before Jean showed us our sleeping quarters. We noticed then that less than half the house was floored. A portion of this served as a bedroom for the Johnsons with their two baby sons, one thirty months old, the other fifteen. The rest was used as a storeroom. There, Mr. Weiss, Mike Ficke, and I were put down for the night.

Weary as I was, I could not doze off, but tossed restlessly in my sleeping bag on the split-bamboo floor. When I turned one way I faced an oval room where visiting Shuara lay around their fires. When I turned the other way I could see the blackness of the jungle through cracks in the bamboo wall. The night was filled with weird sounds. From the forest came a strange symphony of insects, punctuated by the croaking of a frog. From the other side came stirrings and grunts of the Indians. And the snoring around me threatened to drown out all else. I thought of the story Ernest had been telling at dinner of the latest killings between the Shuara and the Atshuara. If an Atshuara were to creep up on this house, might he not think we were all Shuara and kill us in our sleep before he knew the difference?

I groaned aloud, trying to find some new position that would relieve my aching hipbones. My mind flashed back to California and those first missionary boot-camp hikes. What fun we had thought jungle travel was going to be! I had not foreseen that fatigue would take away any thrill at hitting the trail. The glamour had worn off completely since I said goodbye to Marie. This was reality.

An Indian in the adjoining room sat up, coughed, and stirred his fire. This roused another. The two began a lively and, to me, altogether unintelligible conversation.

But if I couldn't sleep at least I could pray. So I prayed for the Johnsons and for their mission until, through the cracks in the wall, I saw the first pale glow of dawn above the black treetops, and the chorus of insects gave way to morning trills of jungle birds.

Rubbing my eyes, I stumbled from our makeshift bedroom into the dirt-floored kitchen to be greeted by a cheery good morning from Jean. Then I noticed she was staring ruefully at a dead chicken lying on the ground.

'Look at what the vampire bats did last night,' Jean said. 'And she was my best layer, too.' She looked up and smiled. 'Anyway, it's a good thing it happened while you were here. Now we can have stewed chicken for supper.'

We sat down to breakfast of cooked tropical wheat. I did not enjoy it because it was full of chaff, even though Jean told us she had spent hours washing and cleaning it.

The mission layout seemed primitive to me. The Johnsons had only such basic utensils as they were able to bring in with them. They had made rough furniture from what the jungle offered. The table was built of bumpy split-bamboo boards. Stumps served as chairs. Two wooden crates had reached them out of the many they packed in Sucúa to be brought in by Indian carriers. One was now a shelf in the storeroom; the other a playpen for the baby.

That morning, to save the remaining chickens and two goats from the vampire bats, Mr. Weiss and I helped line with leaves a small shack where they would be safe.

In the course of our three-day stay, I came to appreciate these missionary pioneers. On first acquaintance one would think them both almost too frail for jungle living. But though slight in build, Ernest had a determined stubbornness that drove him to remarkable accomplishments, such as mastery of the complicated Shuara language. Both were single when they came to Ecuador, Ernest a number of years before Jean. They met in a mountain town and were later married. Ernest had been seven years in Sucúa. From that base he had gone with Indian guides up and down the Upano River Valley to take the gospel to isolated groups of Indians. He had trained himself to live like a Shuara, to eat their diet of plantain and cassava, to sleep on their hard bamboo-rack beds. His leg muscles were as strong as any Indian's and he could withstand the hardships of the trail as well as they.

In January 1944, Ernest walked to Makuma to make final arrangements, with the Indians who lived there, for establishing the new mission station. This location, at a crossroads of jungle travel, was four days' walk from Sucúa. Since he had been here before, he had already decided on the piece of land he wanted to buy: a stretch of virgin jungle on the south side of the Makuma River, several hours east of the last ridges of the Cutucú Mountains.

This land was a piece of neutral territory which he needed so he could be friends with all the Indians. For it Ernest paid the Indians with axes, machetes, cloth, and other trade goods.

"In a year I will come back with my family to live on this

land," said Ernest to the Shuara as he left. 'You will have to plant the gardens, so there will be food for us when I return; and you will build us a small house right on this spot. When I come to live I will bring medicines, clothing, and other items that you will want. I'll have plenty of work, so you will be able to earn these things. I will also bring God's Book to help you know how to live peacefully and happily.' Both Ernest and the Indians had kept their bargain.

After repairing the chicken house I went to watch while Ernest directed an Indian man and his wife who were clearing a space for a garden. As a tree crashed to the ground, the barebacked Indian rested on a fallen log and passed his hand before his face to discourage the swarming gnats. He motioned to his old, unkempt, scowling wife to bring him something to drink.

Noticing he was much younger than I, I asked the missionary how the young man happened to marry such an old woman.

'Because so many of the older men have taken three or four women, there are not enough for the younger ones. They are forced to marry either a little girl six or seven years old or an old widow like Chingasu, as this man, Chumpi has done. He knows he won't always be contented with her and will later want a younger woman to bear him children. Chingasu is already suspiciously accusing him of looking for a second wife.'

Chingasu poured a thick white liquid from a hole in the side of a curved-necked gourd into a small half-gourd. Then she added water from a second gourd and stirred the contents with her fingers. As she brought it to Chumpi, she picked out bits of stringy fiber, licked her fingers, and continued stirring. I wondered how the man could possibly drink the stuff, but he held his hand out eagerly toward the bowl. Shutting his eyes, he quickly emptied it. Then handing it back to the unattractive woman with the drab, ragged piece of cloth only partly covering her body, he picked up the ax. His wife set the gourd on the ground and bent to a squatting position to blow into her neglected fire.

Ernest then called them over to meet me. He introduced me as 'Panchu' (the Spanish nickname for Frank). And 'Panchu' I have been to the Shuara since that day.

When the sun began to drop toward the hills in the west, the Indian workers joined others in the visiting room, sitting around on log stumps while Ernest taught them who God is and what He is like. These Shuara were hearing for the first time the only message that could free them from their fears of witchcraft, wars, and death. The Indians around me gripped their guns in their hands or held them across their knees, mute testimony to their terror of enemy attack. This sense of fear I had seen in the Indians who came with us over the trail. Our guides and carriers had often stopped to examine the remains of a leaf shelter and fire, or strange footprints in the mud. Although I couldn't understand their dramatic-sounding talk, I had guessed that unless they could find out who made the fires and left the footprints, they suspected enemies were nearby. In the Shuara houses too, where we stayed along the way, the men had not slept through a single night without rising to cock their guns and prowl around the clearing.

I watched the Indian men as they repeated in singsong fashion most of what Ernest was saying. They appeared to agree with him. What actors they were!

The women sat inattentively at their husbands' feet, nursing babies or killing gnats. Many were much younger than their men, and were the burden-bearers and the slaves. I knew that most of them unhappily shared their husbands with other wives. They did not recognize that the message of God's love was for them, too.

When the service was over all the women arranged their belongings in heavy loads. Chingasu placed her cooking pots, gourds, and a head of bananas in a woven basket which she lifted to her back and supported from her forehead by a strap of supple bark. Holding sticks of glowing fire in one hand and a machete in the other, she walked away from the house. Chumpi shouldered his gun and followed her. The picture of the burdened, stooped women leading the way for their straight-backed arrogant men stayed in my mind.

In the middle of the next afternoon a large party of Indians arrived. Each carried a box on his back. These were the supplies the Johnsons had paid them to bring over the trail months before. The missionaries, according to Shuara custom, had to spend an hour greeting the newcomers before they could open their packages. We felt for the Johnsons in their disappointment at finding their long-awaited foodstuffs and clothing ruined by jungle dampness. It was plain that supplying the station by Indian carrier wasn't working.

This incident, in addition to the hardships Mr. Weiss had undergone on the long hike, strengthened his conviction that plane service for missionary stations in the jungle was urgently needed.

Just before leaving he suggested to Ernest that he start building an airstrip. He had already urged Mike Ficke to begin one at Sucúa. It pleased me to hear Mr. Weiss say that a former classmate of mine, Bob Hart, had volunteered to come and serve as pilot to help get the program going.

Ernest welcomed the idea, but he couldn't promise when he would be able to finish the job. The labor of clearing land, planting gardens, preparing lumber for a new house, and the daily cares of providing for his family were already putting a serious strain on his rather frail health.

To Ernest the jungle was a living, evil force that he had to fight day by day to keep it from swallowing the clearing with its choking growth. Now, on top of this job, he, with his Indians, would have to chop out of virgin forest a strip long enough and wide enough to accommodate a plane. For implements he had not so much as a wheelbarrow – only machetes, axes, baskets on Shuara backs, and fire – to aid him in this difficult task.

We left that lonely outpost not by the trail over which we had come, but by a shorter one. This led in the opposite direction to a recently established Shell Oil Company camp at a place called Ayuy, some six hours' hike away. Ernest and Mike Ficke came along. At Ayuy, Mr. Weiss and I were flown by Shell Company plane to their main base at Shell Mera where we would find transportation to Guayaquil.

I felt sorry for my missionary brothers, as I looked out the plane window and waved to them on the ground. I thought of the hikes they had ahead of them – Ernest to Makuma, and Mike Ficke all the way back over that hard trail to Sucúa.

I was returning to tell Marie all that I had seen and felt about these adventure packed days, and what the missionary plane would mean to us when we, too, came to live at Makuma.

With the compass pointing northwest, we winged over those formidable jungles toward Shell Mera. Off to the left, I could see the Cutucú Mountains looming up behind the Makuma station. There, standing out against the sky, was the saddle-shaped silhouette I had seen from the trail. Already, in some strange way, it had become a symbol to me of home.

# CHAPTER THREE
# FALLEN HOPE

And we know that in all things God works for the good of those who love him (Romans 8:28).

After I returned to Marie in Guayaquil, we settled down to continue our Spanish language study. On the morning of 19 April, 1946, the first of God's gifts to us, Linda Faith Drown, began her life in a dingy downtown clinic. I stood by while Marie struggled through nausea to consciousness after her first experience with ether. In a screened white crib beside her lay a perfectly-formed baby girl, our own daughter. Marie wept tears of joy and hugged the trim dark-haired young nurse, who cautiously held a kidney-shaped dish under Marie's chin. Not until we had named her did we know that 'Linda' meant 'beautiful' in Spanish. It became our hearts' prayer that her life would be an expression of beautiful faith.

Then, within a few days came a letter from the Gospel Missionary Union in Kansas City, saying that funds had been given to buy a missionary plane for Ecuador, and that there would be no delay in obtaining the necessary entry permit. When this news reached the missionaries at their outposts in the jungle, it stimulated both Mike Ficke at Sucúa and Ernest Johnson at Makuma to hasten the completion of their airstrips.

Now there was a change in our plans. We had hoped to go straight from Guayaquil to Makuma. Instead, we were asked to spend a year in Sucúa, replacing Mike Ficke and his family who were due to go to the USA on furlough.

Although it meant a definite departure from our personal desires, we knew it was what God wanted us to do and we were happy to obey. God was teaching us that to follow Him often meant changing our ideas of what the future would hold. To look ahead one day at a time and trust Him with tomorrow was a lesson we thought we had learned. But it was one we had to relearn – again and again.

Seven months after Linda's birth we completed our basic language studies and missionary pilot Bob Hart arrived in Guayaquil with the plane called 'El Evangelista.' First he made his initial flights to Sucúa and the Shell camp, Ayuy. He left the plane in Shell Mera, gateway to the jungle, and returned to the coastal city. Bob had to play everything by ear in those days; he was doing a real pioneering job. There were no radio communications to guide him. He was not a licensed mechanic himself and had no one to help him, except for one of the Oil Company mechanics at Shell Mera who offered to work on the 'Little Cucaracha' in his spare time. Bob's first job was to get his family and us to Sucúa.

We were ready to move. Our household goods – baby bed, washing machine, books, tools, and utensils – were packed in large trunks and crates. We had arranged for two Christian Ecuadorian girls to go with us – Ester, a schoolteacher, and Raquel, who was to help with the housework.

Together with Bob, we boarded Ecuador's narrow gauge railroad train and spent all day bouncing and swaying over coastal flatlands past banana and sugar-cane plantations, then up the mountainsides covered with a patchwork quilt of neatly-pieced fields. In the bright whitewashed town of Ambato, Marie and I parted company. She and the girls stayed there with missionary friends for a few days while Bob and I transferred the baggage to a bus and accompanied it down the eastern side of the mountains to Shell Mera. Here the Shell Oil Company had built its main base and airstrip to service its camps scattered throughout the jungle. The company had kindly granted us permission to use the airstrip and store our goods in a nearby shack. Bob and I had to open the large crates and trunks and repack our household goods into smaller boxes, which could be flown out, a few at a time, in the four-place Stinson plane.

On the appointed day, Bob and I were still sweating over the repacking in drizzling Shell Mera. From Ambato Marie, Linda, and the girls took a taxi to the town's seldom-used airstrip. They reached the deserted strip at 10:00 in the morning to await Bob's arrival with the plane.

Marie sat down beside the strip and made the baby comfortable on a bed of long, tough, dry grass blown by the mountain breezes and warmed by the sun. Several inquisitive workers from a nearby hacienda drifted by. The many questions they asked were far from reassuring: Did Marie know there had been no regular flights here for months? Did she know they were not expecting any plane? Did she have any idea what the weather was like at Shell Mera? Had she been in radio contact with the pilot?

All Marie could tell them was that she had arranged to meet the plane there that day.

When noon came, they ate the little lunch of sandwiches and fruit they had brought along. Still no sign of the plane. The weather was beautiful at Ambato and she did not know what could be delaying Bob. Marie passed the hours walking up and down the airstrip, carrying Linda, chatting with the girls and the ever-curious passers-by. Never once did she doubt that the plane would come. Her faith was so strong that she did not give any thought as to how she would get back to town in case Bob didn't show up by nightfall.

But the Lord in His faithfulness did not forget us. Back at Shell Mera, around 3:00 that afternoon, the weather suddenly cleared. Bob was able to start out, flying up between rugged mountain ridges to Ambato.

The workers from the hacienda clustered around the airstrip. They were even more astonished to see the plane come in and fly off with Marie and the girls than they had been to see them there in the first place.

Marie's trip – her first experience in flying through narrow, twisting mountain passes – was a thrill to her, but to me it was the definite answer to my prayer. She and the baby would not have to undergo the dangers and sufferings of that horseback-and-foot trek. The flight from Ambato to Shell Mera took twenty-five minutes; then from Shell Mera to Sucúa, forty-five. One hour and ten minutes of comfortable – though sometimes awesome – flight had replaced between five and ten days of miserable trail-slogging. My heart lifted in praise to God for this great blessing.

On our second wedding anniversary we moved into the large frame house in Sucúa which Mr. and Mrs. Olson had built so many years before. Our household was growing. Besides Ester and Raquel, a young medical student, Señor José Andrade, who had been converted through the teaching of the Fickes, stayed on to help us. He continued to run the small medical dispensary for both colonists and Shuara Indians. A couple of weeks later Bob Hart brought his wife Ivy and nine-month-old son Bobby to live with us. Our 'family' now numbered nine.

This was the first time in our married lives that we were not living in a dormitory or someone else's home. The full responsibility for running the house – as well as the mission – was ours. We began to get some idea of what our parents had gone through for us.

We had not been in Sucúa very long when we were visited

by a senior fellow worker, George Moffat, who with his wife had established a station far to the south for the Christian and Missionary Alliance. He had undertaken a long day's journey on horseback to look in on the young missionaries and give us the benefit of his wise and kindly counsel. Among the many helpful things he said was that the tool the devil used most successfully in keeping missionaries from winning people to Christ was just plain hard work.

We came to understand how right he was. There were meals to prepare and the families to care for. Even with Raquel to help with the dishes, the washing, and ironing, our wives seemed to spend most of every day cooking, baking, cleaning house, or minding babies.

All these tasks took much time and effort since we had no such conveniences as are enjoyed in the USA, to say nothing of prepared foods. There was no electricity. We studied at night by gasoline lantern. Our wives and Raquel used a gasoline iron. They cooked on a slow clumsy range for which wood had to be chopped and carried. They did their own canning, and baked all the bread, cakes, and cookies. Water had to be carried in buckets and boiled. I butchered our own meat. There was no refrigeration and no way to keep things. But how we blessed the late Charles Olson for the lovely fresh oranges and grapefruit from the groves he had planted in the front yard so many years before.

I had to give most of my time to chores outside: overseeing the large fields of corn, pasture grass, banana, plantain, and cassava; looking after the chickens, horses, and cattle; and keeping the buildings in repair. There was also the supervision of those who came to work for wages – improving the airstrip, clearing ground, gathering and chopping firewood, and erecting a hangar for Bob's plane.

There were petty annoyances – as with the gasoline-powered washing machine. On many a washday, Marie and Ivy would be ready with the hot water and dirty clothes, only to find that the cranky little engine wouldn't run. When that happened, there was nothing to do but wash the clothes by hand or wait till I got the engine going. I spent hours taking it apart, cleaning it, and putting it together again. The Indians were fascinated by the wringer and by the fact that the motor drank gasoline. I let them smell the stuff just to watch them wrinkle up their noses.

Most of our evangelism activities were with the white population. Even the fifteen Shuara boys who attended the mission's boarding school spoke Spanish. It was good training for me. I preached my first sermons in Spanish at the regular Sunday services while Marie taught both a Sunday School class for the settlers' children and a singing class in the Shuara school. With Señor Andrade's able help we held open-air preaching services in the town square on Sunday evenings. We all sang; Señor Andrade preached; I gave my testimony; Marie played the accordion. On weekdays we visited the townspeople. Señor Andrade helped us improve our Spanish grammar and study the books assigned to us as new missionaries.

Bob Hart's plane was an attraction to both white settlers and Indians. The yard around our house was usually filled with people waiting to see him land or leave. In one way or another, they all wanted to take advantage of it. Bob used to fly the sick from Sucúa, Macas, or other nearby settlements to Shell Mera from where they could go by bus to get medical help. Aside from his missionary trips, Bob had to limit his services to emergency cases, because the insistent colonists asked for more flights than he could handle. Running such a flight program was a first-time experience for us, and there were no rules to go by.

Bob began making regular flights to Camp Ayuy with supplies and mail for the Johnsons. He would detour over Makuma on his way back, both to signal Ernest that his supplies were in Ayuy and to check on the progress of the new airstrip. Early in March, Bob found a note from Ernest at Ayuy saying the strip would be ready in two weeks. When Bob returned to Sucúa with the news, I decided to go with him on that maiden flight. I hadn't been to Makuma since my first visit and I wanted to see how the station had developed since that time.

We came in for the landing. Bob lowered the flaps and shouted, 'This is it, Frank! Watch that log at the other end!' I couldn't take my eyes off it. That log seemed to come up and fill the whole wind shield before Bob slowed the plane to a stop.

From a maze of fallen trees at the side of the strip, Ernest and Jean, followed by several Indians, came running to greet us. We saw the new house he had begun and marveled at all the land he had been able to clear, not only for the airstrip but for gardens as well. Some of the Indians remembered me and called me 'Panchu.'

When we prepared to leave it was nearly noon and the air was hot and oppressive. Bob turned the tail of the plane to the big log and revved up for the take-off. I felt the wheels leave the ground. But as we whizzed by the end of the short rough strip itself, our wings were still below treetop level. Only a few hundred feet of jungle had been cut down for the approach and we were using these up fast. 'Will we make it?' I shouted above the motor noise. The plane seemed to have no lift, which we realized could happen in this still, moist, midday jungle air. High treetops were racing toward us. Bob turned slightly and missed one tall giant, but others were coming at us. Then the wings caught a slight air current and we were up and over. It left me slightly weak, but thankful to be aloft. This experience convinced us that more work would have to be done on the strip to make it safer. But the main thing was that air service for Makuma had begun. This meant much to Marie and me since we were still looking forward to going there to work with the Johnsons.

At Sucúa our dependence on plane service grew from month to month as Bob flew regularly to Shell Mera and back with supplies and mail. Then one day in August this blessing came to an end.

I was out in the yard preparing some duck feed when I thought I heard the sound of a plane motor. Although I couldn't see any plane I set the feed down and listened more carefully. For several days we had been expecting Bob to return from a series of flights to Shell Mera and Makuma. But when he failed to come we supposed, since we had no radio communications, that it was because of bad weather.

I heard the sound again and ran through the yard to the airstrip to make sure there were no wandering cows on the field. Then the noise of the motor faded. 'Why doesn't he come in?' I thought to myself. 'The sky is plenty clear.'

I heard it again. But this time it didn't have the familiar pitch. Suddenly I could see the plane. It was not the little gray-and-maroon Stinson, but a black-and-yellow Grumman Goose, which I recognized as belonging to the Shell Oil Company. What could be bringing it this way? Our airfield wasn't big enough for that plane. I watched it turn toward the ridge at the south, lose altitude, and disappear behind the trees. Then I heard the noise of the motor again. It grew louder; it was coming back. Surely he did not expect to try for a landing. This time it whisked by no more than fifteen feet above the ground. Marie and Ivy ran with the children from the house and stood beside me, watching. Again it came back. This time I saw a man standing in the open doorway of the plane. He looked steadily out – but beyond us – and all around. A sinking feeling hit me in the pit of my stomach. He was looking for the little Stinson.

That meant Bob must have left Makuma – or some other point – on schedule. Now I understood why he had not returned. He had not reached Shell Mera. He was down somewhere in the trackless jungle – I had no way of knowing where. I looked at Ivy and Marie. From the drawn expressions on their faces I knew they must be thinking the same thoughts. They took little Linda and Bobby and walked slowly back into the house.

My heart was troubled. Bob's work meant so much to him, and to those of us who had come to depend on the plane. By this time he was not only serving Sucúa and Makuma, but a neighboring station to the south and another far to the north.

To all of us the plane meant regular mail and supplies of staple foods and fresh vegetables, and even more important, that sense of security when anyone became ill. Medical help was now only a forty-five minute flight and a day's bus ride away, instead of a week or more by trail. If it had not been for the plane, Bobby Hart might have died from diarrhea and vomiting in spite of all that Señor Andrade could do. Bob and Ivy had flown him out to Shell Mera, and then taken him by bus to Quito where they were able to get expert medical care before it was too late. What a relief to us all when they finally returned with a well, happy baby!

Now Marie and I were up against a grim situation. We were expecting our second child. I knew that Marie should be under a doctor's care, and we had planned to go to Guayaquil where Marie would stay until she had her baby. We had delayed our departure so that our visit would coincide with the annual missionary conference. Our plans were to leave this very week. We had allowed our sugar and flour to dwindle, thinking we would be away. We had come to depend so on the plane. And now –

But Bob's safety was our immediate concern. Was he alive or dead? It didn't seem right that he had come all the way to Ecuador to rot in the jungle with no one to help him.

I stood alone for a long time, thinking, forming a plan, then went inside to the others. Marie and Ivy and I sat around the table, first praying, then talking about what steps we could take to find Bob. We wondered if I should organize a search party to comb the jungles along the flight routes. We decided I would first go to the army base at Macas, the provincial capital, to see if I could learn anything there. Several Shuara boys offered to go with me.

The day began with rain and fog. But I knew I faced greater odds than the weather in hoping to find Bob. I said goodbye to

Marie, Ivy, and Linda, with tears in my eyes. I took Ivy's hand. Trying to keep my voice from breaking, I said, 'We'll do our best to find him.' Then I started out on foot.

The much-traveled road to Macas had always been one of the worst of the horse trails. Spurred on by fear for Bob's safety and the urgency of my errand, impatient with the clinging mud that slowed my speed, those twelve miles over hills and through swamps seemed endless.

At the army base, I went straight to see the major in charge. He told me that at seven-thirty that evening he would be in radio contact with his headquarters in Quito and might have some word. He invited me to listen with him.

Seven-thirty came. The operator leaned forward. He could receive by voice, but had to transmit by key. He tapped out his message, then settled back. We all stood with our eyes glued to the radio receiver, fearful of what it might tell us. Then the message came through. Yes, the plane, pilot, and one passenger, a fellow missionary named George Poole, had been missing now for eight days. Missionary Radio Station HCJB, at Quito, had dispatched a sound truck to Shell Mera and were setting up a field communications base there. A search party was being organized at Shell Mera. We were asked to form another at Macas. I hastily scribbled the news and sent it by horse runner to Ivy and Marie, knowing they were waiting anxiously in Sucúa.

The word spread quickly through Macas. Tension mounted. This was a loss in which many shared. The first plane which had come to break the isolation of jungle life was missing. There was no lack of volunteers to help find it, both among local residents and army personnel.

Some time that afternoon, a Saturday, an Indian who lived near Shell Mera arrived in Macas. He reported that on the day of the disappearance he had seen a plane flying very low over a river at what we guessed would be about ten minutes away from the Shell Oil camp. All sorts of rumors started to circulate. But there was nothing trustworthy to be learned until we could make contact with Quito again at seven-thirty that evening. I was watching the clock. The minutes seemed hours: seven-fifteen; seven-eighteen; seven-twenty; seven-twenty-two; seven-twenty-five; at last, seven-thirty.

The operator sent his message and waited. The receiver began to crackle. Straining our ears while the operator fiddled with the knob to cut down the static, at last we heard it:

Stay in Macas ... Stay in Macas ... George Poole has just been brought into Shell Mera by Indians. He says that on a flight from Makuma engine failure forced a landing only five minutes away from Shell Mera. The pilot suffered a leg injury in the crash. Mr. Poole left him by the plane to go for help. But he found none, lost his way, and wandered alone for two days. When he finally circled back to the plane the pilot was gone. He thinks that Indians must have taken him away. A rescue party is leaving from Shell Mera.

Again I wrote the news to be sent back to Sucúa by horse runner.

But our fears were not all quieted. We still did not know whether Bob was alive. No further word was radioed to Macas Sunday night, nor yet on Monday. Then, on Tuesday morning we heard that Bob had been found! The missionary search party was taking him back to Shell Mera. With vast relief and a lighter step I hurried off for Sucúa to take the tidings to Ivy and Marie.

But now, with all plane communication cut off for the foreseeable future, a new ordeal loomed ahead of us. I had been advised to take Marie and Linda, Ivy and Bobby, out to civilization at once. This would mean traveling by horseback over the Andes. Aside from the hardship on the children, Marie was now five months' pregnant and could hardly stand such a trip. Ivy's heart had been weakened by rheumatic fever in childhood and the journey would be even riskier for her.

We talked this over for several days and were still undecided, when one morning a Shell plane roared by overhead to drop us our first direct communication from Bob.

His note read: 'In spite of having spent eleven days in the jungle with nothing to eat but one raw squash, I'm all right. My leg was broken near the ankle, but it is getting better. The Shell directors have decided to send a company plane to Sucúa for our families. Try to lengthen the airstrip.'

Here was new hope. But to stretch out the airfield would require hired labor, and hired labor cost money. Where was it to come from?

I couldn't help thinking of the hundred dollars Marie and I had set aside, a little at a time, to buy a radio which we so badly needed to keep in touch with the plane. We had it tucked away, all in Ecuadorian sucres, in an envelope in a drawer. It didn't take us long to decide to use it.

We rounded up all the men we could find – both colonists and Indians – and put them to work. Each day's payroll ate alarmingly into our fast-dwindling radio fund.

On September 16, Marie wrote in her diary:

Spent the day washing and packing our clothes. We expect the arrival of the Shell plane any time. It is hard not knowing at what hour to be ready to leave. But we are experiencing more of the Lord's grace in teaching us patience. Frank works hard – too hard – every day on the airstrip. The field has been lengthened to 2,300 feet. But now we have spent all the money we had.

We finished the prescribed length in a remarkably short time. One day after another went by – then a week – still no plane. Finally we decided I would have to walk to civilization to see what I could do.

On my way I stopped in the village, hoping there might be mail. There was – a letter from Bob, telling us that the Shell Company had finally decided it would be too risky to try to land one of their big planes on such a small airfield.

I went back to the house to deliver this sad news to Ivy and Marie. Again we talked it all over and concluded that it would be best for me to continue my journey as planned. In my desperation, my head was full of all sorts of wild schemes. Perhaps I could persuade a commercial airline to fly in for them. Perhaps I could organize a group to help me get them out over the jungle trails instead of having to climb the Andes. In any event, I would walk to Makuma, then to Camp Ayuy, and from there try to get to civilization.

The trail to Makuma was no easier to travel than I remembered it from my first trip. Heavy rains had made the mud deeper than usual. On the morning of the third day, our party reached the headwaters of the Makuma River and found it almost too heavily flooded to cross on foot. The four Indians and I joined hands to make the crossing, in true Shuara fashion. In this way, if one slipped, the others would keep him from being washed downstream. What a beautiful lesson for the Christian walk through life, I thought. Just in this way should we hold each other up through prayer. We hiked long hours to cover the five-day trail. When we reached Makuma, after traveling that up-and-down trail, I was exhausted.

I had known for some time that the Johnsons had gone to Guayaquil, since Jean was expecting a baby. Their work was being carried on in their absence by our friends from California boot-camp days, Keith and Doris Austin.

Doris wrote a note to Marie, describing my arrival in Macuma, which she sent by the Indians who were returning to Sucúa:

Frank got here just before dark. Imagine my surprise when I looked out the door and saw him! He had been running for over an hour and needless to say, was all in. He was unshaven, of course, and completely covered with mud. With a bath and some supper he looked a little more like himself. After not having eaten anything all day, he must have eaten too heartily, because the next morning he was sick to his stomach. However, he went on to Ayuy, even though he didn't feel like it. Two of our Indians went with him.

Frank seems to think that if you girls must walk out, it will be easier for you to come this way, rather than by horseback over the Andes. I'm sure you could make it if you took your time. You could stay here and rest as long as you wanted before going the last day to Ayuy.

In a note he sent back Frank said he was leaving Ayuy by plane that same day. He found the last part of the trail the worst of all, because it was so hilly. I think he noticed it more because he didn't feel like himself.

I reached Guayaquil just in time for the missionary conference, thinking sadly that Marie and I had planned to attend it together.

I went first thing to see Bob Hart, who had been in the hospital. He still had his leg in a cast and had lost twenty pounds. He told me the story of his eleven days in the jungle.

Bob had not been taken away by Indians, as George Poole had thought. When George did not come back, Bob decided to try to make his way through the jungle toward Shell Mera. He picked up a stick to use as a cane because he had to drag one leg. Two things he took from the plane: an expensive camera belonging to a fellow missionary, and a yellow, crook-necked squash Jean Johnson had given him to take to us. He got his bearings every morning from the distant roar of the planes taking off from Shell Mera, and from the course of the little streams which he knew flowed into the Pastaza lying between him and the oil camp. He could not handle the squash, the camera, and the cane; so he would throw the camera and the squash ahead of him into the underbrush and hobble along until he caught up with them. Before the first day ended, he found he had to choose between the camera and the squash. He chose the squash. That was all he had to eat for eleven days.

When the search party found Bob, he had come out on the bank of the wide Pastaza River. He was sitting there, chin in hand, trying to figure out some way to build a raft to float him to the other side.

Bob's testimony of God's care thrilled us all at the conference. He said that each day he had prayed it would not rain. But every night he would lie on the bare ground, shivering and soaked with torrential downpours. God had reminded him: 'My grace is sufficient for you, for my power is made perfect in weakness' (2 Cor. 12:9). In spite of the great danger of contracting fever from exposure, God had kept him free from illness and had given him strength to walk a little farther each day until he reached the Pastaza.

When the meetings were over, a group of us including Ernest Johnson and Keith Austin went back to Shell Mera. We were anxious to find the fallen plane. We wanted to see for ourselves how badly it had been damaged and whether there were any parts that might be salvaged. Not one of us considered this accident as the end of missionary air service in the jungle. We knew that others were coming to take Bob's place. We remembered the words of Isaiah 40:31: 'But those who hope in the Lord will renew their strength; they will soar on wings as eagles; they will run, and not grow weary; and they will walk, and not be faint.' Those words seemed a literal promise to us then – a promise which sustained us.

The place where the plane fell was only a day's walk from Shell Mera. We had no trouble finding it. When we parted the branches and saw with our own eyes the miraculous way in which the plane had fallen, we praised the Lord anew. The little Stinson, it seemed, first struck a palm tree, turned over in mid-air, and came down on its back. The wings straddled a gully, leaving the cabin suspended and the occupants unharmed. Fearing the plane might burn, Bob had tried to get out in a hurry. But his foot had caught in the twisted rudder pedal. In the effort to wrench it free he broke his ankle. The motor was resting solidly on a log. One had to see it to believe it could be possible.

We set to work stripping the parts that might be useful. We removed the wheels, front seats, parts of the motor and instrument board and strapped them on our backs to pack them out.

As we turned away, we gave a last look at the remains of the plane that had meant so much to us. It was destined to lie there forgotten, the home of rats and cockroaches. The myriads of umbrella ants using it as a handy bridge across the ravine would never know it had once been a proud bird soaring above the skies, the sound of its approach eagerly awaited wherever it went.

# CHAPTER FOUR
# BACK TO CIVILIZATION

I press on toward the goal to win the prize for which
God has called me heavenward in Christ Jesus
(Philippians 3:14).

While I was still in Shell Mera it became clear to me that
whether I liked it or not, I had no choice but to take Marie, Ivy,
the children, and also Raquel out over the eighty-five miles of
jungle trail. I discussed this with Keith and he offered to help
me.

A month had gone by since I left Marie and Ivy in Sucúa. As
they had no more flour to make bread, they had been living on
corn, corn, corn – corn-on-the-cob, creamed corn, fried corn.

We made plans to leave Sucúa for Makuma. Our sojourn
here was coming to an end. From Makuma we would go to
Guayaquil for Marie to have her baby. Ester would remain with
a woman missionary who came to take our place until the Fickes
would return from furlough.

In spite of all that had happened we were sorry that our year at Sucúa was ending. Our experiences here had begun to give us a love for the jungle and its people. We packed our household goods into fifty-pound loads, and arranged for a number of Indian carriers to take them to Makuma. Even though we knew the journey ahead would not be easy, there was nothing to do but go.

Early on the morning of 27 October, 1947, our curious caravan set forth, some on horseback, some on foot, for the first stretch to Macas. I had Linda in the saddle with me; Señor Andrade, who would go with us as far as Macas, held Bobby Hart. Neither Marie, Ivy, nor Raquel had done much horseback riding. Although their first attempts to guide the horses were frightening, they managed to hang on.

It was muddy most of the way. The horses plunged and lurched. Their legs often sank deep in the muck, and made loud sucking and popping noises as the beasts struggled to pull them out. About noontime we came to a place that was so bad we had to ride with our legs sticking straight out to keep them from dragging and gathering more mud. At one place the mud was up to the horses' bellies. At last Marie dismounted and walked along the outer edge. It was easier for her to plow on by herself than to struggle to keep her balance in the swaying, pitching, uncomfortable saddle.

In Macas we were hospitably received at the military base by the major who had helped us many times during our stay in Sucúa. He even opened a can of artichoke hearts – a rare delicacy in that part of the world – to give the typical meal of rice and meat a luxurious touch. Our beds that night were only bare boards, but we rolled in our blankets and slept soundly.

The next day we left the horses and continued on foot. We tied the children into wooden chairs we had made out of packing boxes and strapped them to the backs of the Indian carriers. Tramping down, down the long steep descent to the Upano River, the Shuara would nearly double over to balance their heavy loads.

The only way to cross the swift, wide river was by dugout

canoe. The ferryman who was to be there with his boats was nowhere in sight. We sat on the bank and waited. Marie freed the children from their chairs and let them run up and down the rocky shore.

A sudden drenching shower came up. We all ran together and made a leaky shelter by throwing our raincoats over some bushes. As we huddled there, Marie recalled that this was Ivy's birthday. We all sang, which delighted the children and made us laugh. Imagine having a party in such strange surroundings!

The ferryman came at last. The Indians went over first with the boxes and baskets. Our wives and babies went next. They all crouched as low as possible to avoid upsetting the unsteady canoe. With my heart in my mouth, I watched the precious load being swept downstream and out onto the rushing waters. I lived a lifetime before I saw them wave to me from the other side. The rest of us were finally ferried over. We then hurried as fast as possible to make up for the long delay. That night we slept at the house of Shuara who lived by the side of the road.

Next morning, when we turned off the road onto the jungle trail, it was rather like leaving a glaring city street for a dim high-vaulted cathedral. The Indians went ahead noiselessly; even the insects and birds were hushed in this awesome forest. But we soon found there was another side to the jungle besides its beauty. Our wives' feet and legs were quite unaccustomed to such abuse as they encountered here. The way was a kind of Pilgrim's Progress – climbing over fallen logs, slipping in the mud, snatching for a steadying branch, being scratched by thorns or tripped by vines, and alternately panting up steep ascents or through oozing swamps. Marie remarked that the United States Army could probably never devise a better obstacle course for the toughening of its recruits.

Mud, mud, mud – always ankle deep and sometimes up to our knees. It stuck to the women's trousers and boots, making them as heavy as lead. Marie had put on a pair of my overalls when we left Sucúa, which served very well while riding horseback. But on the footpath they were more troublesome than helpful. Being much too long, they constantly collected mud. Even rolling them up didn't help since bending down to roll them up was hard for a woman six months' pregnant. I had to stop again and again to do this for her. When they still refused to stay rolled, I cut them off just below the knee. Later, when she got wet up to the hips, the overalls began to bind on her knees and made it harder to climb. She asked for another fitting, and I had to cut them even shorter. The next day she discarded the overalls altogether and continued the trip in comparative comfort, wearing a wrap-around rose print maternity dress.

The days were long and hard for the mothers and Raquel, but the nights were even longer. As they tramped along the trail, they would wish for night to come so they could stop and rest. Then, after lying down a while on leaves spread on the hard ground, their strained muscles twitched and jumped, their bones ached, and they would wish for daylight to come so they could start walking again.

Ivy, Marie, and Raquel were usually so tired by the time we made camp that it took all their strength just to eat and get themselves and the babies ready for the night. Keith and I did most of the cooking, dish washing, packing and repacking of bedding, clothing, and food, besides making the leaf shelters and building the fires.

Our feet were wet every day, all day long. We had two changes of clothing, one for day, one for night. After picking out our campsite, we would go to the nearest stream and rinse the mud from our boots, socks, and trousers. It was always wonderful to change into dry things for the night. But in the morning it took a lot of grit seasoned with good-natured banter to get back into those wet clothes.

I pitied the children most, bouncing along in their chairs, sometimes awake and crying, sometimes asleep, their heads swaying and jerking on the Indians' backs. Although heavily loaded, the carriers would go faster than the women, so Keith usually ran along with them while the rest of us followed. We always caught up with them by noon. Often Keith would already have fed the children some powdered milk mixed with warm sterile water he carried in his thermos bottle.

They gave us a number of scares, one of which particularly sticks in my mind. We had stopped to have our lunch together as usual, this time in a clearing on top of a knoll. Keith had trampled down a spot of brush and weeds and untied the children so they could move around a bit. After enjoying our lunch on the spread-out leaves, the girls and the Indians had started ahead, while I finished packing my knapsack. I stooped to pick up a can of cookies on the ground, but stopped with my hand on the can. A shiver ran up my spine as I saw the bright hues of a deadly coral snake slither away into the bushes around the clearing where the youngsters had been playing.

I could only conclude that God had kept the poisonous reptile dormant. It was only one example of the way the Lord took care of us, protecting us not only from fevers and diarrhea, but also from serious accident.

As we went along, the girls got their second wind. They made a game of counting the number of streams they crossed and the number of times they tripped or slipped. We came to the last day. Keith and the Indians thought that if they hurried ahead with the children they could make it to Makuma before nightfall, and were soon far in the distance. But the worst climb of all lay just before us. Because of Ivy's heart we had to take it very slowly.

At the top of the ridge the view out over the valley was breathtaking. But the way down was so steep that the girls' leg muscles kept knotting in pain, so we had to stop often to rub and relax them.

Finally at the bottom, the sun was sinking toward the Cutucú mountains behind us. We would have to push hard to reach Makuma before night closed in. This was a flat, level stretch and we almost ran. It was now getting so dark we could hardly see the trail. I knew we were quite close to Makuma and I urged the girls to go faster. But the strain was too much for them. Ivy dropped down on a log and sobbed, 'I'm not going to take another step. I don't care how close we are. I'll just have to stay here all night.'

Our blankets and dry clothing were ahead with the other Indians. We could not possibly sleep in the forest. Somehow, the Lord helped Ivy to get up and stumble on. The blackness closed in. I pulled a flashlight out of my pack, but the batteries were almost gone. One of our two Indians lit a bit of tree resin he had found in his basket, thus giving us a flickering beacon.

As we left the trail we found ourselves in the maze of logs and brush that still covered the approach to the airstrip. The Indians and I began to call 'Tu-u-u-u-u-u-u-u-u-u-!' in the hope that someone in the house would hear. Nothing but the sounds of the jungle... We called again. 'Tu-u-u-u-u-u-u-u-u-u-!' came an answering call at last. A few minutes later the flare of a gasoline lantern assured us that Keith was coming to show us the way. Oh, what a moment that was! We saw clearly that the end of the airstrip was only a few yards ahead. Striding down its wide grassy length was pure joy after all the logs and mud we had left behind.

Inside the house was hot water ready for our baths and hot soup for our supper. Doris Austin had already fed Bobby and Linda and then put them to bed between clean sheets and blankets. After chatting a while with Keith and Doris, we retired for the night. How grateful we were that we could look forward to a week's rest in Makuma and that the worst of our trip was behind us.

By comparison, the remaining day's walk to the Shell Camp at Ayuy seemed easy. From there we were soon on our way by Shell Company plane to Shell Mera, then by bus and train to Guayaquil where Ivy and Bobby were happily reunited with Bob. Raquel returned to her family, and Marie and I helped with missionary work here while awaiting the birth of our next child.

# CHAPTER FIVE
# BEGINNING LIFE IN MAKUMA

And surely I will be with you always (Matthew 28:20).

One day toward the end of January 1948, while we were still in Guayaquil, a letter came from Ernest Johnson that caused us much concern.

We knew that he was anxious for us to join him in Makuma soon and that he was doing all in his power to arrange for us to fly from Shell Mera to Ayuy in a Shell Company plane. From Ayuy it would be only a day's walk to Makuma. Without this help we would have to travel over that dangerous horse trail from Cuenca to Sucúa to Macas, then by foot to Makuma through days of that seemingly endless jungle mud.

Now Ernest had learned that the Shell Company was closing their operation in Ecuador. They had found no oil and were closing down their jungle camps, including Ayuy.

'If you were here now,' he wrote, 'you could fly in one of

the empty cargo planes that go to Ayuy every day, returning to Shell Mera with personnel and equipment. It will not be long before this camp is abandoned completely and the flights will stop. You must not delay.'

This meant we ought to leave Guayaquil immediately. But our baby was not yet born. We could only trust God to keep those planes flying.

In mid-February, baby Ross was born. But shortly afterward we were told he had a heart defect. Doctors advised us that he must be kept in Guayaquil for at least three months' medical care.

Another letter from Ernest told us that the Shell Company definitely would not be flying after the middle of April – two weeks away. By then Ross was nearly two months old and we could wait no longer. Although it was entirely against the doctors' advice, we felt led of the Lord to go ahead. We hurried our preparations. Arrangements had been made with the Johnsons to engage a Christian Ecuadorian family named Lopez to go with us to the jungle to help with the material work.

We left by train with them, traveling to the mountain town of Riobamba. There we had to stay a few days to buy supplies. We were counting every hour, because we had no way of finding out on what day the Shell Company would stop its plane flights. Finally one morning in the cutting cold of 4:00 a.m. we boarded a *mixto*, a vehicle that was half-bus, half-truck, in the hope of reaching Shell Mera by nightfall. The only route was a narrow, twisting, one-way road that wound along the edge of steep precipices down the eastern slopes of the Andes to the jungle. Marie, our two little ones, the Lopez family, and I all squeezed onto the hard benches, while our baggage was piled in the back along with gunny sacks of vegetables and assorted boxes. We were thankful for every foot of descent, since we were worried about the effect the high altitude might have on baby Ross. But so far he seemed all right.

Halfway to Shell Mera, our *mixto* ground to a halt. We saw

in front of us another *mixto* stopped before a pile of mud and rocks that covered the narrow mountain road. People standing alongside informed us there had been a landslide. Stepping out, we saw that the road ahead was blocked. Someone said it might well take days before it could be repaired. A delay of a few hours could make us miss the last plane to Ayuy.

But since others around us took the disaster as a matter of course, we did too. We unloaded our belongings, paid the driver, and, carrying babies, sacks, and boxes, picked our way over the muddy debris.

On the other side similar confusion reigned. Here were trucks, buses, and *mixtos*, headed in the opposite direction, unable to carry their passengers and cargo any farther from Shell Mera. The drivers on both sides of the washed-out road were dickering with stranded passengers and switching loads. Marie and I bargained with a driver on the Shell Mera side, and finally settled ourselves, children, and baggage in another *mixto* for the rest of the trip. Although we were assured we would be leaving immediately, we sat for over an hour until every inch of space – inside and outside – was packed with impatient mud-stained passengers and their gear. By this time it was raining and would soon be dark. It was cold outside; the air within reeked of damp clothes, perspiration, and human breath.

At last we started to move, first going backward down the narrow road until the driver found a place where he could turn around. We forgot our discomfort as we enjoyed the changing scene from barren mountain grasses to rich jungle growth. Now and then the incongruous sight of a lovely lavender orchid bending over from the clay banks refreshed our spirits. In the last moments of daylight as we rounded a turn we saw the familiar saddle-shaped silhouette in the Cutucú Range that marked the headwaters of the Makuma. Our destination seemed so tantalizingly near.

Soon it was so dark we could see nothing. But the change from the cool mountain breezes to the humid air of the jungle indicated we were not far from Shell Mera. By the time we arrived it was late and the Shell offices had long since been closed. We would have to wait patiently till morning before learning if the planes were still flying.

Now for a place to sleep; we were all dog-tired. In the town's only boardinghouse there was but one room to be had – four bleak walls with one bare bed and no windows. Here our party of five adults and three children passed the night.

I went first thing in the morning to the Shell office. Bad news: Camp Ayuy had already been stripped; the planes were no longer flying there.

Downhearted, I walked to the hangar to see the pilots in the hope I would find one who was a friend of Ernest. A quiet, reserved young Englishman listened impassively while I told my story.

'You know, I've got a mother back in England,' he said when I had finished. 'It would make her happy to know I'd helped a missionary. I'll fly you to Ayuy.'

I ran all the way to the boardinghouse with the glad tidings. We had to wait three more days for the pilot to schedule the flight. But it didn't matter. We were going to make it.

Ayuy was a dismal ghost town. On my last visit, its buildings and yards had been filled with the cheerful sounds of men at work. Now they were silent and overgrown with weeds. Some structures had burned down. Termites and cockroaches had done their destructive damage on others. But the barracks and cookhouse were still intact. We slept in one and cooked our meals on the big range in the other.

On his return flight, the pilot dipped his wings over Makuma as a prearranged signal to Ernest to send Indians to help us. Although it was noon on the day they came, we left with them at once, in spite of the fact that it would mean spending the night with the babies in a Shuara house on the way. Once more we strapped Linda into the box chair. One of the Indian women carried baby Ross in a sling around her shoulder, just as she would have her own child.

The next morning as we climbed the steep trail up from the Makuma River, we had our first glimpse of the Johnsons' new large bamboo house at the top of the rise.

To move in with the Johnsons was like coming home. Our room was light and airy with bright curtains at the windows. There was a bed with a mattress on a palm-board platform, with two smaller ones for Ross and Linda.

It didn't matter that we would have to sleep under stuffy nets to protect us from the biting vampire bats, that there was no electricity, no fresh milk, and only rarely any meat. This was the place to which the Lord had called us and we loved it.

To watch Ernest and Jean using daily opportunities to make friends with and help the Indians, who were always coming and going, was an inspiration to us. We wanted to be like these missionaries – to talk with the Indians and gain their confidence. We were aware this would take a long, long time, for we could catch only a few phrases out of the Shuara fast-paced conversations. We were eager to have a part in everything they had to do – clear the jungles, build a combined church and schoolhouse, help relieve the sick, visit among the Indians, and teach them the 'God's book' as they called the Bible.

In the evenings, after putting the children to bed, we sat around the kitchen table and talked of our great dreams. By the light of the gasoline lantern, we drank in all the Johnsons had to tell us about their life among the Shuara and what we might accomplish together.

The biggest job was to lengthen the airstrip. We would have to get this done in time for the arrival of the first Missionary Aviation Fellowship plane, which we hoped would be no later than July or August. We wondered if our staple food supplies would last till then.

On one of these nights, Ernest, his blue eyes shining, told me of his vision of training Shuara young men to be preachers and evangelists. My mind flashed back to our missionary training course. This was what we were here for – to establish indigenous churches that would go on long after we were gone – and here was a man, a veteran in the field, who shared our goal. I felt inspired.

After building the schoolhouse, we were ready to start classes. Jean would teach most of the Spanish secular subjects; Ernest would give the Bible lessons in Shuara; Marie would lead the hymn singing; and I would take care of the arithmetic lessons. The next step was to enlist the students. I offered to go along with Ernest to remind the Indians that it was time to send the boys to school. But Ernest, from his experience, understood better than I that getting the co-operation of the Indians was not going to be easy. At best they were indifferent; most were openly antagonistic.

We went first to call on a patriarch named Washicta, who had nine sons. Charles Olson had sometimes stayed at his house during his itinerating through Makuma. Washicta had consistently opposed Bible teaching and the idea of a missionary school. But Ernest accorded him the respect due a Shuara chief by paying him the first visit. Also, Ernest understood that visiting a Shuara family would be a real treat for me.

After a two-hour walk we came to the clearing surrounding the low oval-roofed house. As we stepped into the dim, smoky interior it took several minutes before our eyes could distinguish anything but the bare outlines of the room.

Around the wall was a series of bamboo racks. These were the Shuara beds. At the end of the beds were poles resting on forked sticks to support the sleepers' feet. Underneath were the embers of smoldering fires that kept their feet warm during the night. There were no windows, only two very narrow doors, one through which we had entered, one leading to a room beyond. This, Ernest explained to me, was the *tangamash,* or men's quarters. The *ekenta*, or space for the women and children, lay beyond the farther door.

The head of the house, Washicta himself, sat stolidly in the center of the room on a *cutanga*. This was a very important piece of furniture, a two-legged stool without back or arm rest, its curved seat rubbed shiny from constant use.

Ernest and Washicta began to talk. As they did so, other Indians came and went. I began to get my first clear impression of the Shuara in their native surroundings. They were mostly small in stature, with Mongolian features. The indolence of their movements was in contrast to the alertness of their eyes. It took only a few words to change them from apathy to excitability. Most of them wore long straggly hair and the wrap-around *itipi* (skirt). I was also impressed by the designs on their faces. I learned these were either for decoration or, in the case of hunters, for camouflage, to simulate the shadows of the forest. They always kept their guns at hand, laid across their knees or standing between their legs as though in readiness for an enemy attack. These were old-fashioned muzzle-loaders that they obtained from white traders.

While the men talked, a woman entered from the *ekenta*, bringing clay bowls of *chicha*. This milky-white liquid brewed from the cassava root is the Shuara household drink. The root is cooked, then masticated by the women to speed its fermentation and spewed back into the pot. It is then left until it bubbles and becomes a slightly alcoholic beverage, not unlike beer. At times it is a mild social drink, at times the basis for their orgiastic feasts and revelries. The women served Washicta and the other men. We waited quietly while they drank. Not to drink with them, I found, was not considered an offense against their hospitality.

Ernest and Washicta soon picked up their conversation. They both talked at once, of course. I could not understand anything they said but I was fascinated by the rhythmical, explosive sounds and the dramatic gestures accompanying their speeches. I could have listened for hours. Talking seemed to be the particular pride of the Shuara, their art and form of self-expression. They did nothing else nearly so often nor so well.

Each individual Shuara is a talking repository, not merely of news of the day, but of history, folklore, superstition, tradition, and vital statistics. What people elsewhere in the world get from their television, radio, newspapers, books, and magazines, these Indians get from one another. And they give it out with flair and style. I felt sure no cast of actors on television or the movie screen could be so dramatically arresting as this group of Shuara recounting their simple everyday experiences. As I listened to the two men they appeared to be competing, trying to out-talk each other. Evidently one really had to be able to speak the language well in order to gain the respect of these Indians. I determined to learn it as fast as I could.

My first impressions of these Shuara and others I had met were that they were like friendly, uninhibited children. Also, they were not a downtrodden, beaten people like the Quichua Indians I had seen in Ecuador's mountains, but were independent, self-centered, and arrogant. But although their liveliness attracted me, I was repelled by their filth and personal habits. They always smelled of perspiration, smoke, and rotten food, and kept scratching themselves because of the stinging gnats. Most of these men and women had worn their garments until they were unsightly with stains, then dyed them a deep purple. They regarded soap as a medicine to be used only for skin diseases. After all, soap was a rare item way out here in the jungle.

Outwardly they were an easy going, laughing, careless lot. I could hardly believe that Washicta, now looking like a gentle grandpa with one arm around his naked son, was also a drunkard, wife-beater, polygamist, and murderer.

Now the old man and Ernest rose to their feet as a sign the visit was almost ended. I couldn't tell whether Washicta had consented to send his boys to school or not. I stood with them and recited the two words I knew of Shuara goodbyes before following Ernest out the door.

Washicta still did not want his sons to come to school. He

believed like all Shuara men that it was more important for his boys to become strong warriors and skilled hunters than it was to read and write. The year before, three of them had run away from home to attend the missionaries' school. If they came this year they would probably do the same thing. I could see it would not be easy to establish schools for these jungle children.

A week later, when the classes began with fifteen boys (including four sons of Washicta who had come to us against their father's orders), I understood more of the problems involved. Most of the students were far less civilized than the ones we had known in Sucúa. Few came to us fully clothed or with any conversational knowledge of Spanish. They were completely undisciplined and had little respect for rules. They attended when they felt like it and ran away at the slightest feeling of boredom or resentment. They complained about the food Ernest cooked for them, the clothes we gave them, and about the required two hours of daily weed chopping.

But like children anywhere, they loved to sing and play. I helped fashion for them a long seesaw by fastening a pole to a stump. Sometimes I went to the river with them to fish. Although I couldn't talk much of their language, it wasn't hard to make friends with these responsive Shuara boys.

The schoolhouse was a thatched palm-pole hut. The boys sat on long board benches with a high bench in front of them to write on. Although they were very intelligent, they had to learn everything from scratch. They had never before tried to understand pictures, and didn't always recognize when they were wrong-side up. It took days of practice before they succeeded in writing neat rows of a letter of the alphabet on the restricting blue lines of their notebooks. Jean taught them Spanish, using Ecuadorian primers. They received their first wondering glimpses of the outside world from colored illustrations Jean had cut out of the *National Geographic*. They had not known that any world existed outside their own.

The boys took naturally to arithmetic and liked learning to

count. When we got to numbers beyond their fingers and toes we used beans or corn kernels. They enjoyed naming the months and days of the week.

Some were quicker to learn than others. We wished there were more like Wampiu. His mind was a sponge. Even after school hours he kept asking questions and practiced writing with charred sticks of wood on trees whose bark he had skinned with a machete.

Besides helping with the school, we drew plans and began building our house. For the first time in our married lives we would be living by ourselves in our own home. Working with bamboo, jungle thatch, and long-haired Shuara helpers was an exciting challenge to me. It was great fun to try to imitate these men skilled in picking up vines with their toes and folding and tying leaves on the roof.

When the house was ready and we moved in, we felt as though we were living in a bushel basket. The bamboo walls and springy floors of the same material were filled with cracks. These had both advantages and disadvantages: dust and dirt could easily be swept through them and onto the ground; any spilled liquid quickly disappeared. But very often a table, bed, or chair leg would go crashing through, leaving the occupant surprised and somewhat shaken.

The cracks in the walls also made convenient peepholes for the Indians. Our back porch frequently overflowed with brown-skinned visitors come to satisfy their curiosity about our strange customs. When they couldn't see enough through the windows they walked around the walls to peek through the cracks.

And as they looked they laughed with amusement. They thought their own ways were far superior to ours. They were fascinated by the white diapers hanging in the sun to dry, but wondered why we needed those things. Any Shuara woman knew enough to hold her baby away from her at the proper time and use handy leaves for cleaning up. As for washing dishes and tableware three times a day with soap and hot water – that seemed to the jungle dwellers definitely pointless. How much more sensible to eat with one's fingers from disposable plates of leaves and afterward rinse only the few gourds or clay pots in a nearby stream. Indian mothers could not understand why Marie needed so much paraphernalia just to give Linda and Rossboy their baths. All they had to do was take a mouthful of water, hold it until it reached body temperature, spew it slowly onto their babies, then rub and wipe them dry with their hands.

No wonder the Shuara did not share our high opinion of our own hard-working missionary wives. To them, Marie was a rather useless creature. She could not walk the trail with a load on her back, nor plant the garden, nor peel the tough bark-like skin from the cassava root without cutting herself. She did not even nurse her own babies. She spent most of her time cleaning her house or making strange marks on sheets of paper. But those marks produced neither food nor clothing, so what good were they to anyone? What good was she?

The Shuara world is a man's world. Once he has cleared his land of the trees and brush and built his house he is free of family responsibilities. He may then weave himself a new *itipi* or fashion crowns and ornaments of feathers for his hair. Aside from such duties, he has nothing to do but hunt and fish, loaf and talk about his exploits.

His multiple wives do all the cultivating and harvesting of food and carrying of heavy loads, besides cooking and caring for the children. To a Shuara mother, her children are her chief delight. She never likes to be without a little one in her arms and nurses her babies until they are three years old. As we learned more about them we understood why they felt our way of life ridiculous.

Now that we were in our new house, we began serious study of the Shuara language. Ernest gave us regular lessons from a small grammar he had compiled. Marie spent long hours copying it in longhand and memorizing its conjugations. But I learned more by always being at Ernest's side when the Indians came to work in the morning or when he paid them in the afternoon, and as I listened and watched I would try talking with them myself.

Ernest warned us that the Indians were accustomed to communicating with Spanish-speaking colonists in a kind of trade language, a highly simplified form of Shuara. This was what he had learned during his first year in Sucúa; but when visiting Indian families he found he could understand only a part of what the Indians said to each other. He determined to forget the trade language and master the true Shuara. He also set before us the same goal.

However, we did not gain facility in this language as quickly as we had done with Spanish. That had been simple compared to the complications of learning Shuara. There were not even words to express the spiritual concepts we had come to teach. Their language is rich in terms which describe jungle plants, trees, insects, birds and animals, their own family life, adventures in the forest, wars, and witchcraft. It would be years before we would learn all their varied expressions associated with evil, hatred, murders, lust, contacting demonic spirits, and filth.

But finding phrases to expound the truths of the Bible would be something else. There were no words for salvation, grace, belief, or forgiveness. After long and patient work Ernest had discovered only a few which approximated thoughts of joy, comfort, patience, gentleness, goodness, and the many other virtues named in the Bible. When we spoke of the righteousness of God we had to employ the same word the Indians used to describe a well-cleared garden patch. We had to face the fact that since the Shuara did not know these things they felt no need to talk about them. But the more we studied the more we loved this strange jungle tongue.

Besides helping us with the language, conducting school and Sunday services, our senior missionaries also offered medical care to the disease-ridden Indians. Nearly every day someone would come to the mission with fever or vomiting, diarrhea, a machete wound, or snake bite. Although they always went first to their witch doctors, they were slowly learning that some of their ailments could be better cured by the missionaries' remedies.

One such case was a Shuara baby in serious condition, brought to Jean by his mother. Jungle people generally suffer from intestinal parasites and this child was evidently another victim. Jean administered a shot for dysentery and waited – but without much hope.

About ten minutes later, the mother, moaning with grief, called frantically to Jean. He had begun to roll his eyes and breathe spasmodically. His feet and hands were already cold. Jean applied a hot-water bottle, rubbed him, and gave him a heart stimulant. But it was to no avail. The child died in his mother's arms.

Tearfully, Jean then did her best to comfort the woman by telling her that her baby was safe with the Lord and that she would surely see him again someday if she would just put her trust in Christ.

We could only hope the woman understood, as we watched her go wailing down the path, her dead baby clutched to her heart. We clung to the hope that someday there would be Christians among them who would trust in God in time of sickness, even in the face of death.

There were other cases, though, that had a happier outcome. One day we saw Jean approaching our house running and crying. She wanted Marie's help in treating a baby who had rolled off a bed rack into an open fire and was badly burned. Five days had gone by since the accident before the child's parents, a Shuara named Pitur and his wife, could make up their minds to bring the baby to Jean.

Upon examination, Jean and Marie found one side of his head was literally cooked and smelled putrid. There seemed to be little they could do. They had to wipe away so much of the rotted flesh that the bone showed through. Jean dressed the wound and made the parents understand that they must bring the baby every day to have the dressing changed. For nearly a month Pitur and his wife complied faithfully. Marie sewed caps for his head and helped the mother wash and change them. Slowly, new flesh grew over the scalp until finally the baby recovered completely. But he would always have to wear a cap to cover the baldness and ugly scars.

Another day, about three months after school had opened, old Washicta came for medicine. He had become somewhat reconciled to his sons being in school but was too proud to admit it was good for them. Truculently, he demanded that since four of his boys were in school and working in our gardens, he ought to get medicine free. He wanted more sons and asked Jean for some pills that would give him strength so he could have more children. 'If I have another son won't he come to your school?' he reasoned insistently. I don't know what she gave him, but it must have had the desired effect, because within a year he did have another boy.

During these months with the Johnsons, Sunday preaching services were held in the schoolhouse instead of in the missionaries' home as when I first visited Makuma. Ernest always gave simple Bible lessons with an evangelistic emphasis. Whenever he asked how many wanted to become Christians there would be an enthusiastic response among the thirty to fifty Indians in attendance. But there was more real understanding of the way of salvation manifested by the schoolboys who heard Bible teaching each day than by the older ones who came only occasionally. Even though there was growing interest in knowing God we saw as yet little evidence of changed lives.

But Ernest kept on preaching, visiting, praying, and planning for the salvation of the Shuara. And often we talked of establishing another mission station among the tribe to the southeast, known to the Shuara as their fiercest enemies, the Atshuara. Some of them had lived along the Makuma years before Ernest had moved here. One afternoon while I was building my house, some pieces of broken pottery were brought to me by Indians who had been grubbing stumps from our new yard.

'These were made by Atshuara people,' they had said as they rubbed fresh dirt from the primitive-looking bits of clay. 'Some of them used to live right where you are building your house in the days before our grandfathers drove them away. Now we never see them any more. They live many days downstream hidden in the deep forests like wild animals. It is impossible to get at them, they are so fierce.'

And I had heard stories, too, of the wars between the two tribes. Although the Atshuara did not shrink the heads of enemies they killed, they were hated and feared by all the Shuara. Only a few years before we came, Big Saantu and a young witch doctor named Catani had led a war party against the Atshuara and had shrunk one of their heads.

It was with these Indians that we hoped to make a friendly contact. We prayed that we would be able to win not only Shuara for Christ but Atshuara, too. We knew that the power of the gospel could change their lives and break down the barriers of hatred and revenge that stood between them.

One Saturday afternoon, while Ernest and I were working with a group of Indians lengthening the airstrip, one of our schoolboys named Tiwi emerged from the brush. His new shirt and trousers were tattered and dirty. We leaned on our shovels, brushing the stinging gnats away from our perspiring faces, to rest a minute and visit with him. He laughed as Ernest told him we were doing the job the lazy schoolboys should have finished the day before. Looking out to the hills, Tiwi said he was thinking of going monkey hunting and would like to buy some gunpowder.

'Come along,' said Ernest, shouldering his shovel. 'Let's quit for today and give the fellow what he wants.' His blue eyes twinkled as he said in Shuara, for Tiwi's benefit, 'Next week after Tiwi becomes strong from eating his monkey meat, he'll level that pile of dirt in no time!'

One afternoon a few days later we heard Indians shouting, *'Shuara maayi! Shuara maayi!'* The boys poured out of the schoolhouse at the sound of the piercing voices.

'What are they saying?' we asked.

'Men have killed! Men have killed!' Jean translated quietly so as not to disturb our children playing nearby.

It was not until later that evening while sitting around the kitchen table that we heard the whole story from Ernest.

'Tiwi did not go monkey hunting after he bought that powder and shot from us last Saturday. Instead he went straight to the house of his uncle named Nawich.' Ernest's normally genial face grew angry as he realized how he had been deceived.

This is what happened:

A few months ago Nawich gave his oldest daughter to a young witch doctor who lived downstream in Catani's territory. Soon afterward the girl got sick and died. Nawich thought the witch doctor had cursed her. He plotted his revenge. Nawich sent for Tiwi, and promised him his youngest daughter if Tiwi would help him kill the son-in-law.

Marie broke in, exclaiming, 'To think that our Tiwi who sang the hymns so happily should get caught in that evil trap!'

Ernest continued:

Tiwi accompanied Nawich to the son-in-law's house. They asked him to go fishing with them and he went, not suspecting anything. After fishing for two or three days they visited the house of a relative of Nawich near the Cusutca River. They all sat down to drink chicha. As the son-in-law lifted the bowl to his lips, Nawich shot him in the stomach. He did not die immediately, but lay on the ground screaming and begging the warriors to end his agony. But Nawich would not allow anyone to shoot again.

'Let him lie there and think a while,' he said. 'Did he not kill my daughter? Let him suffer. Let him feel pain.'

Tiwi finally picked up a spear and drove it into the heart of the tormented man, thus earning his bride. Then the other men in the house went wild, threw spears into the son-in-law's body, and tore out his hair.

'But where are Nawich and Tiwi now?' I asked.

'Oh,' Ernest answered in a matter-of-fact tone, 'they're still living with relatives near the Cusutca River.'

As newcomers, we were shocked that the murderers were so well known, yet nobody was doing anything about it. There were no authorities close at hand to call on. We considered sending a letter to our friend, the major in Macas, but Ernest pointed out there weren't enough soldiers to arrest all the Shuara who had taken part in revenge killings. So Nawich and Tiwi would go free – at least until some member of the young witch doctor's family avenged his death.

'There is no end to this slaughter,' observed Ernest sadly. 'And no hope for the Shuara, except in God.'

We four were the only missionaries in thousands of square miles of Shuara territory this side of the Cutucú Mountains. That night, as we prayed together, we felt completely unequal to the task of changing this part of *Shuartica*. Yet we knew that God's power is, and always has been, unlimited. We would faithfully continue our Sunday services, and take daily opportunities to teach the Bible to all. His Word – not force – would someday change their hearts.

Tiwi never returned to school. He and Nawich remained in hiding, fearing revenge from their enemies.

Our days, filled as they were with language study and contacts with the Indians, passed quickly. It soon was the middle of

August 1948, and no plane had appeared. Our salt, sugar, rice, and flour were running low. Still more disturbing, our supply of powdered milk which we needed so badly for our babies was nearly exhausted.

We had been so certain that the MAF plane service would be in operation by now that we had lengthened the airstrip to twelve hundred feet. But shut off in our jungle clearing, we had no way of knowing what was going on. For several months we'd had no contact with the outside world by radio, plane, or foot messenger.

I decided to walk to Shell Mera. I would take a party of Indians to help bring back needed foodstuffs, including the indispensable powdered milk. But just as we were leaving we heard from the Indians that a white man had appeared at one of their houses. Upon investigation we found that he was a Shell Company employee who had flown out to Camp Ayuy and then walked to Makuma to check on some cement markers the company had left behind. I quickly took advantage of the chance to fly with him to Shell Mera.

As we circled for a landing and looked down, I could hardly believe my eyes. There on the long Shell airstrip was a new yellow air plane. The MAF's long-awaited plane had arrived. God had answered our desperate need.

I sought out the pilot. He was a slim, sandy-haired, engaging young fellow named Nate Saint. He was all sympathy when I told him of our plight at Makuma.

A few days later I flew with Nate on the first of several trips to our isolated station. That MAF pilot and plane changed our lives. He brought us mail and food on regular flights. Once, he flew in with our washing machine, bed, and other household items we had left behind in Sucúa. On another trip he brought a small light plant and a generator. At last we would have not only light by which to study, but some radio communication with the outside world. Shortly before Christmas, Nate came with a welcome visitor, Mr. Don P. Shidler, new president of the Gospel Missionary Union.

Christmas had always been a happy time for us. Now we hoped to bring something of its joy and significance to the Shuara, who, for the most part, knew nothing of it. We planned three days of special services, games, and feasting. To our surprise, nearly a hundred and twenty Shuara showed up. With so many there wouldn't be nearly enough meat to go around. Ernest decided to kill some of his precious chickens and ducks for all to enjoy.

Conducting the services and preparing meals for so many people kept us busy. The Indians listened respectfully while Ernest preached; many agreed that God's Word was good to know. But aside from a few schoolboys there were no real converts. There was no joyous spirit, no loving exchange, no singing of carols such as we were used to. Instead, we noted among the Shuara a strong feeling of fear. There was no trust, only suspicion among them. They had come in groups, armed with guns or spears for protection. Their talk was all of murder and threats of killings. For them there was as yet no 'peace on earth.'

But now we began to prepare for an event that would encourage and refresh us. Shortly before New Year we all expected to fly to Shell Mera, a few at a time, to go on to Guayaquil for the GMU annual conference. After the meetings the Johnsons would go to the States for their furlough.

Nate Saint was to come for us on the Friday after Christmas. But although the weather was calm, the plane did not arrive as scheduled. Saturday–Sunday–Monday went by. The weather stayed clear; still no sign of Nate.

On the first Monday evening of every month, the missionaries of radio station HCJB broadcast an off-the-record program of personal greetings to friends. We hoped for some news of Nate and his plane.

We started the light plant and tuned our radio to the frequency. An announcer came on with startling news. Nate

Saint's plane had been caught by a down-draft while taking off from Quito and crashed. Although we were relieved to hear he had not been killed, we were sorry that his back was injured seriously. The brand-new airplane was a wreck.

Marie and I looked at each other. Now what would happen to our lifeline? Our main concern was for Mr. Shidler who was scheduled to speak at the conference. How would he get to Shell Mera? There was no way except on foot. Mr. Shidler himself didn't mind the idea. He wanted to leave the very next day.

Marie and Jean would have to stay in Makuma. This was the second time Marie had looked forward to going to a conference only to be prevented by a plane crash. But she and Jean soon forgot their disappointment in the rush of getting things ready for our departure.

Early next morning, Mr. Shidler, Ernest, and I left for Shell Mera with eight Indians. What a surprise was in store for us when, after six hard days on the trail, we found Jean Johnson there ahead of us. She said she was as surprised as we to find herself there.

MAF had not let us down. Hobey Lowrance, a new pilot, had arrived in Shell Mera just two days before Nate crashed in Quito. He too was concerned about getting Mr. Shidler to the conference, so he had enlisted the help of the Shell Oil Company.

The day after we had left Makuma, a large Shell plane flew over the house and circled the strip. A man stood in the doorway and parachuted down a large box. Marie and Jean, thinking it must contain food supplies, sent Indian boys to get it. For twenty minutes they watched the plane fly back and forth over the strip, and wondered why it lingered. Finally it went away. Back in the house, when they opened the box, they found a note from Hobey to Mr. Shidler, saying, 'If you so desire, I can hire a commercial plane to land at Ayuy and take you and two others out to Shell Mera. If none of you can be at Ayuy within three days, stand on the airstrip with arms extended.'

Not having seen the note, they had not signaled the plane.

Therefore, the commercial plane would be landing in Ayuy after three days. Marie and Jean decided that one or the other of them ought to take advantage of this chance to fly to Shell Mera. Marie was reluctant to go because she was pregnant with our third child. If she went outside now she would not be able to get back until late August after our baby was born. Jean thought this was a reason for Marie's going. But Marie and I were just beginning to win the confidence of the Indians and she knew I would not want to be away from Makuma for the seven months or more. As soon as Jean saw Marie was bent on staying, she made up her mind to go.

Marie was left alone with the Lopez family. She was not feeling very well, but she went about caring for our home and children as usual. She knew the Lord would take care of us somehow, plane or no plane.

Meanwhile, I attended the conference in Guayaquil and after about a month again covered the jungle trail to return to Marie in Makuma.

Without the plane or the Johnsons our jungle outpost was a very quiet place. I had plenty of work: adding on to our house, building a storage shed for gasoline, improving the airstrip, digging drainage ditches, harvesting the tropical wheat, planting more gardens. I worked with the Indians from daybreak to nightfall.

Within a week I was flat on my back with malaria contracted on the trail. I couldn't keep down the bitter quinine pills, so my fever rose higher and higher while I tossed and rolled and wondered why I had to be sick. Marie slept on the floor to give me more room on the bed. She got up every little while to bring me a drink or rub the ache out of my bones.

Marie knew she had to do something further. She thought she remembered having seen a few ampules of injectable quinine on a shelf in the Johnsons' house. She found them and also a hypodermic needle and syringe which she put on to boil. In California boot-camp days we had both had thorough practice, first in shooting a hypo filled with sterile water into an orange, then into each other. But neither of us had given a shot since then. Praying to God for strength, she rolled me over and stuck in the needle. Within twenty-four hours I began to recover, although it was a long time before I could leave the bed.

I had to fight hard not to give way to discouragement. But I had more time to think, pray, and read the Bible than I had had for months. Finally I realized God was teaching me a lesson. I had been neglecting what was most important of all to Him – more important than all the hard work I could offer – time spent in fellowship with Him, praying and meditating on His Word. I thought of the words of instruction given by Mr. Weiss in the farewell message just before we left Kansas City: 'You must build a strong spiritual life maintained by regular and consistent prayer and Bible study habits.'

I did not want to fail as a missionary. I knew why God had put me on my back, and cried to Him for forgiveness and help to do better in the future. God wanted my heart's devotion and my worship and communion with Him more than anything else. Could God ever use such a person as I was, weakened in body and wavering in spirit, to win Shuara for Christ?

A passage from the Bible sustained me: 'He who began a good work in you will carry it on to completion until the day of Christ Jesus' (Phil. 1:6). A battle had been won. I slept peacefully that night.

# CHAPTER SIX
# ALONE ON THE STATION

If a man remains in me and I in him, he will bear
much fruit (John 15:5).

This was the time of our testing. It was February 1949. Before
I left Guayaquil to return to Makuma, Ernest had told me that
he and Jean could not continue in the Shuara work. The rigors
of the jungle had so impaired their health that they were planning,
upon their return from furlough, to live in Guayaquil and itinerate
to surrounding towns to hold evangelistic campaigns. This meant
that we would be without missionary companions until the
resumption of plane service could bring Keith and Doris Austin,
along with a new missionary, Miss Dorothy Walker.

There was no longer the plane to bring us supplies and mail,
and there would not be one until another could be flown down
from the States. We hoped that would be soon because once
again our food staples were getting alarmingly low. We had not
expected such an abrupt end to the service. The boys' school
had been closed since November, as there was not enough in

the gardens to feed the youngsters. Few Indians appeared to work, visit, or attend our weekly Sunday service.

We realized how much we had depended on the Johnsons. Up to this time they had taken the responsibility; we were only learners. Ernest understood how the Indians thought, as well as what they said. He was always there to listen to their woes, give them counsel, and teach them God's way. Jean, although not a registered nurse, had skillfully and lovingly cared for the sick. Now the responsibilities were ours and only ours. There was no one to turn to but God. But as He promised, He never forsook us. On one of those rare days when we could get a letter out by an Indian who was going on a visit to Sucúa, Marie wrote to her folks:

> Without the Johnsons, our spiritual work among the Shuara is somewhat at a standstill. Aside from our prayers and the witness of our daily lives we cannot do much. We cannot open school again until we have a Christian national schoolteacher. Frank cannot hold preaching services until he knows the language better.
>
> But we are neither discouraged nor longing to leave this place. We hope folks are praying for us but that no one wastes any time feeling sorry for us because we do not have the same ease of living that we could have in the States. We have all that is necessary for complete happiness – the love and fellowship of our Lord, and a real goal in life that keeps material things in proper perspective. I need not mention the blessings we share of unbroken harmony between Frank and me, and of the laughter and tears of two babies to make each day interesting and different...

We never had time to feel lonely or sorry for ourselves, even if we'd been so inclined. Rot and decay necessitated continual repair and reconstruction of the thatch and bamboo buildings. Before we finished harvesting one garden of plantains and bananas two more needed planting.

I had planned a full work program and needed all the help I could get. But the Indians didn't see things the same way. Those who walked back with me from Shell Mera and knew I had brought some store goods spread the word around. At first they were all eager to earn new clothes, machetes, and fishhooks. But when I wouldn't give them the coveted goods on credit, many lost interest. Only a few returned to work in the days following.

We held a service on Sundays for any Shuara who would come. We were pleased that enough usually turned up to fill our back porch. Marie played her accordion and we all sang hymns. Then with the help of pictures in a Sunday School paper, I related to them, in my limping Shuara, stories about Jonah and the whale, and Jesus healing the sick. I learned more from their comments than they did from mine.

My bout with malaria stopped the work program and even the Sunday services. Some Indians came every day to sit with me on the back porch. I couldn't understand nearly all they said, and therefore could not be of much help to them. But I was glad they were beginning to bring me their problems, just as they had done with Ernest. As my strength returned, I went with them to their homes and so learned more of their everyday lives. Slowly they accepted me and invited me to go on hunting and fishing trips with them.

One such trip stands out in my mind. I had gone on a monkey hunt with two Indians and their wives.

Late the second night as we sat around the fire after eating the stringy chunks of monkey meat, a squat, hook-nosed, heavy-browed Shuara named Jeencham ('bat') hunched forward and began to tell me how the Shuara seek help from the spirit world. His object is to make contact with his dead warrior ancestors. They believe that the dead become demons who may appear in the shape of certain beasts, birds, or reptiles. Having induced a cataleptic state by drinking a brew of *tsaangu* (tobacco leaves) or *maicua* (belladonna), his mind is free to communicate with the spirits of departed forefathers to gain strength or ask questions which will later be confirmed by the witch doctor.

But in serious matters, as when a relative is very ill or when a group is deciding whether to go to war, Shuara summon the witch doctor who has the strongest contact with the spirit world.

Before the witch doctor arrives, the family will have cooked up for him in a big black pot a narcotic of simmered vines. This is called *natema* (Banisteriopsis caapi). The witch doctor drinks the liquid until he attains a state of delirium.

Now the ancestors appear to him, in the guise of water boa, fer-de-lance (snake), toucan, deer, owl, jaguar, or ocelot. As the witch doctor sings his chant, he waves before him a handful of leaves to protect himself from the demons who are writhing toward him. They advance and retreat and advance again, drawing ever closer. They are a hideous, nightmarish sight, a fact which the witch doctor makes clear as he describes to his audience what he is seeing. Gradually, he surrenders his own willpower and gives himself up to the power of the demons. They, in turn, will reward him by revealing the cause of the illness and the name of the enemy witch who has sent the curse.

The witch doctor loudly and dramatically sucks on the afflicted part of the body, then proudly spits out the 'arrow' that caused it all, which may be a stone, a bone, a bug, or a bit of glass.

To prepare young boys for manhood, or older warriors for battle, the patriarchs will take a group up into the mountains, where they will bathe in clear streams at the foot of certain waterfalls. There they drink the *tsaangu* or *maicua* and talk with the spirits of their dead, distinguished ancestors. This communing with the spirits gives special power to the supplicant. A strong contact produces such a conviction of invincibility that a Shuara will unhesitatingly go to war in the face of the greatest odds, certain that he cannot be killed.

The firelight flickered eerily as Jeencham, in his excited voice, described these rites. I thought how intoxicating with power, yet how hard, short, and dangerous, is the life of a witch doctor. Of the many killings among Shuara in our neighborhood, most of them happened to witch doctors. Jeencham's accounts aroused in me a lasting desire to learn all that I could about their weird religion and folklore.

As I look back on my convalescence, I can see that what appeared to be an affliction was really the working of God's will. Those apparently wasted hours spent visiting, talking, and wandering through the jungle when I could not work brought nearer by many months the day I would be able to preach God's Word to the Shuara. It helped me to learn the language in the easiest way possible. It helped me to understand their belief system. Above all, it paved the way as nothing else could have done for them to accept us.

In time I was able to do more work each day building the house and improving the airstrip. Still using our radio and generator, we listened weekly to radio station HCJB. We had been notified to tune in every Friday night for a special broadcast, for there might be news about the replacement plane. The Friday night broadcasts were bright spots during those long weeks. We didn't have much gasoline, so we rationed it, denying ourselves other uses of power so we could go on listening to these newscasts.

Finally, one Friday evening came a message we knew was especially for us. Robert Savage, one of the station directors, was speaking from Quito: 'Now a special announcement for all our colleagues working in the Oriente (eastern jungle). The new MAF plane is on its way. It should be seen over these towers within two weeks...'

This filled us with great rejoicing. Now we had something definite to look forward to.

Then we both faced emergencies that drove all thoughts of the plane from our minds. Marie was about to perform her first delivery of a baby. I was called upon to deal at first-hand with the murderous feuding of the Shuara. These things happened almost at the same time.

It was early in the afternoon when Graciela, our Ecuadorian helper, came running breathlessly to our door. Her mother, Señora Rosa, who lived in her own house nearby, was about to give birth. This daylight delivery was an answer to our prayers, for there was no light in Señora Rosa's house by which to manage a night delivery.

'It's really happening,' exclaimed Marie. She began to make ready according to Jean Johnson's instructions. This birth had to be a success. Señora Rosa had suffered sad misfortunes in childbirth. She had lost three babies. One had been dropped; two had died from infection of the umbilicus. In her great faith, Señora Rosa looked on Marie as God's instrument to bring her safely through this one.

But Marie's only experience had been the births of our own two children. She was outwardly calm as she moved about efficiently, but I knew how she must be feeling inside. Graciela built the fire in the stove and put water on to boil. Marie gathered some old magazines which she had sterilized in the oven to serve as bed pads. She got out a pan with scissors and tape to cut and tie the umbilical cord, and a syringe with which to give the ergotrate after the delivery. As a last-minute refresher between all of these operations, she once more consulted the obstetrical book Jean Johnson had given her.

The children, Linda and Ross, were clamoring to go with her. They wanted so much to see the new baby. But Marie said no. She persuaded them to stay with me on the promise that they could come the next day and watch the baby being bathed.

Marie gathered all her paraphernalia and set out. My heart went with her, and my prayers, as I stood in the doorway with the children, watching her go.

I had barely sat down on the log bench on the porch when I saw a crowd of Indians coming up the hill from the river. They were all shouting at once, hoarsely and out of breath, as though they had been running for some distance. At the head of the band was Nawich, a tall, gaunt Shuara, his black eyes blazing, his hair flying. He had a gun in his hands.

At first all I could get from their rapid-fire conversation were a few familiar phrases:

'You'll see! You'll see! He'll pay! He'll pay!' Then I heard them shout, *'Shuara maayi! Shuara maayi!'* which I remembered meant 'Indians have killed!'

I directed them to sit down on the porch in the hope this would calm them. Ross crawled into my lap; Linda sat down beside me. First we hurried through the familiar, usually long-drawn-out salutations.

Slowly I drew out their story, which I had them repeat many times before I could understand what they were saying. Juang, a witch doctor who was Nawich's brother, had just been killed by a Shuara named Uyungara and his band from the Upper Makuma. They had attacked at night, under cover of a rainstorm, shooting through the walls of the house into Juang's sleeping form.

As soon as I could get a word in I asked, 'But why did Uyungara want to kill your brother?'

I learned that Nawich and Juang and the Cusutca River Shuara had long been enemies of Uyungara and his Upper Makuma gang. A relative of Uyungara's had died of an illness. Uyungara blamed Juang, the witch doctor, for having caused his death by putting a curse on him. Uyungara had sworn never to rest until he got his revenge on Juang. Now, in turn, Nawich was bent on avenging himself on Uyungara.

At this point, the purpose of the visit became clear. In his peculiar, twisted Shuara way, Nawich had come to enlist my help in his war against Uyungara. He fixed me with his burning eyes.

'You're against the Shuara killing each other, aren't you?' I admitted that I was.

'All right. Then you mustn't let Uyungara go free. If you do, he will finish us all off.'

I asked him what he wanted me to do.

'Send for the soldiers. Get them to come and put Uyungara in jail. Ah, they'll make him suffer there! Then he can think about the evil he has done!'

'You hypocrites,' I thought to myself.

The distraught Indian was pacing up and down the porch, wildly waving his arms as he talked. The split palm-wood floor bounced under his step. Linda, looking at him wide-eyed, was afraid, since she was unable to understand a word he was saying. She cuddled closer to me. 'He naughty, Daddy?' she said, 'He naughty?' I gave her a gentle squeeze.

'Yes,' I answered, 'He is very naughty. He needs the Lord Jesus to change his wicked heart.'

This seemed to satisfy her enough for her to slide down and run to play in the kitchen with Ross tagging at her heels.

I had to do some hard thinking. Nawich's demand, on the face of it, wasn't altogether unreasonable. But there was a trap here. If I wasn't careful I would find myself siding with one group of Indians against another. I had reason to thank God then for my recent outings with the Shuara which at least enabled me in Shuara style to ask a few questions and deliver a few imperatives.

Turning to Nawich, I told him to sit down and be quiet. Then I asked him, 'Many moons past, did you not go with young Tiwi and kill your son-in-law? Did you want the soldiers to come then?'

He had no answer for that one. I began to gain some confidence. 'You go on back to your home. Perhaps I will send for the soldiers and tell them about Uyungara. When they come, shall I tell them about you, too?'

Seeing in Nawich's uncertain look that my words were having their effect, I jumped to my feet and shouted:

'You want others to quit warring with you? Then you quit warring, too. Maybe you can't do it by yourself. But God can help you. Listen to Him. Obey His Word.'

The Indians' response was to cover their mouths with their hands and laugh noisily. I knew by now that they did this to cover their embarrassment at having been out-talked by a white man. I had won their respect.

As they got up and shuffled away, I resolved that I would never take sides in these Indian wars, but treat everyone the same. I would try to teach them all to learn the love of God and give up their bloodthirsty ways.

Just then Marie appeared. I was so flushed with my triumph, I had to tell her all about it. She took me right down to size.

'Oh, you're just like the Shuara,' she said, 'full of hot air. You know good and well you won't send for those soldiers.'

Now it was my turn to listen to her experience. She recounted:

I found Señora Rosa lying on her bed. She was trembling and breathing irregularly in her pain. She didn't think it would be long before the little one would be born, so I quickly opened the bundle of clean papers and spread them over the foot of the bed and a table. Graciela brought the water, scissors, tape, and baby clothes, then left the room. I bathed the mother, tried to soothe her, and got everything ready. Having a few minutes left, I hurriedly consulted the instruction book to see if I was forgetting anything.

I was deep in the book when I heard Señora Rosa calling my name very softly. She said the baby's head was through. I hurried to the bedside, hardly believing it was happening as easily as that. There on the paper at the foot of the bed lay a tiny mucous-covered baby girl, gasping for breath. I could scarcely see for the tears that filled my eyes. But somehow I managed to find the cord, cut it, and with shaking hands lift the little life to the table for its first bath. Graciela came back in then to help me care for her mother. Soon both Señora Rosa and her child were resting comfortably.

We recognized that the Lord had helped us in both of these situations.

MISSION TO THE HEADHUNTERS

Once more our thoughts centered on the plane. The day on which it was supposed to reach Quito was drawing near. The plane's coming would change everything. When the hour we were to receive final word arrived, we sat by the radio, straining our ears through the squeakings and squawkings for the news. Then we heard Robert Savage's familiar voice. The plane had not arrived. He didn't know what had gone wrong. It just wasn't there.

What a blow! We had built up to such a terrible letdown. Up until now our confidence that the plane would come remained so unshaken that we had not made any alternate plans. Our situation was getting worse. Our rationed gasoline was running out and we did not know how much longer we would be able to operate the radio. Our staple foods were just about gone. Soon there would be no more powdered milk for the babies. We kept all our staples in tight tin cans to protect them from the insects. When we bumped them together, oh the dismal effect of their hollow sound! Heavy rains further depressed us. Everything we touched was soggy and damp. For ten days it was either darkly overcast or streaming with rain. We resented the bad weather the more because we thought it was keeping the plane from coming.

Alternatives had to be considered now. I paced the porch, trying to make up my mind what to do. I thought of hiking over the trails to bring back fresh supplies. But if the plane should come while I was gone, I would not be on hand to receive it. Every avenue was blocked. There was nothing to do but sweat it out, and put our trust in the Lord. It cheered us a bit to remember that April 19, two days away, would be Linda's third birthday. We made up our minds that whatever our troubles, nothing would spoil the day for her. She would have the best birthday party we could manage.

With the very last of our flour, Graciela baked her a big three-layer banana birthday cake. Marie, rummaging among the forgotten belongings left by the Johnsons, produced three fat candles. Linda would have some presents to open: six marbles wrapped in tissue paper from Ross-boy; an outfit of doll clothes for her favorite doll Larry, which Marie had sewed; and a set of wooden tinker toys. The final touch was added when, as we were sitting down to the table, in came Señora Rosa, her arms loaded with flowers. Graciela's little brother ran along beside her, bringing Linda his pet baby rooster with a gay red ribbon tied around its neck.

Linda's eyes were big and round as the birthday cake was brought in glowing with its three candles and we all sang 'Happy Birthday.' For a few precious moments, losing ourselves in her joy, we forgot the empty food tins and the silence in the sky.

The next day the weather lifted and the sun came out, bright and clear. Now, I thought, the plane will surely come. But it didn't. The day passed and there was no sign of it. The following afternoon I was working outside when I heard a faint sound overhead. Could it be the plane? Yes, I said to myself, it is a plane. Without waiting to hear any more, I took off in one leap, like a wild deer, for the airfield. My heart was pounding for joy to think the plane was coming at last, after so long a wait. I shaded my eyes and stared upward, eager for my first look. But I could see nothing. Even what I had thought to be the hum of the motor faded. I began to think it was all an illusion, that in my anxiety I had been hearing things. I turned away from the airfield. Then, like the strains of sweet music, I heard the plane again, far in the distance. Only this time it was coming from a different direction. It grew louder. It might be a military plane, I thought, or even a Shell Company plane. Could it be just passing over? No, it was coming closer now, headed right for our mission station. It must be our plane. Before I could get to the airfield, I saw the little craft, bright yellow against the blue and white of the sky. It circled the field several times to have a good look, then lowered and came in for a landing.

I shouted to all within earshot. Marie and the children were already running, along with a number of Indians. We greeted those MAF pilots, who were strangers to us, as the dearest friends on earth.

The strain was off. There followed one of the happiest occasions of our lives.

The MAF pilots staggered into the house under loads of such delicacies as we had forgotten ever existed. They piled on the kitchen table hams, cheese, cocoa, raisins, potatoes, and fresh vegetables. We just stood and looked at them.

Thoughtful Marj Saint, Nate's wife, had even sent us trays of ice cubes from her kerosene refrigerator at Shell Mera. Tepid lemonade we drank almost every day – we had lemons in abundance at Makuma from trees Ernest Johnson and the Indians had planted years before – but lemonade with ice cubes was something out of this world.

As in a dream, we walked into the front room with our guests to sit and drink lemonade and talk, talk, talk. It was so good to hear other voices again and the news of the outside world.

Our mood of celebration did not last long. In the stack of mail the pilots had brought was an urgent letter for me. I went off to one side, opened, and read it. The letter was a reminder that I was to attend a session of our missionary field council which was meeting in Riobamba. The plane was to leave again within the hour. My instructions were to fly to Shell Mera with the pilots. Our happy social hour came to an end all too soon, as I packed my bag for leaving. Marie made it easier for me by being such a good sport about it. In a few minutes I was walking out to the plane with the pilots, suitcase in my hand, having tasted no more of the goodies than my delicious glass of ice-cold lemonade.

Within a week I was back again. This time I brought with me Keith and Doris Austin, our close friends from Bible school days in Minneapolis. With us also was Dorothy Walker. Sparkling-eyed, witty, and friendly as well as talented and trained, she was coming to do Bible translation and language analysis.

The plane was on regular service now. On successive trips it brought in one-hundred-pound sacks of flour and sugar, cans of powdered milk and gasoline, and even plastic pants for Ross-boy.

A happy time of working with friends – new and old – was ahead. As soon as Keith and Doris Austin and Dorothy Walker were established in Makuma, Marie and I left for Guayaquil to await the birth of our third child.

Hobey Lowrance flew us to Shell Mera where we stopped to spend a few days with Nate and Marj Saint. Nate greeted us with his characteristic grin, wanting to know how the 'yardbirds' were doing in the backwoods. Marie and Marj met for the first time and were soon chatting like old friends.

They were all busy people. The MAF had established headquarters here. Hobey did the flying, Nate the building, repairing, and odd jobs, although his back was in a cast and he could not stoop. Marj operated the radio with which they maintained contact with the plane. Receiving sets had not yet been installed in the mission stations.

Their house was almost always filled with guests. When Marj was swamped with tracking the plane flights by radio, or doing the bookkeeping, bread-baking, washing, or entertaining, Nate often gave her a hand with the housework or tending the baby.

Shell Mera was a new experience for our children, who had no memory of anything beyond our settlement in the green jungle. Reluctantly, we all left the warm oasis of hospitality and traveled to Guayaquil. On 10 August, 1949, Irene Marie Drown was born. Within three weeks we were on our way back to Makuma.

During our absence, Hobey Lowrence with the help of HCJB radio technicians had placed short-wave radio sets in each of the jungle stations. Regular morning contacts were maintained between MAF at Shell Mera and each of the isolated outposts serviced by the plane. The two-way communication was an invaluable addition to MAF's operation. Now we could relay weather reports before scheduled flights and keep in constant touch with the plane. Never again would a plane go down without its position being known.

The Austins and Dorothy had moved into the Johnsons' house and done some remodeling. We all began working with the Indians in an earnest effort to learn the language, recording long lists of words and phrases and discussing better ways of writing down the strange sounds. The vowels gave us particular trouble. We discovered that under certain circumstances they were nasalized and under others they were whispered. Such minute variations could change the entire meaning of a word. 'Oh,' Keith would say upon hearing a Shuara word ending in a voiceless vowel, 'there is one of those things you don't hear and you don't say, but you have to write.'

Keith and I carried out the manual work of the station, clearing more land and building a schoolhouse for Shuara girls. Dorothy ran the dispensary, worked on language analysis, and helped with the routine housework. Marie and Doris looked after the little ones and helped sew clothing for the Shuara school children.

Ever since I had been shown the pieces of pottery I longed to take the gospel to the neighboring Atshuara tribe. Now I had a companion who would go with me. Keith and I had many talks and prayed for the day to come. But any mention of this plan to the Shuara was met with dismay and fear. None in our area had friendly relations with the Atshuara; in fact, they regarded them as their most hated enemies. We heard repeated references to the head-shrinking of an Atshuara named Chiriapa by Big Saantu and his gang.

One day Pitur, the Shuara whose baby had been so severely burned, came to see us after having been away on a long trip. He had cautiously traveled over the 'no-man's land' that lay between us and the Atshuara, and visited an influential Shuara leader named Taisha who lived on the very edge of Atshuara territory.

When I heard this I eagerly asked him to tell me more about Taisha. Did he know any friendly Atshuara? And would Taisha consider taking me to visit them?

To my delight, Pitur stated that since Chief Taisha jealously maintained his neutrality in order to carry on his somewhat shaky trade relations with the Atshuara, he might consent to take us to some of their homes.

This was our first indication of a possible contact with the Atshuara and we were quick to take advantage of it.

# CHAPTER SEVEN
# WHERE CHRIST
# HAS NOT BEEN NAMED

It has always been my ambition to preach the gospel
where Christ was not known (Romans 15:20).

Keith and I had been waiting for a lull in the demanding routine
of Makuma station's growing activities. As soon as we found
one we prepared to leave to carry the gospel to the Atshuara. I
could not have asked for a better comrade. Keith was quiet,
studious, and uncomplaining about the rigors of jungle life. We
laughed together to think how it would have sounded, back when
we were students in Minneapolis, if someone had told us that
one day we would be fellow voyagers in a dugout canoe headed
down the Makuma River.

Having already bid our families goodbye, we stood watching
on the river bank that steaming morning while the five Shuara
that were to go with us lowered our crafts into the water. These
consisted of a cargo raft with an elevated platform on which
would go our food, bedding, clothes, phonograph, records, and
goods for trading; and a dugout canoe in which two Indians,

Keith, and I would follow.

We couldn't help admiring the workmanship of the sturdy raft which the Indians had put together with only a machete, stones, and the strength and skill of their hands. It consisted of five twenty-foot balsa logs lashed together with tough vines and strips of inner tree bark wound around hardwood pegs. They hadn't used a nail or a screw anywhere.

The Indians managing the raft were Saantu, Naicta, and Tangamash. In the case of Saantu – the Shuara corruption of the Spanish word Santo, meaning saint – the name was ironic; this slender boy with the black unkempt hair and hollow eyes was anything but saintly. We called him Little Saantu, so as not to confuse him with Big Saantu, the witch doctor. We had heard that Little Saantu, too, was studying to be a witch doctor.

We stepped gingerly into the canoe and shoved off behind the raft. What lay in store for us? We did not know.

In the canoe with us were Pitur who knew Chief Taisha, and Jeencham. Pitur stood in the stern, paddling and watching for rocks and rapids ahead. Jeencham poled the canoe along from the prow. A son of old Washicta, he was a very good hunter. He often came to the mission, bringing wild tapir, deer, or monkey meat to sell to us. None of these men were Christians at the time and it had taken some persuasion to get them to go along.

We started out peacefully enough. Both raft and dugout slid smoothly and quickly over the deep quiet pools of the Makuma. But the river was not always peaceful. Every few minutes the pools dissolved into the white waters of angry rapids swirling over sharp-toothed rocks. Whenever we could, we kept our seats and shot the rapids as we came to them. But there were times when we had to jump overboard and guide the canoe through from alongside.

We had not gone very far when at the end of a long narrow gorge we came to a falls four feet high. The Shuara took the raft over first. They lashed tough vines to the sides, maneuvering the raft from either bank, and began to inch it slowly over the falls. Their grip could not falter an instant, or the swift waves pounding against great rocks could beat the raft into matchsticks. All was going well, when suddenly the raft caught. One side reared upward and the other tipped down until our cargo was nearly under water. At this point Naicta gave an almost superhuman tug. The raft righted itself once more and our cargo was saved from a soaking. Getting the canoe across was much easier by comparison.

As nightfall approached, our muscles were quite sore and we were glad to stop and make camp.

We built a fire and put some rice and beans on to cook. The Indians went off into the brush to find the right kind of leaves and poles to build a good shelter. We tried to impress on them that they must bring enough leaves to build a big one with a thick roof to keep us dry in case it rained.

I had too many memories of wet and miserable nights spent under poorly made shelters. At first the musical and rhythmical sounds of raindrops falling on the leaves have a soothing effect. You welcome them, thinking they're going to help you fall asleep. But as soon as the leaves are soaked, the drips start coming through and the cold water splashing on your face isn't exactly conducive to sweet dreaming.

This time the Indians brought plenty of leaves; we built a rainproof shelter and settled down for the night.

On the next day's travel we left the hills behind. The river widened. There were fewer rapids and longer quiet pools through which our canoe and raft sped swiftly. In the course of the afternoon I shot a wild turkey and Keith caught a fish; we had meat for supper that night.

Afterward we sat by the campfire along the river bank and pored over a map given us by the Shell Oil Company. We were trying to see where we were. The Indians were uneasy, as they knew we were close to Atshuara territory. Naicta, the most talkative of the five, insisted that he knew our position better than our foreign-made map. 'We're not in white man's country now, and only we Shuara can tell exactly where we are,' he said. 'Didn't I go through this very spot years ago on my way to Atshuara Chiriapa's house?'

'Oh,' Keith said, 'were you not perhaps with that group of Shuara that went with Catani and Big Saantu to avenge the deaths of Catani's father and brothers? Tell us about it.'

Though Naicta at first was reticent about revealing this dark episode from his past, he gradually opened up and told the story:

Just upstream from this spot where we are sitting, Catani took us to the house where his father and brothers had been killed. The house had been abandoned; it was now a resting place of the dead. We were almost sixty men who entered that ghostly room. We stood staring in silence at the four mounds in the center of the dirt floor. Here were buried Catani's relatives who had been killed by enemy Atshuara warriors.

The sight of those graves made everyone so furious all they could think of was killing. We hurried on to Catani's house. Our leaders repeated the war challenge many times in neighboring houses until nearly a hundred men were ready to go. Three of the witch doctors in the group passed the night drinking *natema*. Under its influence, evil spirits appeared to them, making it plain that an Atshuara named Chiriapa was the one they should kill.

As the roosters crowed the next morning, we started down the trail. After walking two days without coming to any houses, we knew we were getting close to our enemy. Being hungry by this time, we shot and roasted wild turkeys that were easy to find around there.

The next morning, we couldn't go on without making sure that the spirit beings wanted each of us to take part in this war. Fearfully we asked each other, 'Have you seen anything in your dreams that assured you that you can go on safely?'

One said, 'I saw the *pangi* (water boa) come up out of the river. He appeared to me, promising that in his might I would win.'

Another said, 'I saw the devil himself, looking like a mighty Shuara warrior. "It is I, the leader of the spirit world," he said. "I will help you. With my power you will be victorious."'

Others said they had seen spirits in the form of the ocelot, the jaguar, and different kinds of birds, which told them that they would be the victors.

But there were also those whose dreams revealed danger and defeat. One such said, 'I dreamed maggots were eating a hole in the calf of my leg. Therefore I must get back to my own home.'

Another said, 'In my dream a dog ran at me and bit me. So I'm going back, too.'

Another, 'I saw myself rolling into the fire and burning my side. I cannot go on.'

Many left the party then. Only half of us remained to carry on the war. We could not disobey the commands of the spirits. If those with bad dreams had gone on they would surely have been killed.

We found the *sua* tree. From its small fruit we made a black dye in which we dipped balls of cotton and painted wide stripes and designs on our faces and bodies so it would be harder for our enemies to see us against the shadows of the jungle. We chanted back and forth to each other:

> Now we've become black, black with the sua;
> It won't be long now, we're getting close.
> Tomorrow we'll arrive
> Because we're black.

One of our men, named Anang, did not blacken himself as much as the rest. Foolishly thinking he did not need it, he used only a little.

Walking down the trail we came to a stream that flowed by Chiriapa's house. The seasoned leaders said, 'We're on the Wild Pig's trail now. It won't be long.' We snickered at this insult to our enemy.

When we came to three trails, all of which led to Chiriapa's house, we hid ourselves and crouched in the brush the rest of the day. Even though our food supply was gone and we were very hungry, the hope that Chiriapa would come walking down one of those trails and into our ambush kept us from turning back. As the sun dropped below the trees we closed in around the clearing. Silently and with trembling knees we approached the house only to discover no one was at home.

As it began to get dark, we felt like giving up the hunt. Someone said, 'Let's go back. Let's go home.' But Catani shamed us into staying as he snarled, 'Why did you think I called you here? Are you weak women? No one is going back until our brothers' deaths are avenged!' Even though I wanted to go home, I couldn't.

Anang did not have any shirt and he felt chilled in the cool early evening. He put on someone else's shirt but soon took it off again, saying, 'I don't feel right. This shirt makes me weak and short of breath.' Everyone wondered why he should talk like that.

By the light of palm-wood torches we searched the surrounding jungle until someone found footprints leading away from the house. Assured that Chiriapa and his family had made them, we followed slowly and silently, stopping often throughout the night to rest. But since we couldn't see well we kept stepping on thorns and tripping over vines. Our feet were badly cut and bleeding before the night was over. Just before dawn we came to a banana and cassava patch and, knowing the house was nearby, we snuffed out our torches.

A lone cock's crow startled us all. 'We're here now,'

Catani whispered. 'Let's rush them. If you see a woman, catch her. If you see a man, shoot him. But don't shoot his head. We want that whole. All right, you men from the hills, don't lose your nerve! Give it to 'em!'

We surrounded the clearing and waited, shaking not only from the cold but also from fear. Through the brush and banana leaves we could see the stockade wall. In the morning stillness we could hear the slight creaking of a bamboo bedrack. Someone was beginning to stir.

Suddenly the dogs started to bark. Then a man's voice gruffly shouted, 'Woman! Get up! Don't you hear the dogs? Our enemies must be outside. The Hill People are after us. The Mura Shuara have come. They have come to avenge the death of their brothers. Get up! Do you not hear their footsteps?'

We looked at each other as we thought to ourselves, 'Chiriapa's home all right.'

Then we heard a woman's voice saying, 'Why do you always talk like that? There are no enemies outside. The noise you heard was only a possum knocking a papaya from a tree. Even the dogs have stopped barking.'

Feeling relieved at her words, we looked at each other, hopeful of not being discovered.

But again Chiriapa shouted as though he knew we were just outside. Ever since the killing he had been fearful we would retaliate.

'Listen, you head-shrinkers, I hear you! Come on, if you want to fight. You'll find out who is the strongest. Have I not killed many of your men? I will finish off the rest of you.'

'Oh hush!' snapped another of his women. 'You are always saying that the Mura Shuara are after you. Wasn't it just a short time ago that you killed some of them? They are too cowardly to come again so soon. No one is outside now!'

'Well, if you're not afraid, step outside and see if anyone

is there,' retorted Chiriapa. Then he must have changed his mind for we heard him say, 'No, you better not go. You'll surely get it if you do!'

The women laughed as they chorused sarcastically, 'You mean you love us and don't want us to get killed, ha?'

Chiriapa's only answer was the chilling sound of bullets clicking into place in his Winchester .44.

'What kind of gun does he have?' whispered one of our men.

'A carbine,' answered Catani, 'but that doesn't matter. Don't men die from shotguns, too?'

Then we heard the Atshuara call again to his women, 'Is it not broad daylight already? The cowardly Shuara will not attack us now. Let's go to the river where the chonta fruit is ripening. Bring your baskets and we'll fill them full.'

We could hear someone push open the heavy door and move toward the stockade gate. Others followed. We watched women and children file out the gate. Then came Chiriapa.

Unpainted Anang fired the first shot. He boldly stepped into the clearing and lifted his gun to fire again when Chiriapa dropped him with his big Winchester.

Then the Shuara shot from all directions. Chiriapa, realizing he was outnumbered, fled toward the house screaming, 'Mura Shuara! Mura Shuara! They have come to kill me! They have come to k—'

He fell in the doorway as a bullet tore into his back. Shuara warriors swarmed into the yard and filled the Atshuara's body full of gunshot and spears. I heard the women and children shriek as we burst into the *ekenta*.

'Take the pig's head!' shouted an old witch doctor from the Chiwasa hills. But no one stooped to touch the body. The hesitant younger men began to offer lame excuses.

'I can't cut off the head because my wife is too young. She isn't able to cook the victory feast for such a big crowd.'

'My wife has just given birth to a baby. If I touched this

dead body my newborn one would die!'

None of us wanted to do it. But the old Mura Shuara from Chiwasa who was wearing a white man's black suit coat knelt beside the dead man. With a machete he slashed the neck first on one side and then on the other. It was so hard it would not cut easily. He wrenched the head back and forth with his hands, then finished cutting it off. Taking hold of the long hair, he slung the head over his shoulder and started out the door. Everyone gasped as he turned his back. The warm red blood was running down his new coat.

The veteran witch doctor commanded us all to follow him. The enemy was dead now and we had to leave quickly. The body on the ground still seemed to breathe but no one paid any attention to it. Before following the bloodstained one, the Shuara hurriedly ransacked the house of everything valuable: bead necklaces, blowguns and quivers, ammunition, dogs, children, and women. When one of Big Saantu's sons picked up a young girl, no one had to force her mother to go, too. 'Don't take my little girl alone!' she cried. 'Her father was killed by his enemies and now you killed my third husband. Don't take away my only child. Take me also.'

We let her come with us. Then someone noticed one of the women was missing. We knew she had gone for help and that we could not stay there any longer.

I ran outside the house, wrapped Anang in a length of cloth, lifted him to my back and fled as quickly as I could from the Atshuara clearing. Moans from the suffering one and wails from the old mother filled our ears as we hurried over the trail. Before noon the moans ceased and some of us stopped long enough to bury Anang along the road. Fear that pursuing enemies would overtake us conquered our hunger and weariness and forced us to leave Atshuara country faster than we had entered it. By noon we caught up with the rest alongside the river.

There knelt the old man with the head. He was cutting at the neck in an effort to separate the skin from the skull. Turning the soft fresh skin inside out as he cut, he pulled it over the jawbones, chin, nose, and eyes, being careful not to cut the nose cartilage from the skin. Quickly he threw the skull into the river and filled the head-skin with sand and small stones. Although he would have preferred to build a fire to cook it then, we dared not delay that long in enemy territory. Wrapping the skin in leaves, he placed it in a basket on his back and ran with us through the forest.

The next day, when we arrived at Catani's house, the old man placed the head-skin in a cooking pot filled with water and brought it to a boil, holding it by the hair all the while. Allowing it to simmer only briefly, he pulled it out and laid it on a leaf to cool. Then with a sharp thorn he pierced two small holes on top of the scalp through which he securely fastened a long piece of jungle fiber. Carefully searing the lips with a heated machete, he pinned them shut with slivers of black palmwood and used more of the twisted fiber to tie them in place. With an air of pleased triumph the old man stood to his feet and carried his trophy to a stream to wash and scrape off any loose flesh. Then he handed it to one of the younger men who took it up the bank to the clearing. There the younger Shuara filled the head-skin with hot sand and stones and closed the neck opening with a tough vine. Then, grasping the end of the vine, he swung the head in circles. After he repeated this process several times with changes of hot sand and stones, he rubbed charcoal into the face and neck and ears.

As we began the trip back to Saantu's house, all the women except the one little girl were left with Catani. Big Saantu insisted he have this one as his fourth wife and also insisted the head be taken to his house for the first feast.

Along the journey the head was carefully wrapped in rags and carried in a waterproof basket. At night the men unwrapped it to see if the spirit of the dead man had eaten part of it. Each day the hot sand and charcoal treatment was repeated and each day the head grew smaller, drier, and blacker. The eye and ear openings, now less than a third their original size, were nearly closed and the neck hole would barely admit a man's thumb. With each passing day our pride in the shrunken trophy increased. The *tsantsa* was a symbol of our triumph and victory instead of a loathsome, terrifying head of our Atshuara enemy. No one was afraid to touch it now.

We sent runners to Big Saantu's to tell his wives that we were on our way home with the *tsantsa*.

Shuara from all over the valley and hills arrived to help prepare the feast and share in it. The day we victors returned to Big Saantu's house the women, having heard us call from a long way off, stood in the doorway eagerly awaiting the first glimpse of the *tsantsa* and the victorious warriors who were bringing it. One of the men from the house hurried to the edge of the clearing and placed a stool on the ground and a large wooden shield on top of that. As the men began to appear from the forest trail, the women sang:

The victors have arrived:
The victors have arrived.
The *tsantsa* they have brought
The black trophy is ours.
Now our hearts will be happy and at rest
Because our enemy is no more.
He is dead and we have won the victory.
Great is the one who took his life.
Is he not a Shuara?
He is the victor.

When we all gathered in the clearing, the oldest warrior took the *tsantsa,* still wrapped in rags, from the basket and placed it on the shield in the center of the group. The wives in the doorway continued to chant as four of the victorious warriors took their places beside the shield.

The old man solemnly chewed some *tsaangu* and spit a little into the nostrils of each of the four men.

These are the ones who overcome the enemy!
These are the strong, victorious Mura Shuara!

sang the wives of the ones who had killed Chiriapa. The old one took the hand of Big Saantu, and touched the *tsantsa*. Big Saantu then loosed the trophy from its rag covering and tied its fiber string around his neck, allowing the small black head with its long hair to rest on his chest. The ritual continued with the women chanting in more excited tones.

The *tsantsa* is coming, let it come in.

As the men slowly approached the house, the group stopped at intervals while the old one spit more *tsaangu* in the victors' nostrils. Finally inside the house the old witch doctor pushed Big Saantu to the center of the *tangamash*.

The old one from Chiwasa also wanted to take the little captive girl's head, but as he and the others were concentrating their attention on the ceremonies, Big Saantu's brother hid her in the *ekenta* and charged an old haggard grandmother not to let the girl out of her sight.

Meanwhile, in the *tangamash* Big Saantu lifted the *tsantsa* from his neck and raised it high in the air. All the women formed a line behind the killer and his wife in the center of the room. Each of the women wore narrow belts with innumerable dangling pieces of snail shells and hollow dried seeds tied in rows around their waists. Placing their hands on the belt of the one in front of them, they began to jump and dance a few steps forward, then backward, in time with the chanting. The shells and seeds on the forty jiggling belts clinked and rattled with the accented rhythm. The rest of the men sat and watched while the dance continued with each of the four victors and their wives taking turns holding the *tsantsa* and leading the dancers.

After the dancing, the feasting began and continued with much drinking and sexual revelry for three days. The *tsantsa* was fastened to a stick and placed beside the narrow doorway to the *tangamash* where all who entered or left the room brushed by its long hair.

Only the main killers could not take part in the riotous celebrating. Since the spirit of the dead enemy would be especially angry with those who had led in the murder, they needed to stay alert and in their right senses lest an evil curse befall them. Such a curse would rob them of victory in succeeding wars and make them easy victims of some disaster. A tree might fall on them, or a snake bite them, or lightning strike them.

After the days of riotous feasting, visiting Shuara kept coming to the house to see the *tsantsa* and the captive Atshuara girl. Although accounts of revenge killing were common talk among Shuara, few of them had the courage and the time during a killing raid to take their victim's head. And none had kept a captive Atshuara girl as his wife. They pointed and laughed at the frightened child as she blew the fire for Big Saantu's women, who were bitter with jealousy and hate. Hunching her shoulders in imitation of the enemy captive, one of them sneered, 'Doesn't she look like a turtle?'

'She is afraid and draws her head into her shell!' jeered another amid uproarious laughter.

Hearing angry voices from the *tangamash,* the women stopped to listen. The old black-coated man who had cut off the head was determined to take the trophy to his house in the even higher hill country.

'If you do not give me the *tsantsa* then I will make another from the head of the captive girl,' he threatened.

After much arguing Big Saantu and his men finally consented to give up the head. 'But first we will cut off some of the hair,' they said. 'Then we can fasten it on a gourd with some tar and make another *tsantsa*. We must have another big feast after a year with the gourd *tsantsa* in order to insure continued help from the spirits and future victories in war!'

Naicta added that Big Saantu and his men prepared a gourd *tsantsa* and planted large gardens in preparation for another big feast. All but the 'Little Turtle' looked forward to it. She cried continually during the first weeks she was in Big Saantu's house. But gradually as Big Saantu showed her special favors and the other wives begrudgingly accepted her, she became a part of the household. Later she bore him a little daughter and became almost contented.

But Keith and I knew Big Saantu's fourth wife still lived in a cloud of fear. She would never walk the trail with anyone but her powerful husband, and rarely came to our side of the river for fear some Indian from the hills might see her and try to kill her. And we also knew that the war between the Makuma Shuara and the Atshuara could flare up again at any time.

After hearing these terrible incidents we did not blame our Shuara companions for being afraid. Did we dare hope that one day so many Shuara would go into Atshuara territory, not to make war and shrink heads, but to share Christian love with their one-time enemies? Knowing that with God all things are possible, we determined to keep on with our efforts.

That night we could not get to sleep without praying both for the Shuara and the Atshuara.

The next morning we had gone only a little way when we sighted a canoe with a lone paddler coming upstream. Since setting out on our journey we had not seen an Indian or a house along the banks. Our Indians gave the familiar Shuara call 'tu-u-u- u-u-u-u-u-u-u.' But the paddler did not answer. Instead, he did a quick right about face and sped away out of sight. Perhaps he thought we were enemies on our way to stage a surprise attack. We wondered if this were a sample of the reception we might expect.

A short distance downstream we saw a house. We hoped this was Chief Taisha's place, since, according to our map, we should now be approaching it. Here we planned to make our headquarters.

We moored our canoe, 'tu-u-u-u-ing' loudly to announce our arrival. After making our way through gardens of plantain, cassava, and sweet potatoes, we had a chance to study the large house before us. The first thing that attracted our attention was the roof. The leaves were woven much closer together and in a different pattern from the Shuara roofs around the Upper Makuma. Otherwise it looked just the same. We felt this must be Chief Taisha's house.

Swinging aside the four poles of bamboo hanging in the narrow doorway, we stepped out of the glaring sunlight into a large room so dark it took a while for our eyes to get adjusted. We saw before us a figure seated in the center of the *tangamash* wearing only a knee-length loincloth. Long wavy hair hung loosely over his plump shoulders. This was Chief Taisha. Without a word he motioned us all to be seated on the various stumps and platform beds scattered about the room. Two women entered from the *ekenta* with clay bowls of *chicha,* which they proceeded to serve to everyone but Keith and me.

Continuing to ignore us, the chief turned to Pitur, the only one in our group he knew. Their salutations were long and explosive. Both men talked at once, sometimes repeating the words the other had just uttered, sometimes introducing new phrases. It sounded as though each knew in advance what the other was going to say. But when we heard Pitur giving an account of our trip, we knew that it was not altogether rehearsed.

Chief Taisha then addressed each member of the group by turn, indulging in the same long-drawn salutations with each one. The singsong pattern was the same for all five, although the details differed.

When he had finished, the Chief turned toward Pitur and asked him to interpret for me, but Pitur told him that Panchu could speak Shuara for himself. After a couple of false starts, the head man slowed his pace of speaking to match mine and from then on we had little trouble understanding each other. I told him we had come down the river as friends to bring him a message from God; that it was our aim to take the same message to all the Atshuara people. For this, I said, we would need his help to guide us and to introduce us as friends. He seemed agreeable enough to the idea, but hastened to point out that since the Atshuara families he knew had all been warring with each other recently, he couldn't very well take us to visit them. The people were too nervous and fearful at this time. We were dismayed. Had we come all this way for nothing? The chief was silent. Then he seemed to have a happy afterthought. He did know a Shuara, he said, who had married an Atshuara woman. He suggested that we get that man to take us to his wife's family.

This possibility cheered us considerably. But not our Indian companions. They had talked bravely enough in faraway Makuma, but now with news of war just across the river it was a different story. They flatly refused to leave Chief Taisha's house. After having listened to their stories on the trip down here, even Keith and I began to have our doubts.

Chief Taisha promised to put us up, so our Shuara went back to the river bank to bring our gear, while we settled in. By nightfall some fifteen men had come to have a look at us and at the goods we brought for trading.

When they were all gathered after supper, we got out the portable phonograph and began to play the gospel records that Ernest Johnson and fellow missionaries Mr. and Mrs. George Moffat had made in Shuara. Then we began to sing some hymns and choruses we had learned. After we had their attention, I tried to tell them who God was and what He had done for them. Like all Shuara, they were curious to know what God's Word had to say about how their world began. The Genesis account was quite different from the fantastic stories in their own lore of how the rivers and forests, the sun and the stars, had been formed. They were especially interested in the story of their ancestors, Adam and Eve, and how they had sinned against God.

But I had to explain very slowly. Since they were hearing these biblical truths for the first time, they could not grasp too many new thoughts at once. Besides, there were not enough words in my limited Shuara vocabulary, nor in all their language, to express some of these ideas clearly. They knew the devil as ruler of the world of evil spirits, and they feared him. Hell, they believed in as a place of punishment and torment for the souls of men after death, and to all of them it was inescapable.

Through all this, Pitur, Naicta, Tangamash, Saantu, and Jeencham sat listening with smug piety. By their remarks to the members of Chief Taisha's household we could tell they were giving the impression that they already knew and believed in everything the missionaries were teaching. They had sung loudly with us and pretended to great saintliness, although most of them had not attended services regularly at Makuma nor professed to be Christians there. Nevertheless, when I had finished they were surprisingly helpful in making my message clearer to my listeners. How I longed for the day when they would truly be able to preach the Word with real understanding and power!

We spent the next day visiting other houses in the area, repeating the creation and Adam and Eve accounts and God's forgiveness wherever we went. In every house we asked the men if they would take us to the Atshuara. But nobody would. Late that afternoon we had just returned to Chief Taisha's house and were making ready for another evening teaching time when a new group of Indians appeared in the clearing. They were picturesquely dressed. The men were clothed in new, brightly-striped *itipis*. Their hair at the back was twisted into ponytails, wrapped with hand-woven belting, and decorated with the brilliant red-and-yellow feathers of the toucan bird. They had bound their long sideburns tightly with string so that they stood out stiffly from their faces like front pigtails. In their ear-lobes were pieces of reed about ten inches long.

Again we had to wait through the customary salutations which took about an hour before we could learn who they were. Finally I found out that the key man of the group was the very one I was looking for. After visiting with him a while he readily consented to take us to his brother-in-law, an Atshuara named Timas.

The Bible teaching and discussion that evening continued for a long time. There were more questions to be answered, more truths to be explained. The Indians were impressed by the fact that we had left our homes and families and undertaken a journey of several days, neither to exploit them nor to attack them, but only to bring them God's Word and the good news of salvation. Although they did not understand all we had to say, they accepted us as friends.

Early next morning we reloaded some of our gear in the canoe and started downstream again with the visiting Shuara brother-in-law, our new-found guide. I mentioned to Keith that I could feel the opposition of the evil spirits. A feeling of heaviness seemed to oppress us. Jeencham, unable to overcome his fears, stayed behind in Chief Taisha's house. Without him we pushed ahead.

We must have traveled about six hours when our guide gave us the signal to beach the canoe by a barely noticeable trail. It took us about an hour of steady walking before we came to the typical Indian clearing which told us we were approaching a house.

Suddenly, out of nowhere, came a high-pitched shout:

'Don't come any closer! Go back where you came from!

We don't want any strange Shuara or white men here!'

We stopped in our tracks. Our guide, who knew the voice, went ahead to see what was the matter. The rest of us followed. Since we could sense trouble ahead, we felt it would be better to gather in the house than to be scattered outside.

The house was on the other side of the clearing. We approached it cautiously and went in. Inside were a lone young man and several women and children. An ominous silence greeted us. There were no singsong salutations. The women made no move to serve any *chicha*. Timas, the head of the house, was not to be seen. Something seemed to have gone wrong. Our guide looked at us nervously and motioned to us to sit down. Then, turning to the frightened young man beside him, he began to talk very fast:

'Don't be afraid. These men have not come to kill. They want to make friends with you. They have brought some cloth and knives to trade. But more than that, they have come to tell you what the great Creator God has written in His Book... Now send for Timas. Let him know what I have told you and ask him to come back into the house. Tell him I have brought friends to visit him.'

As soon as he had finished, one of the young women slipped out of the house. She was gone for quite a long time while we all sat around and looked at each other in silence. Presently she returned, went straight up to the young man, and whispered something in his ear. The young Indian looked even more terrified than before. Haltingly, he relayed to our guide what the woman had told him.

She had seen Timas who informed her flatly that he would not receive us and ordered us to leave immediately. If we did not, he would come back and kill us all.

That was enough for our Makuma Shuara. They did not need to be told twice. They all tore out of the house and started running back to the river and the canoe. But our guide stood his ground and Keith and I stayed with him. After a time he sent another messenger to Timas, again trying to convince him that we were friends and meant no harm. Again the word came back. He was angry now with his brother-in-law for having brought strangers to his house; and if he did not take us away at once, he would kill him, too.

I was fearful now myself. I had the impulse to run, like our Shuara. But if I ran, it would indicate to the Atshuara that we had really come to kill them. Only by walking slowly could we show them that we had come on a friendly mission. We did so, all the way to the river bank, even though it took plenty of willpower.

When we reached the river we found that the four men from Makuma already had the dugout pointed upstream. Our guide stood on the bank to bid us goodbye.

I took a new knife from my pack and handed it to him. 'The next time you see Timas give him this,' I said. 'I want him to know that I am his friend.'

We cast off. Naicta paddled the canoe away from the bank and out into the middle of the stream. 'Why give him that good knife?' he muttered in disgust. 'Why not give him a few bullets from the end of your gun instead?'

'What he needs is to be shown the love of Christ,' I answered. Naicta did not seem to understand. He just shook his head and paddled faster.

By nightfall we reached the house of a friendly Shuara about halfway back to Chief Taisha's. Five men with their wives and children were at home, and we used the opportunity that evening to play our records and once again tell of man's rebellion and God's love. We doubted that they would ever have the chance to hear God's Word again.

Shortly before noon next day we found ourselves back at Chief Taisha's house. That evening we made the most of our last opportunity to explain salvation and sing to Chief Taisha and his friends.

Now we had to prepare for the long trip home. But Pitur, knowing better than we how impossible it would be to paddle upstream, had sold the canoe. We therefore gave the raft away, packed our gear on our backs, and started off on foot. Soon we found ourselves in the swampy jungle 'no-man's-land.'

Three days of steady walking and we were back once more at the mission station. Our wives and children came running to meet us. In spite of our muddy, bedraggled appearance and our twelve days' growth of beard, they smothered us with happy hugs and kisses. Disappointed though we were about not having made friends with any Atshuara, we could only think then how wonderful it was to be home!

Several months later we learned of the narrow escape we had had on our visit to Timas' house, and of how only God's protection had miraculously intervened to save us from death. Timas had told the story to another Atshuara, who in turn repeated it to a Shuara. It was a long time reaching us, but we listened with amazement as the Shuara related it:

On that afternoon when we were walking down the trail from Timas' house to the river bank, Timas himself was crouched in ambush in the underbrush. He was so fearful of us that he had made up his mind to kill the last man in our party to walk by. This was common practice, as it was easier for the killer to get away. First he saw the Shuara fleeing, then Keith, followed by our guide. I was the last man.

'I waited with my gun cocked,' ran Timas' story. 'As I saw the forms of the Shuara and the white men through the bushes, I tensed my muscles. I was ready to pick off my man. I pointed my gun to his head. Then my arm went weak. My finger would not move. I could not shoot even though I wanted to.'

God who stopped the mouths of the lions for Daniel had stopped the trigger finger of Timas that day on the Atshuara trail.

# CHAPTER EIGHT
# NEW CREATIONS IN CHRIST

Therefore, if anyone is in Christ, he is a new creation;
the old has gone, the new has come!
(2 Corinthians 5:17).

The Indians looked at me in wonder and disbelief. Some laughed. One asked: 'Why do you need another house, Panchu? Do you not already have one for yourself and your family, one for the single lady, one for the church, one for the boys' school, others for the chickens, the wood, and the gasoline? Why do you need a new one?'

'This is not a house for me,' I replied. 'This is to be a school house for your girls.'

'Our girls?'

'We want them to come live here, to learn to read and write and know God just as your sons are doing. We will give them new clothes and medicines and good food. They will learn to be happy, as God wants them to be. That's why I am building this house.'

More explosive laughter and rude comments from the Indians. Clearly, they did not want their girls to go to school.

'Don't you know we give our girls in marriage when they are very young?' said one. 'Why should they learn to read and write? They only need to know how to work hard in the garden, to cook and serve their husbands well.'

'What good will it do them to learn about God?' put in another. 'Girls are like dogs who have no souls anyway.'

'We will build this house,' I insisted, 'because I know it is what God wants me to do. I have talked it over with many of your people. Two have promised to send their girls. Even if no others come we will build this house.'

When the building was finished and ready for opening day, seven little girls came. They slept and ate and attended classes all in the same building. Their teacher, a young Ecuadorian student from the Berean Bible Institute in Guayaquil, had her room at one end of the schoolhouse and cared for the girls day and night. Señor Segundo and Señora Rosa took charge of cooking the meals for both boys and girls, who ate separately.

The girls came to us wearing the only clothes they owned – a single ragged dress apiece. One barely had enough rags to cover herself, so Marie quickly snatched up one of her own dresses and put it on her. We soon gave them bright, ready-made print dresses that we had bought for them.

The girls, unlike the boys, were no disciplinary problem, since they were used to submitting to constant watchfulness over their lives and were not inclined to run away. But because of their backgrounds, they were extremely shy. If a girl in a Shuara household opens her mouth in the presence of men, she is considered bold. At first it was hard to get them to say so much as *buenos días* to the teacher. They had never had any freedom of choice nor any chance to think for themselves. In the presence of boys in joint chapel sessions they shriveled into silence. Whatever they did learn had to be drummed into them, over and over again. They responded somewhat to the white chalk, blackboards, and colored pictures, and they enjoyed singing hymns. They loved playing with each other. For the first time in their lives they had a chance to laugh and be carefree.

The next year our enrollment of girls increased to ten. But running the schools was not without its handicaps. For one thing, our missionary staff was suddenly reduced to ourselves and Dorothy Walker. The Berean Bible Institute was moving its headquarters from Guayaquil to Shell Mera and was in desperate need of more teachers. Keith and Doris Austin felt called of God to go and help in training Ecuadorian youth to know and preach the gospel. From among these students would one day come missionaries to the Shuara. We missed the Austins' help and fellowship greatly.

There were other problems. We could hold sessions for only four months of the year, both because we were not producing enough food from our gardens and because of the restlessness of the Indian boys. Their fathers taught them hunting and fishing, house-building, cloth-weaving and basket-making, fashioning combs and feather decorations for their hair, and the strategy of tribal warfare. Otherwise, they did as they pleased. They had never been used to following any set routine or taking any home responsibilities. Most of them had never had a spanking. Selfish, independent, and irresponsible, they came to school when they felt like it and ran away when anything displeased them.

When the weather was dry, the rivers were low and they played hooky to go fishing. When the weather was wet, they stayed home by the fire to keep warm. They would disappear if they didn't like what they had to eat, or if they thought the teacher was too hard on them. The parents didn't think enough of the school to force them to come and we had to keep constant pressure on them.

It was difficult to get either boys or girls to speak up in class. If they weren't completely sure of the answer to a question by the teacher, they'd rather keep still than shame themselves by making a mistake in front of the others.

Then there was the food situation. Half-starved most of the time, their appetites were insatiable. We cleared more land and planted more gardens. But plantain and cassava take a whole year to mature. Any strong wind would blow down the plantain trees and foraging animals would dig up and eat the cassava. Our efforts were continually frustrated. We didn't get much help from the Indians. They seemed to us too lazy, for the most part, to grow enough for themselves, let alone any extra to sell to us.

Food, clothing, and medicines were persuasive factors in getting the Indians to send their children to school. We gave them meat more often than they had at home. Rock salt and brown sugar were attractive delicacies. So long as we fed and clothed the youngsters, the parents didn't care what we taught them. None foresaw that in time their children's *shuartica* would give way to *Yus shuartica* (Christian custom).

At the end of the second year of school came a heartening sign of progress – something for which every missionary strives – the first baptismal service. It would be held in the waters of the Makuma River at the close of three days of Bible teaching for everyone.

This was a real turning-point. To us it was a fulfillment of our purpose in coming to Ecuador. For the first time in the history of the Makuma mission there were Shuara Christians who wanted to be baptized. These jungles had never before witnessed such a ceremony. There had been times when we feared we would never hear a Christian confession of faith from the lips of a Makuma Shuara. But now here in our midst were five young men and women who had renounced the evil ways of their people. They wanted to make plain that their lives had been changed and that from then on they would live for Christ.

From our own point of view, it was the climax of our first five-and-a-half-year missionary term in Ecuador. From the point of view of the Indians, it was a strange white man's ritual that had no meaning, except to those being baptized. The home life and tribal customs of the converts had been a constant hindrance to their relating to Christ with love and obedience. *Shuartica* was really ingrained into them.

Wampiu, the oldest convert, was one of the most intelligent Indian boys I knew. In both school and church service he would fix his alert eyes on the speaker and never allow anything to distract him. It was a joy to me to watch his face while preaching, and to see mirrored there the light of understanding of scriptural truths.

The oldest son of a witch doctor who had died when Wampiu was very young, he had moved to Makuma from the Upano Valley with his mother Chingasu and stepfather Chumpi. When Mistira (as he called Ernest Johnson) first talked about God the Creator, Wampiu was on familiar ground. Most Shuara believed there was a God, and that He had made the world and all the people in it. But they had never heard that God loved them and wanted them to be with Him through all eternity. When Mistira told that God's Son, Jesus Christ, died on the cross to pay the penalty for man's sin, and how He wanted to give men new life and power to overcome sin, Wampiu did not easily understand. These words were new to him and he did not know what they meant. So he came to school daily, learned to read and write in Spanish, but above all he learned more of God's desire to forgive his sin if he would accept Jesus as payment. He now learned to know and please God the good Spirit. His faith, however, was often severely tried.

Shortly after Wampiu's conversion his younger brother fell ill with chills and fever. He was the disciple of an established witch doctor and for that reason would not yield to Wampiu's pleas to avail himself of God's help and the white man's medicines. He feared losing what power he had already attained as a novice witch doctor. An older witch doctor visited him and insisted that he keep using the *natema* drug which would increase his power as a witch. This made him even sicker, so Wampiu's mother, Chingasu, demanded that he take the dying boy to see another witch doctor. She could not understand Wampiu's refusal and kept at him with tongue-lashings until he gave in. Wampiu then set out. He carried his brother on his back over difficult jungle trails, grieving and praying for his brother and mother all the way to the house of the witch doctor.

But the brother died soon afterward. Chingasu, convinced that the first witch doctor must have put a curse on her son, demanded that Wampiu kill him to avenge his brother's death. But this time, in spite of all Chingasu could say, Wampiu steadfastly refused. *Yus shuartica* was taking the place of *shuartica* in Wampiu's life.

The other two boy believers, Tsamaraing and Jimpicti, had also been in every year's session of school. Quick-witted and given to ready laughter, they sang the hymns and choruses with gusto. They were sons of old Chief Washicta. From him they had learned to hunt birds and monkeys with a long blowgun through which they shot poison-tipped darts. They knew the names of all the creatures of the forest, winged and four-footed, and could imitate their calls. They were full of tales of the wars which dominated the conversation at home and gave accounts of the visits of witch doctors and of how they had called up evil spirits to heal the sick. When their father found he could not keep them from adopting Christian practices, he stubbornly ignored their new-found faith.

The two girls who were to be baptized were Tirisa and Pakesh. Tirisa had been in school only during the last session and showed a remarkably quick response. But she was the only Christian in her family and life was very hard for her. As a little girl she had already learned to make and serve *chicha*. Now she did not want to do it any more, because it led to drunkenness. Nor did she want to take part in the immoral feasts that followed *chicha* drinking – feasts that seemed to bring such pleasure and excitement to the rest of the family. She preferred to pray and sing and try to win her mother to faith in Christ. This set her apart from the others and made her life rather lonely. Pakesh was having similar trouble with her family. She had wanted to go to school from the time she first heard about it, even though her parents objected.

Puanshira, her father, had come home one day from the mission holding his sides with laughter. 'Guess what!' he said to Pakesh's mother in the child's presence. 'Panchu is paying me to help build a new schoolhouse for Shuara girls. Can you imagine? I told Panchu none of our girls would go. It would only make them lazy to spend their time reading white man's words.'

But Pakesh, who was then about twelve years old, listened eagerly to what her father had to say. Her two younger brothers had been going to the boys' school and often talked to her about the things they were learning. And now there was to be a school for girls! As soon as she was alone with her mother, she said: 'My brothers have told me a little about God who loves everyone and about His Son who is much more powerful than the spirit beings we know. Isn't that hard to believe? Oh, how I would like to go there and learn more. And perhaps the white people would give me a new dress the way they gave my brothers pants.'

Her mother shook her head. 'You know your father won't let you go. Neither will your grandfather, Washicta. And I'm not in favor of it myself. Don't you forget that long ago your father sold you in marriage to Icam from across the river. Three times we have gathered and eaten the fruit of the chonta tree since he and Big Saantu settled the bargain. Icam is nearly old enough now to take you as his own. Don't even think about going to school. You must stay home and learn to be a good Shuara wife.'

But Pakesh reasoned to herself: 'My father and mother know only *shuartica*. Yet they are not happy. Doesn't my father mistreat my mother? Long ago he bought a second wife and brought her to live here, then beat my mother when she cried about it. Now he has bought a third wife, one who is smaller than I am. And to pay for her, he has traded me to her brother,

Icam. When Big Saantu gave his daughter to my father, he made him promise to give me to his son. But I do not want to marry Icam. I want to go to the missionaries' school.'

When the school for Shuara girls started that year, Pakesh came with the others. What had made her parents change? Why had they let her come? It might have been because Icam was going to school and they thought it would be a good idea for her to learn to read and write as well as he. Or it might have been the new dress or the prospect of Pakesh's eating food which they wouldn't have to work for.

Whatever their reasons, Pakesh was in school and very happy to be there. She was having many enjoyments besides learning to read and write: blankets to wrap up in at night when it grew cold, instead of having to shiver by the fire; regular meals three times a day, instead of just whenever there happened to be food on hand; the weekly washing of clothes with soap, instead of letting them get stiff with dirt. And best of all was the singing about God.

'At the school they sing because they are happy,' she told her mother one Saturday on a visit home. 'Our people do not have any happy songs, do they? The witch doctor sings while treating the sick. The older men sing about hunting, or killing their enemies in war; and the women wail over the dead or dying. Are not all our songs sad or bad? The missionary songs are so happy it makes me glad to hear them.'

One morning in chapel service she knelt in prayer to confess her sins and accept Christ as her Savior. She knew God had forgiven her. Now she wanted to be baptized.

On the day of the ceremony, everyone was on hand. Some of our fellow missionaries who had played a part in preparing the young Shuara for this event traveled from far away to be with us. Ernest and Jean Johnson came from their ministry on the coast, and Mike and Ella Ficke from Sucúa. The many Indians who had arrived from different parts of the jungle were curious to know what baptism was, although some were derisive and full of distrust.

'This is not *shuartica*,' one of them remarked disapprovingly as he left the church at the end of the Bible teaching sessions and started down the steep trail toward the river bank.

'What good will it do our children to lie down under water and then come up again?' asked another.

'None at all,' retorted a third. 'Surely it won't give them any more strength to overcome their enemies. They should do as our old leaders have taught us – go up the mountain and drink the *maicua* and *tsaangu*, so that in their visions they would see the spirits of our ancestors who would make them strong warriors. If they become God's Shuara they will never go to war. What a shame!'

'Oh, they're only doing what Panchu tells them,' came another voice. 'Now that school is over they'll soon forget the white man's words and be like the rest of us again.'

'But what are the girls being baptized for?' inquired another. 'It will only make them lazy and disobedient. Look at the trouble Puanshira is already having with his daughter, Pakesh. All she wants to do is go to school and learn more about the foreigners' ways. Now she's even saying she won't marry Icam, Big Saantu's son, even though she was promised to him years ago. That shows how foolish a girl who goes to school can become.'

'We'd better be there at the ceremony,' put in a more practical-minded one. 'If we don't do what Panchu says, he might move away. Then, I ask you, where would we get our medicines and clothing and our machetes?'

So the conversation went all the way to the river bank. Then, with an audience of about a hundred Shuara lined up watching, I stood beside the three boys and two girls on a sandbar along the cool waters of the Makuma, and instructed the crowd as to the meaning of baptism. Each believer took his turn speaking to the Indians in clear voices, to tell of the experiences that led them to Christ. Although few of the older Shuara hearing their testimonies understood the power of the gospel, they could not deny that these young people had been freed from the fears of witchcraft and death and were happy in their new faith in Christ.

One by one I immersed the radiant young believers and lifted each again to a standing position, repeating five times as I did so the phrases I had memorized in Shuara for the occasion: 'On confession of your faith in Jesus Christ, God's Son, and on your promise to walk in God's road, I baptize you in the name of the Father, the Son, and the Holy Spirit.'

When Pakesh's turn came, she was watched from the bank by her father and mother, her grandfather, Washicta, and Icam. They heard her say that Jesus had died for her and that she wanted to live in obedience to Him. They could not have anticipated how much her testimony was to change the plans they had for her life. Just as Pakesh was about to be immersed, her father, Puanshira, stepped into the water at her side, evidently to satisfy his curiosity about this strange ceremony. There were a few whispers and suppressed giggles from the crowd on the bank. But mostly they were quiet with awe. They had never heard such words before.

Ernest Johnson closed the service with a prayer that God would manifest His love and power to the rest of the Shuara through these first Makuma Christians. We climbed back up the hill, confident that the One who had begun His good work in Wampiu, Jimpicti, Tsamaraing, Tirisa, and Pakesh would go on developing it until the day of Christ Jesus.

The baptism of the first converts in Makuma did not mark the end of their struggles; rather, it was the beginning of even harder battles against the customs that surrounded them.

One who adhered stubbornly to her new faith through many trials was Pakesh. A few days after the baptismal service, Big Saantu and his son Icam visited her parents. This could only mean that the time had come to complete the bargain made so long ago. Tonight she would be expected to prepare the cassava root with her own hands and enter the *tangamash* to serve Icam his portion, thus initiating the marriage process. She detested the thought of approaching this young man especially because he was learning to be a witch doctor like his father.

When she brought the steaming bowl into the *tangamash* she handed it to her father and refused to serve the visitors. Her father, with just one more exchange of command and refusal, picked up a stick and beat her until she managed to squirm from his grasp and run sobbing outside. She hid for a few days only a short distance from the house, but one night, fearing her father's continued anger, she ran through the forest to find refuge in the house of the missionaries. Pakesh knew that Dorothy Walker loved her and would try to help in any way possible. When she reached the house she called softly through the bamboo wall until Dorothy let her in.

The next morning the girl's father, who had been searching for her since she left, arrived at the mission. He suspected she was there and demanded his daughter. 'Send her out so I can teach her how a Shuara woman should act!' he shouted.

Dorothy noticed his third wife, who had accompanied him, sitting smugly under a grapefruit tree. Her heart ached for both girls, who were the pawns in a bridal arrangement. She refused to turn Pakesh over to her father. Later in the day when Pakesh's mother appeared along with her father and asked for the girl, Pakesh agreed to go with her.

Instead of turning to the right from the road by the school, Pakesh's mother grasped her daughter's arm and started down the trail toward the river. With her father pushing her, they entered the canoe and crossed the river to Icam's house. But rather than become Icam's wife, Pakesh ran away again. This time she hid for nearly three weeks until her parents and even the missionaries believed she had died. Icam declared that since she had twice run away he now despised her and would not marry her even if she were still alive.

'Let her live alone as a thrown off one. No other Shuara will marry her either,' declared Icam.

But to everyone's surprise she appeared one Sunday morning

at the missionaries' door, ragged and thin but still confident that God would keep her from becoming a witch doctor's wife. Since Icam had lost face and refused to have anything to do with her any more, Puanshira could let the matter drop and still keep his new wife. He allowed her to live quietly once again at home and even to return to the next session of school. Our hearts were full when we heard the story – full of praise to God, Who had helped this Shuara girl.

Not long after the baptismal service we left for the United States on furlough. Dorothy Walker, with the help of another young lady missionary, courageously continued helping the Shuara choose God's way of life. Dorothy started a weekly Bible class especially for the women and also a weekly prayer meeting to encourage the young believers. But because it was not *shuartica* for a woman to teach men she did not lead the services herself. Nor did she always give the Bible messages, but encouraged the new Christians to learn to tell their people what God says. Upon our return we were thrilled to see the growth in zeal and understanding on the part of the believers.

We felt the need of a separate building for church meetings rather than holding them in the boys' school as we had been doing. The Christian Shuara were enthusiastic about the plan and gave freely of their time to put up the simple bamboo-walled structure which they promptly named 'God's House.' With great pride they spread the news of this first church to be built among the Shuara in the Makuma area.

The Indians would say with wonder: 'No one eats or sleeps here. When we gather together do we talk of war and witch doctors' curses as we used to? No. We pray to God and listen to more of His Word. No one need be afraid to enter God's House. We want everyone to come and learn with us.'

We prayed and began to hope that more would come and that other churches could soon be initiated throughout the jungle.

And come they did. At times the attendance reached nearly one hundred. It was almost becoming *shuartica* to attend church on Sundays.

Although we sang God's praises and preached His Word, these services were seldom carried through to the end without noisy disturbances or interruptions.

It was not unusual for Washicta or other respected chiefs to come stomping into the Makuma church in the middle of a prayer or a hymn. He would proceed to extend greetings to everyone present in a loud, deep voice; at the same time he would expect everyone to take notice of him and respond in kind.

Quite often a small bird would unwittingly fly in under the leaf roof and be unable to find its way out. It would dart and swoop back and forth while all eyes followed its flight, and rows of heads moved back and forth in hypnotized rhythm. Often an Indian boy, forgetting he was in church and not out in the jungle, would take after the bird. Then all praying would stop until it was either caught or made its escape.

Vampire bats were also frequent disturbers of the peace. One never could tell when a bat would decide to leave its hiding place in the thatch of the roof and swoop down among the heads of the congregation. A hubbub would ensue as the boys assailed the ugly creature with sticks. When it had made its retreat everyone would settle down again to listen to the Bible lesson.

Every service was conducted under the constant threat of dogfights. Most Shuara families brought their mangy half-starved mongrels to church, sometimes tying them outside, sometimes allowing them to lie under the benches. All dogs were highly suspicious of one another. A sniff, a growl, an answering snarl would be the signal for general bedlam as a whole church full of dogs howled their defiance of one another.

The Shuara women preferred to sit at their husbands' feet, rather than on the bench beside them. Shielded in their bosoms were pet pigs, monkeys, chickens, or parrots which they fed and cared for as the sermon progressed. They would further divert themselves by picking gnats from their husbands' legs and exterminating them between their teeth.

We learned to take these distractions with patience and good humor, knowing they did not seriously interfere with the growth of the true Church of Christ among the Shuara.

# CHAPTER NINE
# MEDICAL MISSIONARIES

I am the resurrection and the life. He who believes in me will live, even though he dies (John 11:25).

Whenever a plane took off from our airstrip bearing a sick or wounded Indian to the hospital at Shell Mera; whenever we went on early morning radio contact to describe symptoms or to ask for a diagnosis, we gave thanks that we were part of a fast-growing team dedicated to bringing the miracles of modern medicine to people who formerly had known no succor but the witch doctor's chants.

We were indebted to a host of others: hard-working pilots, doctors, radio operators, and fellow missionaries, who were prompt and faithful in their support.

But in the beginning we had to learn by doing. We had no radio and no planes. Our first dispensary, set up by Ernest and Jean Johnson, was in the same small room as our store. Our meager supply of medicines shared shelf space with trade goods. There was no running water. We carried our water in buckets and boiled it on the kitchen stove. Most of our patients came in the daytime, so it did not matter much that there was no light. Since there was no examining table, patients lay on blankets on the floor. The waiting room was the porch.

The dispensary was improved over the years until it had its own space in part of a five-room building which we called the 'pentagon.' The walls were painted; there was running water, and an examining table with a pad on it. By comparison with earlier arrangements, this was the acme of modern efficiency.

Jean Johnson, when she was with us, then Dorothy Walker, Marie, Gladis Gibson, and others took turns running the dispensary. The Indians were suspicious at first and not many came for treatment. But as some were cured and told others, more and more came.

In our innocence, we thought that once they had been healed by our medicines they would turn their backs on their witch doctors. We soon found it was not that simple. With our days so taken up with the routine work of dispensing shots, worm medicine, and aspirin, so trivial and so demanding, there were moments when we wondered whether this medical side of our work was worth the effort. But just as often, God strengthened our hands and hearts to continue.

Our medical successes slowly brought us a good name throughout the jungle. Through this work we came to better understand the Indians and their ways. Eventually, many whom we first reached through caring for their diseased bodies came to know Christ. And we were heartened to see changes for good worked by God in many lives.

Since Marie did more of the medical work than I, she tells here some of her own experiences:

One morning as I opened the dispensary door, I saw an Indian, Mr. Hummingbird, and his wife, Tsetsempu, waiting outside. They were bringing their ten-year-old boy for treatment. Tsetsempu had carried the boy on her back over a five-hour trail, bearing also a machete and a basket of cassava roots. Breathing hard and moving slowly, Tsetsempu stepped to the center of the room, got down on her knees, untied the cloth that bound the boy to her back, and gently eased him onto her lap.

Two things were striking about the boy: the extreme emaciation of his wasted body; and the expressiveness of his enormous black eyes, framed by long, beautiful, curling eyelashes. At once I named him 'Big Eyes.' He could not walk or even stand erect. His hands, hanging limply at his sides, were nothing but bony structures with transparent skin stretched over them. His neck could hardly support the weight of his head. Although his face at first glance looked full-fleshed, it was only because it was swollen.

Weeks earlier, Mr. Hummingbird had come to our mission from his home along the Cusutca River, seeking medicine for the boy whom he had at that time left at home. He told me the child had suffered from diarrhea for many months. After guessing his weight and height from the father's description, I counted out some sulfa pills and told him he could let the boy come to our school as soon as he was better. Mr. Hummingbird looked slightly shocked at the idea, shook his head vehemently until his ponytail waved back and forth, and said it would be impossible.

Now I understood why and was filled with remorse that I had not taken the boy's condition more seriously. I began to question the mother.

'He vomits,' she answered. 'All the time he vomits. No food stays in his stomach. He doesn't want to eat and when I do feed him a little, he vomits. I chew his food myself and give it to him from my own mouth just as I did when he was a baby. But it doesn't do any good. And he has diarrhea. Terrible diarrhea. And he says his head always hurts. Don't we Shuara know that when anyone can't eat he won't live? Give him some medicine for the sickness that has made him so weak and so thin.'

I kept asking questions while bringing an aspirin and a little

Kaopectate in water. 'Big Eyes' just turned away and said, 'I don't want it.' The low hoarseness of his voice, as he spoke for the first time, startled me. This, too, must be the result of his disease. With gentle coaxing from his mother, he finally swallowed the medicine – only to bring it up a few minutes later.

Tsetsempu fixed me with accusing eyes.

'You see. I told you so. That's why he couldn't take those other pills you sent. Now what are you going to do?'

There was no hope either in the tone of her voice or in the hardness of her gaze.

I was trembling inside, but I tried hard not to show it. At that moment I had no confidence in myself whatsoever. Here was another case I was probably powerless to help. These not-too-friendly Indians had no doubt tried every witch doctor in the neighborhood; then only as a last resort, when the child was nearly dead, had they brought him to the missionary. Yet I took some comfort in the fact they had come at all.

'What are you going to do?' the mother asked again.

'Before I do anything else, I'm going to talk to God in prayer and to the doctor by radio.'

Mr. Hummingbird and Tsetsempu looked at each other uneasily while I prayed: 'May this experience bring mother and father and child to understand how much they need You – not only for physical healing, but for forgiveness of their sins, too.'

Then I went to the radio and called the missionary doctor in Shell Mera. He prescribed the shots for 'Big Eyes,' antibiotics in the morning and vitamins in the afternoon. I could hardly find enough flesh on his shrunken buttocks to accommodate the hypodermic needle. After several injections I was fooled into believing I had found a little patch of flesh on one hipbone. But when I expressed hope to his mother, she pointed out to me that it was swollen only because I had tried to stick him with the needle so often.

For two days a Shuara woman named Ana and I took turns

feeding 'Big Eyes' a formula of a little salt, sugar, and paregoric mixed with much water. We began with a half teaspoon every half-hour and increased the dose according to what the child could keep on his stomach. We dared not depend on the mother because she refused to give the solution. 'He doesn't like it, so I won't make him drink it,' she would declare. 'He says it stinks.' Then an expression of undiluted disgust would pass over her face. Yet, sometimes under my supervision she would encourage him to open his mouth and accept the mixture from the spoon in my hand.

Every morning when I'd ask how much liquid he'd kept down during the night, she'd show me the partially filled quart jar by the bed. This always made me wonder how much she'd poured on the ground. Although I insisted that she give the child nothing to eat in my absence, I knew her fear of his starving to death would drive her to feed him whatever he asked for. She did not trust me or my methods. I did not trust her or her methods. A silent war went on between us.

But in spite of her lack of co-operation, the diarrhea and vomiting gradually subsided. When 'Big Eyes' was able to eat a little bit of banana, I would carefully peel one and mash it with a fork before giving it to him. This involved the use of three utensils, the fork, a spoon, and a small plate, all of which had to be sterilized. The mother's method was much simpler. She merely kneaded the banana between her fingers before peeling it, opened one end, and allowed him to suck between his lips as much as he wanted. I had to admit that her way was not only much simpler than mine, but more sanitary.

I had a hard time getting him to take other foods I knew his body needed. Milk he refused altogether, protesting that since it came from a cow it must be fit only for dogs. I prepared a chicken broth, but he found it too salty. Then I prepared it unsalted, and put a few crumbs of rock salt alongside. He would smack his lips over the latter with as much relish as any American child with a lollipop.

One day, in desperation, I named every single item of food I had in the house. He refused each one of them in turn until I mentioned bread. This he seemed willing to consider.

'I have heard that white people eat bread and that it is very good,' he said solemnly. 'I would like to try some.'

Highly pleased, I went to the house, cut a slice of home-made bread, wrapped it in a piece of waxed paper, and took it to him. His eyes shone with pleasure as he fingered the package before opening it. The smooth soft paper seemed to fascinate him. Finally he opened one end, broke off a corner, and put it experimentally into his mouth. He chewed it thoughtfully for a moment. Then he exploded with as much force as his limited strength would allow. Spitting it out as he spoke, he unwittingly taught me two new expressions in Shuara: *'Yajesmaiti! Yuchatainti!'* ('It is abhorrent! It is inedible!') His mother, thinking this a great joke, laughed and laughed. Then taking the slice of bread from him, she ate it herself. But 'Big Eyes' still clung to the piece of waxed paper. He folded it carefully and put it in his shirt pocket.

For ten days 'Big Eyes' with his father and mother remained at the mission, living in a small building only two minutes' walk from our house. Mr. Hummingbird worked faithfully in the mission gardens to help pay for the child's mounting medical bills. Tsetsempu kept the fires smoldering, prepared their food, and cut down weeds around the house. 'Big Eyes' himself sat or lay on the bed wearing a shirt I had given him that had belonged to our son Ross and using an old dress of his mother's for a blanket.

Soon visitors came from around Cusutca; they brought 'Big Eyes' news of his sisters and neighbors.

And strange were the things I heard them say, as I listened to them belittling me and my foreign ways of treating their illnesses. I knew enough Shuara now to understand them. But they seemed purposely to ignore the fact that they knew very well my ears were taking in most of what they said. I could have been hurt by them if I had been willing to let myself.

I heard them make many remarks such as these:

'What's that she gives him from the bottle? ... Just water with salt and sugar in it? How can that help? It's not *shuartica* for a person with diarrhea to drink so much water ... Doesn't she know that the more water he drinks, the worse his diarrhea will become?'

'Oh, my heart hurts to see how sick he is ... Tsetsempu, take him home ... You can't let him die here. See how thin and weak he is. He's dying for sure.'

'Don't we Shuara love our children! Won't we cry and suffer when he dies! Oh, take him back home! Don't let him die here with the white people!'

Every setback the child suffered was always blamed on me and my treatment. His lips and the inside of his mouth and tongue broke out with sores which the mother attributed to the paregoric. When he couldn't urinate for a couple of days she told me it was the fault of the shots. But when he did succeed, she took pride in showing me the exact spot on the ground at the foot of the bed.

In spite of everything, we were becoming friends. The mother's hostility and distrust lessened each day. She tolerated me; then I felt she almost began to like me. 'Big Eyes' grew to look forward to our visits together. He would ask me to come back soon and not stay away so long. At my first visit in the morning and the last in the evening I included hymn singing, a Bible story, and prayer along with the doses of medicine and the shots. 'Big Eyes' always listened attentively, repeating and even singing some of the words after me. At first his mother seemed to pay little or no attention. She busied herself blowing and arranging the fire, washing and peeling food to cook, and even talking with other Indians.

I had a little wordless booklet with green, black, red, white, and gold pages which represent created life, the sinful heart, Christ's blood, the redeemed heart, and heaven. It was helpful in explaining God's love and plan of salvation for mankind. 'Big Eyes' loved it and asked immediately if he could keep it. He had reacted the same way to the colored plastic cup and spoon and the empty injection bottles he was given. I gladly added the booklet to his collection, instructing him that he was not to tear it up or throw it away but rather to 'read' its message to himself and any other Indians that would listen. Each time I came he would take it from his pocket and ask to hear the wonderful story again.

These were busy days in our dispensary, for 'Big Eyes' was not the only patient. One afternoon a young Shuara named Tsungi had brought in his fourteen-year-old wife, Juani, in labor with her first child. She had been in labor for two days and was still unable to deliver. I gave her castor oil in lemonade, but it did no good. The next night, feeling sure the baby was about to be born, I sat up with her, her husband, and her ever watchful grandmother. I wanted to time the contractions. Although they came with three-or-four-minute regularity, the distraught child-wife suffered in vain. Tsungi kept bringing her food and drink (including beaten egg white with a peppery jungle spice) that, according to *shuartica,* would hasten birth.

The wrinkled grandmother told me over and over again throughout the night hours that Shuara women never deliver while lying on their backs on a table and that Juani would certainly die in that position. Once, to humor the old lady, I helped Juani down from the table to the newspaper-covered floor where she tried to give birth to the baby in a squatting position. The grandmother sat behind, holding her tightly around the waist as she pushed and squeezed with her hands and arms, but it was no use. Finally, at 2:00 a.m. I settled the group with blankets and told them to try to sleep for a few hours. I did the same, resolving to call for a missionary doctor to be flown from the Shell Mera hospital as soon as the 6:30 radio contact should begin.

At 3:00 a.m. the father called, saying that his wife was surely ready to have the baby. I cleaned up the delivery room and table again and lay the suffering girl in place. So far as I could tell, the baby was no closer to being born than it had been the day before.

Suddenly my attention was arrested by the alarmed voices of Indians running up the dispensary steps. It was still too dark to identify the panting, perspiring runners, but their words presented a frighteningly clear picture.

'He's been bitten by a snake! He's been bitten by a snake! Get the medicine ready quick!'

Before I could ask who, when, where, or by what kind of snake, a Shuara dashed wildly into the dimly lit area of the dispensary. Collapsing on the floor, he managed to gasp hoarsely, 'I'm dying.' It was our convert Tsamaraing, who had become one of the church preachers.

I fully believed him; but fortunately I had enough presence of mind, in spite of my panic, to give him shots of antivenin and morphine. Shortly, he sat up and began vomiting blood-streaked bile into a pail. His lips were swollen double size, his eyes bleary and bloodshot, his hair disheveled. The dreamy young fellow who had stood in front of the church and preached a good sermon just three days before was beyond recognition.

He blurted that a bushmaster, one of the deadliest of snakes, had bitten him on the top of the foot. He groaned that he had been running for two hours through the black jungle night.

Now I had three critical patients on my hands: 'Big Eyes,' an expectant mother, and Tsamaraing. All of them desperately needed a doctor's care; with or without it they might be dead by nightfall.

I looked at my watch. There were still a few minutes before the radio contact. I could not wait; I decided to take a chance on getting through. I ran to the house a short distance away and turned on the set:

'Makuma calling Shell Mera ... Makuma calling Shell Mera ... We have emergency traffic ... We have emergency traffic...'

The hum of voices told me that the round of contact between Shell Mera and other stations had begun. But at the words 'emergency traffic' all other voices died away. I heard Marj Saint answer me. I was getting through.

'Send a doctor and a pilot as quickly as you can.' Then Marj's voice: 'Right away. We have a doctor here visiting from the States.'

I hurried back to my patients. Since Tsamaraing had been running for some time, the snake poison would already be circulating through his system. He kept sitting up to vomit and I tried to keep him as quiet as possible.

This past hour had been one of the longest I'd ever lived through. Other missionaries of whom I had read went into a room by themselves at such dark times, and got down on their knees. But there was no such chance for me; I had to do my praying on the run.

And the Lord answered wonderfully.

By 8:30 a.m. the plane came, bringing Dr. Murray Weaver, a distinguished surgeon from California. He just 'happened' to be visiting the missionary hospital in Shell Mera. From there he brought truly marvelous equipment: an intravenous set for 'Big Eyes'; an obstetrical kit for the mother-to-be; more antivenin for Tsamaraing; and his own great kindness, understanding, and skill. To me, this was all the answer to my prayer.

Dr. Weaver knelt down beside Tsamaraing on the floor, gave him morphine to quiet him, administered the antivenin, and a shot of vitamin K. He joined me then in praying for our young preacher. We could see Tsamaraing's muscles relax. He stopped vomiting; and presently, he slept.

The doctor turned now to his patient on the delivery table. He comforted her with soothing sounds so that she stayed on the table in spite of the grandmother's lamentations. But the worried old woman insisted on climbing up on the table and sitting with her granddaughter's head in her lap. In less than half an hour, Dr. Weaver brought into the world a beautiful four-pound baby boy.

At her great-grandson's first cry, I laughed to see the old grandmother reach into her bosom, produce a piece of freshly cut and peeled sugar cane, and push it into the younger woman's mouth. Judging by the ensuing chewing and sucking noises, the sweet juicy cane satisfied a need at that precise moment.

After cleaning up, we checked the snakebite patient still on the floor in the adjoining room. Then we went to the little house where our third patient, 'Big Eyes,' was staying with his family. Throughout that day and the next Dr. Weaver administered two bottles of saline solution slowly into 'Big Eyes'' blood stream. Then he diagnosed the child's main affliction as the last stages of tuberculosis. He predicted that even with the best of medical care he had not long to live.

Although it took a good deal of effort, I told his parents exactly what the doctor had said. I assured them that we would do all in our power to help prolong his life. I knew God was giving the child and his hardened parents an opportunity to know Him.

By the next afternoon when the doctor had to return to Shell Mera, all three patients (not to mention the missionary) were feeling much improved and grateful for his help. The proud young parents named their baby Araas after our son Ross. The following Sunday we were thrilled to hear the young father accept Christ as his Savior. He turned his back on his newly chosen witch-doctor career to become instead a Yus Shuara. As for Tsamaraing, he improved so rapidly that two weeks later he could stand again in the church pulpit and testify how God had saved his life in answer to prayer.

But 'Big Eyes' showed no lasting improvement after the doctor's visit.

Later, as I walked toward the house to care for him, his mother met me on the path outside their door. She wanted me to listen to what she had to say before going in.

'I was getting some branches for firewood,' she said, 'when "Big Eyes" called to me to come quickly. I sat down on the bed and talked to him. But he said that my voice sounded a long way off. Then he told me that he couldn't see the walls or the roof of the house any more. He found himself in a place of beautiful light. I was afraid he must be dying; but in a few moments he could see and hear me clearly again. I think it must be because he drank a little of that milk you brought him this morning. I'm afraid. What can you do?'

Ana, our Shuara helper, was with me, so I asked her what she thought. 'God is calling him to heaven,' she answered unhesitatingly. Although I was quick to express my agreement, the mother was unable to accept such an explanation. Nevertheless, as I talked more of God and His ways with people she sat still and quietly listened and she even bowed her head as I finished praying. The next day both of them prayed and sang with me, asking the Lord for forgiveness. They thanked Him for the sure hope of a home in heaven.

The following afternoon was suffocatingly hot. As I approached the little house, all seemed unusually quiet. The three hollow bamboo poles were placed straight up and down blocking the doorway instead of slanting toward opposite sides as they usually were during the day. Although I announced my arrival in the customary Shuara manner, I barely heard the response from within giving me permission to enter. Tsetsempu was giving her son a bath. He sat quite naked on a log next to the fire. He was turned backward and then forward to receive full benefit from the insect-repelling smoke and the heat of the glowing coals. A small pot of warm water sat balanced over the embers and from that Tsetsempu filled her bowl made of a half-gourd. For washcloth and soap, she used the two halves of a lemon. Squeezing the juice into the warm water, she refilled the lemon halves and gradually poured and rubbed the solution over her son.

No mother anywhere could have been more tender or careful

of her invalid son as she wiped the eyes and ears, and dried him fondly with the same dirty dress he used as a blanket. She proudly put on the shirt I had given him, fastening the buttons over his sunken chest and around his thin wrists. Then she gently helped him lie back on his bed, leaving him as refreshed and contented as any patient in the best of hospitals.

That Sunday the little house was filled with visitors as Indians dropped in before and after the church services. Some of them carried leaf-wrapped packages of a real jungle delicacy – large edible ants. September is the time of year when thousands of ants leave their old nests in search of a new environment to start another colony. The Indians knew that on the morning after the first heavy rains that followed several weeks of comparatively dry weather, the ants would swarm. Most of the Shuara in church that morning had passed the night out in the brush, crouched beside an ant hill and waiting for the first sign of dawn and flying ants. Then, attracting the insects with their flaming reed torches, they burned off their gossamer wings. Gleefully they all dropped to their knees and scooped up handfuls of the now-crawling creatures. They then wrapped them in leaves and took them home to be toasted in the glowing fire.

'Big Eyes' seemed to enjoy having the visitors. The house soon filled with the nut-like smell of toasted ants and the sound of crunching, popping insect posteriors. The ant's pea-sized abdomen is supposed to be the most delicious part. I registered first surprise and then alarm as I saw 'Big Eyes'' chin resting on his knees, his mouth and fists full of toasted ants and pieces of cooked cassava root. But he only laughed at my shocked expression. There was nothing I could say. The whole group was in such a party mood that I could only make the best of it and try to join in the fun.

Suddenly 'Big Eyes' held out a handful of toasted insects and invited me to have some. Ever since I had come to the jungle I kept telling myself, *This year* I am going to eat one of those ants and try to find out why the Indians think them so delicious!'

But I had never had the courage to put one into my mouth. This was my perfect chance – indeed, one that was unavoidable. I accepted his offer and raised one to my lips. With the round end actually between my teeth, I bit hard and fast. Then I exploded, spitting and sputtering in as noisy an imitation of the Indian fashion as I could manage. *'Yajesmaiti! Yuchatainti!'* I said. 'Big Eyes' laughed to hear me use the same words to describe his ants that he had said about my bread. The others joined in, evidently amused just to hear me utter the words. It all came off very well. But on the way home one nagging thought persisted. I still didn't know for sure what those ants tasted like.

The following morning, Monday, things really began to hum. It was the opening of the fall term of school. The sudden arrival of more than a hundred Shuara boys and girls kept us missionaries and two new schoolteachers just arrived from civilization busy. All these children to care for in addition to our medical patients left us very little time for anything else.

In the midst of all the boisterous activity, the greetings, and excitement, I suddenly saw a contrasting scene. A family group was making its lonely way down the road that leads to the river. It was Mr. Hummingbird, his wife, and son. 'Big Eyes' was again carried in a sling on his mother's back, his head resting wearily against her shoulder. He looked just as pathetic as when they had brought him here. They were taking him home to die. I ran after them to have a few last words. They told me that 'Big Eyes' had had another attack of diarrhea the night before. And now that the school children were coming, they were afraid he might pick up some new disease from them.

I had come to know the boy so well that my heart ached to see him go, especially since I knew I might never see him again on this earth. As I stood looking at him, he took from his pocket his simple treasure, the wordless book, still wrapped in the shiny piece of waxed paper. He smiled wanly. Then as I watched the family continue down the road, I waved sorrowfully at the child.

About two weeks later we heard the news. Death had at last

brought release. Although we had tried to resign ourselves to the inevitable, we felt as though we had lost someone very close to us. But at least there was the consolation that he had lingered with us long enough to come to know Jesus Christ as his Savior.

# CHAPTER TEN
# THE FATEFUL TREES OF
# CANGAIMI

As you hold out the word of life (Philippians 2:16).

'Panchu, the Shuara around Cumai need your help,' Tsamaraing, a believer who had married a girl in Cumai, said to me. 'There are many sick who should have medicines and many children who should be in school. I am the only one among them who knows about God's forgiveness, but I cannot make them understand. I tell them to come here to Makuma. But they say it is too far and the wide Pastaza River lies between. They want you to come to them.'

In obedience to *shuartica,* Tsamaraing had to live with his in-laws for a period before he could bring his new wife to his own home in Makuma. As the only Christian in the neighborhood, he was having his troubles.

'Here it is easy to live for God,' he said, 'but there it is hard. Do I hear the preaching of God's Word every week? Do I sing and pray with other Yus Shuara? No. I am alone, and I cannot read the Spanish Bible well enough to learn from it.'

I asked him what I could do. His eyes lit up. 'If we had an airstrip, you could fly over often to preach to us. The doctors could come with their medicines. We could have schoolteachers for the children. I have spoken to the other Indians. There is a wide flat place along the river. It would be fine for an airfield and would not take much work. We will build it without pay if you will just tell us how long it should be.'

This was another answer to prayer. We were not satisfied to confine our efforts to Makuma and had long looked for a quicker way than itinerating on foot to reach Indians separated from us by miles of jungle trail.

Later I discussed this plan with Marie, Nate, and Dorothy. All agreed that with the help of the MAF plane and our Makuma Shuara believers, we should take this opportunity to spread the gospel faster and farther. Makuma would be our main base from which to reach other groups. Cumai would be our first outstation.

We made our initial visits on foot. With us went Chumpi and old Chingasu, the strong-minded Shuara woman who had once used her biting tongue and strong will to try to keep her son Wambiu from becoming a Christian. The couple had been Christians for over two years. Both now wanted to share in teaching the gospel to the Cumai Shuara. In January 1954, a new missionary couple, Roger and Barbara Youderian, came to join us. They had helped us the year before while we went to Quito for the birth of Timothy Frank, our fourth baby. Now they were in Makuma to stay and were studying the Shuara language. These young workers, filled with the love of God, and enthusiastic in all they did, provided the impetus to launch our outstation program in full force.

Just before noon one day shortly after the Youderians arrived, an Indian runner came from Cumai to tell us their airstrip was finished. We contacted Nate at Shell Mera and arranged for him to make a trial landing. Roj insisted that he walk in first and check on the strip. He would stay to guide Nate in. He would have to leave right away if he was to make it by nightfall, so he started out, not taking time to eat or to let us pack him a lunch. This tall ex-paratrooper did everything with a sense that 'the King's business requires haste.' He always worked as if his days were numbered, although he had no way of knowing then that he had only a few years in which to win others to Christ.

At Cumai, he inspected the strip, ordered a tree cut down that was standing too close to the airfield, and sent word that all was ready.

With great skill and care, Nate landed the Piper cruiser, and congratulated Roj on his helpful teamwork. We had promised the Indians a visit from the doctor and a hundred-pound sack of salt as a reward for finishing the strip. They were disappointed, therefore, to see the pilot fly in alone. Roj assured them there would be other flights and returned with Nate to Makuma.

The doctor and the salt were soon flown in, along with Dorothy Walker and me. The excited crowd of Shuara that had gathered for their arrival regarded us as secondary benefits. Everyone wanted the salt; they smacked their lips over it like children. Everyone's head or body needed the doctor's attention. The day passed rapidly in caring for all these patients. In the evening we celebrated with a praise and prayer gathering. The Cumai outstation was begun.

With Cumai a reality, we laid plans for establishing a second outstation, close to Atshuara territory. There was an airstrip already in existence at Wampimi, about thirty miles southeast of Makuma – one that had been built and abandoned by the Shell Oil Company.

'Maybe a dwelling of sorts could be made from the old company buildings,' I suggested one night. 'If some of us could stay there from time to time, we could preach to the Wampimi Shuara; and when any Atshuara hear we are there, with our medicines and trade goods, they might come to visit us.'

Roj was so excited by the idea that he made the first visit on foot, staying just long enough to enlist the Indians to cut down the tall grass on the strip. Within a few days I flew to Wampimi with Nate to talk over our plans with the Indians. One night there was enough for us. We tried to sleep in an abandoned shack, but chiggers ate us alive. We spent most of the night hunched up in the cramped seats of the plane. Before we left we got the Indians started clearing land, planting gardens, and cutting away the thorny vines that had swarmed over the paths and broken-down buildings.

Roj and Barb made ready to move to Wampimi. Before his family arrived, Roj patched together several buildings standing in a row, to make a home. One had been a shower room and had a cement floor. He fixed this up as a bedroom. Another building, forty feet away, which also had a cement floor, he changed into the kitchen. He walled in the space between with various boards and odds and ends. He covered the whole structure with a kind of crazy-quilt roof which he made of thatched leaves, tile, tar paper, corrugated iron – anything he could find.

The lower altitude made Wampimi hotter than Makuma, and the place crawled with biting ants and bugs. Their water, except for what could be caught in a rain barrel, had to be carried from a stream several minutes walk away. Roj and Barb did have a hand-crank radio, so the MAF plane made regular landings on that good strip with food, mail, and whatever else they needed.

They were happy. Their days, filled with language study, treating the sick, and trying to talk about God, passed all too quickly. When I went to help with a special greeting and teaching session a few weeks later, I found forty Indians in attendance – a real crowd for this less populated area. For most of the next six months, the Youderians continued to live at Wampimi. They never gave up hope that one day Atshuara visitors would come.

As the outstations at Cumai and Wampimi were getting under way, a third one was opened up on the banks of the Cangaimi River – one which was to involve us in new crises. The Cangaimi station was about as far to the south of Makuma as Cumai was to the north.

Interest in establishing a missionary station there had been encouraged, as in the case of Cumai, by two Shuara boys from our school. This was another tribute to Ernest Johnson, who had foreseen that the training of Shuara boys in a Christian school would one day result in a corps of evangelists to their own people. Now his vision was becoming a reality.

One day the two schoolboys invited me to visit some of their relatives at Cangaimi. They were anxious that I bring a doctor along, as there was considerable disease there. I arranged for Dr. Paul Roberts, one of the HCJB missionaries, and Dr. Ralph Eichenberger of Wycliffe Bible Translators to fly to Makuma and accompany us.

With the boys as our guides, we all started on the eight-hour hike. They took us to the home of the leading patriarch named Tuitsa. He turned out to be a rough character. Judging by his long gray hair, his straggly whiskers, and his bent-over body, I thought he must be one of the oldest Indians I had ever met. But he was vain about his age. He kept up a running fire of filthy, boisterous talk, obviously trying hard to give the impression that he was still as tough and active as any young warrior.

Tuitsa and his large family group were friendly, perhaps because they were so anxious for the doctor's help. I was amazed that here, on our very first night in the home of a strange Shuara, we could give medical help to this group. We could only surmise that it was because our schoolboys had been such good ambassadors on our behalf.

One small need paved the way for further contact with these people. It was nothing more than a boy with a toothache. I had learned that a big handicap to the Indians' appreciation of modern medicine was the lapse of time between treatment and cure. The Indian expects his witch doctor to heal him pronto. If he doesn't, he is no good. The same demonstration of mystical power is looked for from the missionary doctor. Unfortunately, much of the doctor's routine work, such as dispensing worm oil or cleansing infected wounds, offers little opportunity to demonstrate magically quick results.

But treating a toothache could be different. Dr. Roberts explained, through interpreters, that he was about to give a general anesthetic. All twenty-five Indians living in the house gathered to watch.

At first they were merely curious. But as they saw the boy go to sleep, panic seized them. The Shuara greatly fear the unconscious state. Some began to cry out that the boy was dying and begged us to do something. Dr. Roberts calmly continued with his operation.

When the boy woke up, he did not even know, until Dr. Roberts told him, that his tooth had already been pulled. He couldn't believe it because he had felt no pain. This made the Indians shake their heads in wonder. Afterward they sat quietly while we sang hymns and spoke to them of Jesus and His love, though many of them had not so much as heard of the gospel before.

That night the doctors, in their turn, had an eerie experience in what it means to live and work among the dark and mysterious forces of the jungle.

The household had settled down. Fires burned lower as the Indians stretched out on their bamboo racks and began to fall asleep. Suddenly and without warning, a strong wind ripped through the forest, tearing leaves from the thatched roof. Outside, giant trees swayed and groaned. Within, Indians jumped from their beds, stirred up their fires to give more light, and ran wildly about the house, all talking at once.

Old Tuitsa, yelling above the storm, dashed to the door. He kept pointing outside to some unseen danger. I ran over to see what was bothering him. He told me that a large tree, quite near the house, was likely to come crashing down on us at any moment. He could have been right; jungle trees do not have to put their roots very deep into the ground to find water. A wind as strong as this could very easily blow this one over.

Now the pounding of the rain, with the whining of the wind and the cries of the Indians, created a frightening din. I sensed in their voices a new note of terror. Tuitsa ran for his gun and returned trembling and shrieking to the door. He stood there shaking, straining his ears.

I understood what terrified him. The Indians were convinced that the storm had been sent by a witch doctor to give their enemies cover for a surprise attack. Shouting, howling, running about or standing rigid, listening, the Indians were suffering from memories of previous attacks as well as from fear of another. They knew by experience what might happen.

Meanwhile, the doctors were also racing up and down as excitedly as the rest of us. Since I had forgotten to interpret for them, they didn't have the slightest notion of what was terrifying everyone. At last when the storm subsided into a steady downpour the Indians grew quieter and I had a chance to explain to the doctors. They were deeply shaken by this contact with the powers of evil. None of us could get back to sleep. We talked long into the night about the destructive practices of animism and how the power of Christ could stop the revenge wars, the witchcraft, and the terrible fear of death that gripped these dear people.

A few months later we learned that the Cangaimi Shuara had picked a site for their airstrip. Our two schoolboys asked Roj and me to come down and have a look at it, inviting us to stay at the house of a pleasant young man named Mayacu, uncle of one of the boys.

We were hopeful that Mayacu might become a Christian like his nephew. He listened eagerly as we told him that God not only created him, but wanted him to live with Him both now and forever. He did not say much. But we thought we detected a hunger in the eye he kept fixed on us.

The airstrip site was breathtaking. The Indians had picked a place at the edge of a 350-foot bluff, thus eliminating much of the work of carving one of the approaches out of virgin forest.

Roj and I stood there now, drinking in the view. The terrain at our feet dropped down to the shifting channels and sandy banks of the Cangaimi River. Spread lavishly before us was endless dense green jungle, edged on one side by the dragon-tail humps of the Cutucú Range, cut through the middle by the sweeping curves of the Cangaimi and stretching to the southeast horizon.

There was no more time to admire the view. Turning in the other direction, we faced the immediate job. Half a mile of tough tangled trees still had to be cut down.

With the help of some Indians we began hacking away at the undergrowth. We had made only a small dent in it by sundown. It was now too late to walk back to Mayacu's. An Indian named Jintachi lived not far from the airstrip. We went to his house and asked if he would put us up for the night.

Jintachi was a cocky little man who reminded me of a banty rooster. Grudgingly, he allowed us to stay. But he wanted us to know he was against the airstrip. Judging from past experience, he feared the plane would bring white people to claim his land. He would have nothing to do with outsiders. When supper time came, he refused to give us, or even sell us, anything to eat. In our exhaustion, however, going to sleep with empty stomachs didn't bother us a bit.

The work got underway. We saw enough indications of enthusiasm among the other Indians to make us believe they'd go on with it; so the next day we hit the trail back to Makuma.

Late in November of that year, 1954, an Indian runner reached our mission with the announcement that the airstrip was ready for use. I set out on the trek to Cangaimi with a light heart. I could imagine Nate Saint coming in to make the first successful landing after I had checked out the strip, then flying me back to Makuma.

What a shock it was to find many tall trees still standing at the jungle end of the approach. There was nothing to do but help cut them down. The Indians were even more unhappy about this than I, as they thought they had finished it. Silently, they picked up their axes and followed me. All that day and the next, the air rang with the whack of blades and the groan and crash of giant timbers thundering to the ground. We were pushing back the solid wall. Again I imagined myself taking off out over the Cangaimi River with Nate.

I was lost in such daydreams when the crack of a tree followed by sharp, anguished cries pulled me back to reality. Picking my way over the criss-crossed logs, I ran to the spot where the cries were coming from. The figure of an Indian loomed up before me. It was Jintachi, the banty rooster. I had not expected to find him here at all. He had just reported for work because he didn't dare lose face by refusing to help with a project so widely supported by the other Shuara.

Jintachi glared at me defiantly and almost gleefully declared, 'A falling tree just killed one of the men. It's Jisma, he's dead.'

There was no mistaking his implication: 'It's *your* fault – it's all *your* fault.'

I ignored Jintachi and turned to the others. 'Where is he?' I called.

'Here – pinned down by the tree trunk!' someone shouted back.

I vaulted a log and headed in the direction of the voice.

Hurdling one log after another, I reached the scene just as the Indians were dragging a limp, skirted form from the brush into a clearing. I knelt down and examined the injured man. His nose was smashed; some teeth were gone; his head was all bloody. I wondered if he could still be alive. Then he groaned. I gave thanks that there was still breath in his body.

I had brought no medicines or bandages. Suddenly I remembered that I did have some long strips of torn white sheets to mark out the length of the landing field so it could be seen from the air. I sent one of the Indians to get the bundle.

I needed help badly, but in emergencies, Shuara Indians seem totally useless. When one of them faces the mere prospect of death, the rest give him up. Even while the afflicted one still lives, they start plotting vengeance against whoever had caused him to die. This was no exception. Superstitious taboos kept anyone from touching the doomed man. No one would give a hand in bandaging Jisma's wounded head. No one would bring water, nor any clean leaves for him to lie on.

An angry muttering arose. I heard one Indian say, 'If this, my brother-in-law, dies, the man who cut down that tree will never eat again. I am strong enough to finish off the one responsible for this awful deed. And I will do it.'

The threats increased. They all started asking one another who had felled the tree. It never occurred to them that it might have been an accident. Somebody had done it purposely and they were going to find out who.

To my consternation, I heard the name of one of our Cangaimi Christian schoolboys being mentioned more and more. Was he not the one who had first proposed the idea of the airstrip? Was it not he who had persuaded the Indians to work on it? Then was not he the one who cut down the tree?

This was the moment Jintachi had been waiting for. He was going to prove his point. He began to talk the loudest, his voice coming out above all the others: 'Have I not been saying right from the beginning that to build such an airstrip was all foolishness? Are we Shuara being paid for all our sweating? Now look what has happened! See what those who have toiled so hard can expect for their labors!'

He pointed to Jisma lying on the ground.

'Will he ever eat again?'

Jintachi's words were having their effect. The muttering became a chorus. If Jisma died, I feared for the life of the Christian school boy.

But I had to turn my attention to the victim. His breathing sounded a bit more normal. His wounds were beginning to clot. But he couldn't stay here. He would have to be taken to a house.

And how could this be done, with the Indians feeling as they were? Summoning up my willpower and drawing strength from the Lord, I literally forced the stubborn Indians to improvise a stretcher from poles and borrowed shirts, which I then covered with leaves. I made them carry him to the nearest Shuara house, although it was half an hour's walk away.

There I checked his condition again and found it fair. But he needed medical care. If I could just get to Makuma in time to catch Nate and his plane, I could tell him to fly over Cangaimi and drop at least sulfa powder and clean bandages, since the airstrip wasn't yet fit for a landing.

I never walked so fast in my life. On the way, I thought through the situation from every angle. Matters at Cangaimi had come to a crisis. If Jisma died, it could set off a new wave of vengeance killings. Our hopes for evangelizing the Cangaimi Shuara would be blasted.

To make things worse, I could not go back to help Jisma myself. I was already committed to attend the regular meeting of the mission council in Quito. I had also promised to bring Linda and Ross home from school for Christmas and was due to leave Makuma the following morning. I could only cling to God and pray that Jisma would not die.

Most important now, beyond seeing that remedies got back to Jisma, was to impress on the young Shuara walking at my side the immediate need to get the remaining trees chopped down and the airstrip in usable shape, in the event Jisma had to be flown out to the hospital. But could the Indians, gripped by superstition, be persuaded to resume the work after such an unfortunate accident?

When I reached Makuma, I learned that Nate was grounded in Shell Mera by rain. Since there was no way to fly the remedies to Cangaimi, I sent them, with instructions as to their use, back with the Shuara guide. The next day the skies cleared and Nate flew to Makuma to take Dorothy Walker and me to Shell Mera. Marie would be left alone during our ten-day absence. She promised to inform Nate of Jisma's progress.

I had been in Quito about three days when I was wanted on the radio. It was Nate calling from Shell Mera. He had just heard from Marie. Jintachi had showed up at Makuma with the news that Jisma had taken a turn for the worse. He had developed a high fever and was out of his head. Jintachi, knowing the sick man would die unless he got help from the missionaries, had put down his antagonism to come and beg Marie to have Jisma flown out to a doctor at Shell Mera. He kept assuring her that the rest of the trees were now down and the strip safe for a landing.

Nate was willing. But should I let him go ahead? Was the strip actually ready? While I was trying to decide what to do, Roj called from Wampimi. He volunteered to hike to Cangaimi and check the airstrip himself.

It was then 10:00 in the morning. Roj arranged to meet Nate in Cangaimi at 4:00 that afternoon. Roj was to start some small brush fires to indicate the wind's direction.

Roj's hike was something of a feat. He made it over eighteen miles of that tough jungle trail in slightly less than six hours.

No one could appreciate what Roj had done better than Nate who later wrote of it:

At 3:55 p.m. I was approaching the new strip, a mere cut in the matted jungle and it was almost invisible until you got right over it. My heart rejoiced as I spotted smoke drifting skyward from the cliff end of the clearing. There was Roj running from one smudge to another, stirring them up so they'd throw more smoke. He signaled 'Okay' on the condition of the strip. The wind was almost calm, slightly favorable. No downdrafts. I went in, committing the operation to the Lord.

The landing surface was the roughest I've been on for a long time, but firm and perfectly safe. Roj was the ghost of his usual self. He was haggard and pale and sweating profusely. His shirt was in shreds. His heart pounded visibly and he panted for breath as he shouted to the Shuara, instructing them to bring the wounded man as quickly as possible. I had some food for Roj in the plane ... but he had no appetite for anything but a ripe pineapple which he promptly finished off. He hadn't had anything to eat since we had talked on the radio in the morning. Why? Because he could not stop even a minute ... could not spare himself and still arrive in time.

Off through the jungles I could hear the excited calls of the men who were bringing the victim. They carried him on a bamboo pallet slung between shoulder poles. His face was horribly mutilated ... bones broken ... one eye was opaque, probably blind before the accident ... the other was blood red. He looked so dead I was shocked to see him move.

Nate reflected:

Here was one of the hopelessly lost ones that the Lord Jesus had come to seek and save ... a poor old one-eyed killer who rarely had seen or shown any expression of pity. He probably trusted me only because his own people had given him up. Death to him was the horror of the unknown; the anguish of a starless night forever. He knew nothing of God and less of Calvary. If only I could make it to Shell Mera maybe Doc Fuller could pull him through the night. The Lord willing, he might still be snatched from the brink.*

The Lord was willing; Jisma lived. A few months later he was back at Cangaimi strong and well. I gave praise that impending tragedy had paved the way to victory for the gospel.

If one were to attend church in Cangaimi today, there, listening attentively to the service from the front bench, would be seen the cocky Jintachi himself!

---

* Russell T. Hitt, Jungle Pilot: *The Life and Witness of Nate Saint,* pp. 246-48.

# CHAPTER ELEVEN
## CRACK IN THE WALL

Always be prepared to give an answer to everyone who asks you to give the reason for the hope that you have (1 Peter 3:15).

When I left Quito to take the children home for Christmas of 1954, I had no inkling of what was in store for me.

We stopped to spend the night in Shell Mera with Marj and Nate. Marj was on regular radio contact next morning when she suddenly summoned me to the set. Roj was calling from Wampimi.

'I have traffic for Frank. Is he there? Over.'

'He's right here, Roj. Over.'

'Tell him to stand by. I have a visitor, a very important visitor who wants a word with him. Over.'

Bursting with curiosity, I asked Marj to find out who it was. Roj wouldn't tell her. He would only say, with an air of great mystery, that this was a friend very dear to me, but someone I hadn't yet met.

'Ready. I'll put him on. Over.'

It was against the general rule for anyone but missionaries to use the jungle network. With some misgivings, Marj handed me the microphone. I called Roj and waited. It was not Roj's voice that I heard, but the resonant tones of a stranger, speaking in Atshuara.

'Panchu!' said the voice, 'I am Tsantiacu, Atshuara chief.'

I could hardly believe my ears – a leader of the tribe I had been trying to reach was calling me on the radio!

'We have heard much about you,' he continued. 'We want to be your friends. My people hope you will come to our land. They are waiting to see you. I invite you to stay at my house.'

The chief and I talked back and forth for a few minutes; he was perfectly at ease with the microphone. My heart was full of thanksgiving for this unexpected opening to the Atshuara people.

His voice faded. Roj told me later that Tsantiacu had kept on talking even though Roger had stopped transmitting because his arm got tired cranking the generator. Marie, listening in from Makuma, was overjoyed to hear the Atshuara's message.

This opportunity had come about only because Roj and his family were willing to endure the discomforts of living in that hot primitive outpost. A few days later, when Roj brought Barb and the children to spend Christmas with us, he told us how God worked to bring this contact about.

Tsantiacu lived three days by trail to the northeast of Wampimi. He hadn't been this deep in Shuara territory for years.

The Atshuara, however, carried on trade relations with some Wampimi Shuara who lived not far from Roj and Barb. These Shuara had plenty of wild pig skin. The Atshuara were more skilled than any other tribe at making blow guns and poisoned arrows. The Shuara traded their pig skins for blow guns, and the Atshuara in turn traded the skins with commercial traders farther south, for cloth, machetes, guns, and ammunition.

Word went through the jungle that there were missionaries at Wampimi who had medicines. Hoping to find a cure for his illness, Tsantiacu had come as far as the home of Chief Taisha, a neutral Shuara from where he sent word to Roj that he would like to see him.

Roj found Tsantiacu both impressive and friendly. He consented to come to the mission house. There Roj gave the chief and his party medicines and presents of food, played Shuara gospel records, and arranged for him to talk to me on the short-wave radio. Then he discussed plans for us to visit Atshuara country.

At the right moment, Roj spoke of the trip Keith and I had made several years before. He told the chief how Timas had threatened us and wanted to know if he were likely to make trouble again. Tsantiacu then revealed for the first time why Timas had tried to kill me.

'Did not Timas fear both white men and Shuara from Makuma?' the chief said. 'Did he not think Panchu had come to spy, so that the Shuara could come back later to kill him? But since that time he has learned more about missionaries. He knows you are his friends and only want to help us.' He grunted. 'Anyway, he lives now in another part of the country, so he will not make trouble for you.'

Roj tried not to let his eagerness to take advantage of this opportunity blind him to the dangers involved. He put another question to Tsantiacu: 'If Panchu and I decide to travel to your house soon, will you come back to Wampimi to take us over the trail to make certain no other Atshuara warriors try to hinder us?'

Without hesitating, Tsantiacu said he would. He was a man of quick, sure decisions. Having given his word, he would keep it. The two men set a date for the trip.

'By the time two moons have passed I will be back,' promised Tsantiacu, 'unless the rains swell the river so we cannot cross, or you send me word you cannot come.'

The two moons had nearly passed when Roj returned to Wampimi after having stayed to help us for a while in Makuma.

There the Indians brought him discouraging rumors. They were all saying war would break out at any moment between Tsantiacu and Timas. The latter's little son had died. Timas claimed the baby had been cursed by Shuunta, a young witch doctor who was Tsantiacu's nephew and who had accompanied the chief on his recent visit to Wampimi.

Roj had every reason to fear that the looming war would make our going impossible. But he did not change his plans. Believing God was directing him, he sent Indians to Tsantiacu to let the chief know he was back in Wampimi and ready.

After two days the Indians returned. They had not been able to reach Tsantiacu's house, as the lower Makuma was too swollen to cross. Roj didn't believe the Lord had brought Tsantiacu to Wampimi in vain; the baby's death, the flooded river, were only the devil's work to keep us from taking the Gospel to the Atshuara. He instructed the Indians to try again later.

Roj said nothing of this to us in Makuma, but only reminded us that by the middle of February the 'two moons would have passed.'

And sure enough, on February 16, Tsantiacu, with one of his wives, appeared at Wampimi. War had not broken out; the river had receded; the Indians, on their second trip, had reached Tsantiacu's house and found the chief ready to come.

Roj sent word to us in Makuma and to Nate in Shell Mera that everything was going according to plan. He also asked that Marie go with us as far as Wampimi in order to stay with Barb and her children. Dorothy offered to care for our Timmy, who was then twenty months old, and also our new baby, Laura, so that Marie could go. Nate flew to Makuma to take Marie, myself, our six-year-old Irene, and a visiting friend, Dr. William Reyburn, to Wampimi. Dr. Reyburn, a cultural anthropologist working with the American Bible Society, was eager to meet Atshuara Indians.

At Wampimi we packed our loads to go on the backs of

Shuara carriers. These included a phonograph, records, blankets, medicines, food, one change of clothing each, and a compact short-wave hand-crank transceiver. The Wampimi Shuara would never have ventured through 'no-man's-land' and into Atshuara territory by themselves. Reluctantly they went with us for pay.

I saw Tsantiacu for the first time at Roj's. The chief was a man to command respect. His piercing eyes could be steely cold with hate or warm with friendliness. The Winchester .44 which never left his hand was as much a part of him as the geometric designs painted across his high cheekbones. He wore no shirt, but a new striped *itipi* that reached from his waist to his ankles. His black hair was cut in even bangs across his forehead and hung down his back in a long ponytail adorned with toucan feathers. His sideburns were twisted into forward pigtails, bound with string and also decorated with bright feathers. Ten-inch hollow reed plugs stuck through the lobes of his ears.

Just before our party left the clearing, Chief Tsantiacu, deftly and without embarrassment, changed his costume. First he took off all his brilliant feather ornaments and tucked them into his shoulder bag. Then he fastened an old dirty *itipi* around his waist, at the same time dropping the new bright one to his feet. As he fell in line behind his pudgy little wife, he no longer looked the chief, but like any other Indian on the trail.

Late in the afternoon we came to the last house on the Shuara side of 'no-man's-land'. We set up the hand-crank radio and watched the Indians fasten the antenna in the trees. In a few minutes, from that remote spot we were talking to Marie and Barb in Wampimi, to Marj in Shell Mera, and to Dorothy in Makuma. By now we took the radio contacts as an everyday affair; even the Indians no longer marveled at them.

But it brought joy at the other end to hear our voices. Marie wrote in her diary:

February 20. Praise the Lord for radio contacts. Barb and I take turns on the hand crank. It is so hard I cannot turn it sitting down. By leaning my left leg on the seat, standing on my right leg, and turning the crank with all my strength, I can barely produce enough power to transmit for a minute or two at a time. But it is well worth the effort to know how the fellows are.

And Dorothy wrote to friends:

One of the Indians came to chat before the Sunday service. He asked me, 'Do you suppose the Atshuara have killed Frank and Roj?'

'No, they have not,' I said, 'because I talked to them by radio this very day. They are well and will soon be at Tsantiacu's house.'

'What a joy to be able to reassure them – and myself.'

We had two more days of hard travel through virgin jungle, jumping over logs, fighting thorns, often crossing flooded rivers. We slept on the hard ground which was cold and damp, with no mattress but a thin layer of tropical leaves. Then, unexpectedly, we came out into a clearing and saw before us Tsantiacu's huge oval house.

In all my travels I had never seen a larger Indian dwelling. It was about forty feet wide and must have been ninety feet long. It was arranged like a Shuara house: The *tangamash* had six bamboo sleeping racks; the *ekenta* had eight or ten, with bamboo partitions between. Smoldering fires at the foot of every rack in both sections filled the house with a thick blue haze. The roof, about forty feet up at the highest ridge, was beautifully woven in an intricate pattern of folded palm leaves, and was sooty black from the smoke of many fires. The longer we stayed the more our eyes smarted and our throats burned.

We sat down and changed our water-soaked socks and shoes. Tsantiacu showed us our bamboo racks. Then he called to the women to bring us some food. They filed in from the *ekenta*, bearing pineapple, papaya, bananas, plantains, boiled eggs, cooked meats, and sweet potatoes, more than I had ever been served in any Shuara home.

Looking around us, we could see how the Atshuara lived. Large bundles of unhusked corn, along with rolls of dried pig skins, hung from the rafters. A signal drum made from a hollow log stood against the wall. Above the men's racks were blow guns and quivers, small snare drums, a hand-made violin and flute, monkey-skin bags, and many baskets of brilliant feather ornaments.

The *ekenta* crawled with assorted children, dogs, parrots, and monkeys. A pet pig squealed and skittered behind one woman's skirt as she worked. The floor was littered with pots, vegetables, and fruit. The women were not nearly so strikingly dressed or lavishly adorned as the men. They all wore simple outfits of the same dark, coarse cloth, in the same two-piece style. Their wrap-around skirts were gathered in a big roll around their hips, resting on their protruding abdomens. Their loose blouses were purposely cut short to easily nurse their babies.

Because many warriors had been killed by enemies, more women than men made up this jungle family. As visitors came throughout the day, there must have been at least twenty adults, almost that many children, and fully as many dogs.

The Atshuara appeared more industrious than the Shuara. Their gardens were larger and better kept. They were always on the lookout for chances to trade.

They appeared healthier too, although there were plenty of signs of the usual diseases – tropical ulcers, skin trouble, and the distended bellies among the children that indicated worms. We looked forward to the day when we would come back with a missionary doctor.

For two days and two nights we lived with the Atshuara, amid the smoke, heat, bugs, and strange smells, sleeping on their racks and eating what they ate. They were almost embarrassingly friendly and inquisitive. They could hardly keep their hands off us or our belongings, apparently they were even more curious about us than we were about them. We had long prayed for the opportunity to get to know these people and understand them. It had come; we made the most of it.

The conversation was especially satisfying. They never seemed to tire either of talking about themselves or of listening to us. The differences in pronunciation from Shuara weren't hard for us to grasp, although every once in a while they lost us in the intricacies of their grammatical constructions.

We did better than we had hoped on a first visit in getting through to them. Every morning, afternoon, and evening we called them together to listen to the gospel on the phonograph, to hymn singing and Bible lessons. Like the Shuara, they thought of God as Creator of heaven and earth but now unreachable. They had never heard of Jesus, God's Son, or of the forgiveness of sins offered to all people.

Alternately standing or sitting on the hard stool, I would begin with the biblical account of creation, go on through the fall of man, and the redemption accomplished by the death of Jesus for our sins. Each time I finished, Chief Tsantiacu would look at me with emotion and say, 'Never have I heard such beautiful words. I want you to tell them again.' The others would nod their shiny black heads in agreement.

My voice grew hoarse. My bones ached from my cramped position. But we were so delighted at their interest that I told the story again and again. They never seemed to get enough.

Once, when I had finished, Roj whispered to me, 'Just to see the expression on their faces is reward enough for plowing through all those mud-holes. Praise the Lord for bringing us here!'

We made a point of getting acquainted with the members of Tsantiacu's household. We learned their names, tried to keep straight their relationships to one another, and listened to long tales of their experiences.

Tsantiacu had three wives, one daughter, and one young son.

I asked him which of his wives was the mother of his children.

'None,' he answered. 'Their mother is dead.'

'What caused her death?' I asked, thinking perhaps it must have been some illness.

'Oh, she was bewitched. But the witch that killed her isn't alive any more.'

'What happened to him?'

Without the slightest trace of embarrassment or guilt, Tsantiacu said, 'I killed him.'

This was a healthy reminder that, in spite of their fascination with my Bible lessons, conversion of the Atshuara would not be a quick or easy task. Their own talk, like that of the Shuara, was filled with tales of wars, of violent death, and of curses inflicted by the witch doctors. At no time were their guns far from their hands. Their feeling of fear was especially noticeable at night. I have always been a light sleeper, even at home on a comfortable bed. Here, tired though I was, I had trouble dozing off on the hard bamboo rack. Through all the hours until dawn I was conscious of the noiseless step of one Indian or another, prowling about, gun in hand, his eyes and ears alert for sight or sound that would betray the surprise attack of some unseen enemy.

We had a reminder again in the morning of the crudeness of the Atshuara way of life. Before the first rays of daylight sifted through the cracks in the walls, we were startled by awful sounds of retching, vomiting, and belching. Then there would be light bantering conversation and even laughter interspersed between repulsive gargling and the sound of splashing on the hard dirt floor. We realized that this must be the voluntary 'stomach washing' which we had heard they practiced. For them it signified nothing more than the start of a normal day in this household.

During the last afternoon of our visit, Tsantiacu invited Roj and me to stroll with him over the land he called his own. As we walked we came to a stretch of road, about half a mile in length, which was remarkable for its width and straightness.

How had it ever come to be here, right in the heart of the jungle? Why had it been made so straight? We asked Tsantiacu.

'It is just a trail we used while bringing leaves for our new house,' he replied.

Roj and I looked at each other. We both had the same idea. This would make a perfect site for an airstrip!

We sounded out Tsantiacu. The instantaneous smile that brightened his rugged face told us that the same idea had already occurred to him. He started talking.

'Do you mean that if we made an airstrip here you would come to visit us often and tell us more of God's Words?'

'Yes.'

'Then that is what we want to do. If you will tell us how to build an airstrip, we will make one.'

Roj didn't lose a moment. He started right out, pacing off the desired length and breadth. Then he stripped branches and stuck them in the ground to indicate the boundaries. We promised that as soon as we got back to Wampimi we would send in shovels and axes to help speed the work. As inducement to push ahead, we assured him that we would fly in a missionary doctor as soon as there was an airfield fit to land on.

We left with the chief's declaration of friendship and warm invitation to come again ringing in our ears. I couldn't help contrasting this experience with my first visit to the other Atshuara chief five years before. That one had ended with our being ordered to get out or be killed. There had seemed to be no hope of ever making contact with these strange people. But now, in God's mysterious ways, He had opened the door to make it possible for us to bring them the gospel.

# CHAPTER TWELVE
## A VOICE FROM THE SKY
All things to all men so that by all possible means I might save some (1 Corinthians 9:22).

The witch doctor went into his trance. The demons in the form of anaconda, fer-de-lance, and jaguar writhed and danced toward him. He gave up his will to theirs. In return, they disclosed to him the name he was seeking.

'Catani!' he moaned. 'It was Catani who put the curse on your nephew and caused his death!'

That was all Tsantiacu needed. He organized a war party, descended on Catani's house, and killed one of his relatives for revenge.

Catani then secretly summoned a large group of Shuara to his home. There they drank the *chicha*, whipped themselves to a frenzy by their hypnotic war dance, and departed en masse for Atshuara country.

Wampiu brought us this news with a stricken look on his

face. Full-scale warfare was breaking out again. We should not have been so optimistic about quickly establishing good relations with the Atshuara.

Everything had been proceeding according to plan in building the airstrip to reach Tsantiacu's people. The axes and shovels had been sent as promised. The clearing of the strip was going along; Roj and I were planning another trip soon to check on progress.

Now we faced a setback.

'Catani and his men mean to get Tsantiacu's head and bring it back for a *tsantsa*,' Wampiu whispered. 'And if they can't get the chief's head, they are bent on making a *tsantsa* of some other Atshuara.'

His report filled us with consternation. Tsantiacu and his people would blame us for Catani's attack. They would look on us as spies who pretended friendship only in order to help our Shuara neighbors destroy them. It was clearly our Christian duty to stop this attack. But how? We did not have much time. It would take Catani and his party, at the most, three days more to reach Tsantiacu's house; and according to Wampiu, they were already on the trail.

I racked my brain but nothing came. At the next contact I turned on the jungle network radio and put in a call for Nate Saint at Shell Mera.

Nate, I knew, had great ingenuity. He did not fail me this time. His first notion was to fly over Tsantiacu's house, lower an aerial telephone in a bucket at the end of a long cord, and warn Tsantiacu of the coming attack. But Nate quickly discarded that one, pointing out that Tsantiacu, never having seen a telephone, wouldn't know what to do with it. Then he hit it. Why not rig up a loud speaker in the plane and warn Tsantiacu from the skies? I agreed. Nate signed off, saying he would get right to work on it.

The weather turned against us. All that day it remained too rainy for flying. The second day, the same. The third day dawned murky and threatening. Along toward afternoon I advised Nate that it was wide open at Makuma. He said it was still heavy at Shell Mera, but he'd take off anyway.

Nate brought another missionary, Bill Gibson, with him. The three of us took the cabin door off the plane and set up the loud speaker in its place. Then we left for Tsantiacu's house.

We found it without much trouble and began circling overhead. Now my efforts at learning the names of Tsantiacu's family paid off. I could see the Indians running about down below. When I took the microphone and called them by name, they knew it was Panchu speaking. One woman dropped her basket and streaked for the brush. Several men remained, jumping up and down and waving their arms like college cheer-leaders. I warned them that Catani and his men were on their way to take them by surprise. Nate cut the motor and we glided over, so they could hear my voice free from the engine noise. 'If you hear me, lie down on the ground.' I wanted to be sure they heard me: though we did this several times, no one lay down, but we hoped they understood.

Now we had to let Catani know that Tsantiacu had been warned.

We flew back toward Makuma to Shuara country until we saw the house where Catani lived on the edge of 'no-man's-land.' Again we circled. There was no one in the clearing, no smoke coming up from the house, no sign of life anywhere. But we knew that even if Catani and his men were there they would not show themselves. Again we broadcast our message from the plane. 'Tsantiacu knows you are coming. He and his warriors are ready for you.' We had no way of knowing whether Catani heard us. But we had done our best. We headed back to Makuma, and just in time, for darkness was coming in.

Through succeeding days we waited apprehensively for news of the attack. But we heard none. Later, we learned that the Lord had worked through us. Catani had been along the trail that day within earshot of my voice. He had heard our message, and as a result had given up the attack and sent his war party back home.

But the respite in the bloody warfare was not to last very long. About six months later, another relative of Tsantiacu's died from illness. Again the witch doctor named Catani as responsible. This time it was the Atshuara who organized a raiding party and set out to avenge themselves on the Shuara.

For several days Tsantiacu and his men lay in ambush along the trail leading to Catani's house. They grew jumpy with waiting. At last they heard footsteps on the path. Tsantiacu's Winchester split the air as the first shadowy figure appeared. An Indian crumpled to the ground. The attackers, thinking they had got their enemy, fled.

The man they shot, however, was not Catani, but his brother-in-law Mangash, who would later attend our school in Makuma and become a Christian. Miraculously, he had not been killed. Tsantiacu's bullet had cut through the flesh of both arms and grazed his chest, just missing his heart. Mangash had fallen to the ground more from fright than from injury. A week later he came to us for treatment. His wounds were almost healed by then. We told Mangash that only God in His mercy had preserved his life.

Mangash had had enough of feuds. He moved from his old home near Catani's house to Makuma to be near his brother. But the attack set off a new series of killings. The Shuara knew it was Tsantiacu who had shot Mangash – how, it was hard for us to say: perhaps by the sound of his gun; perhaps by his footprints, for the Shuara can read footprints as they can faces. They even knew how many Indians Tsantiacu had brought with him. The war was no private affair between the two chiefs. All their followers were involved; and even we missionaries had difficulty staying neutral.

This time it was Catani's turn to set out with a raiding party, bent on killing Tsantiacu. Then a strange thing happened, unknown to us until some time later.

One afternoon we flew over Tsantiacu's house to show the new airstrip to a distinguished Ecuadorian army officer. We found, as we expected, that the airstrip was not yet in shape. So we circled the house several times, dropped some clothing to encourage the Indians to continue working, and turned back. As we dipped for the drop, we noticed a newly-built high stockade wall which Tsantiacu had put up around his house as further protection against his enemies.

While we were flying back over 'no-man's-land,' Catani spotted us from the ground – so the Shuara told us later.

'It's Panchu! He's gone to warn my enemies again!'

When Catani and his party sighted the plane they were going to turn back. But they were now so near to Tsantiacu's house, and so worked up with rage, that they decided to press on.

They crept up as far as a little stream that flowed just outside the stockade. There Catani hid in the bushes, waiting for the moment when an Atshuara would come for water. Soon a woman appeared, carrying two large water gourds. She stooped, filled them, and was starting back to the house when Catani fired, killing her instantly. Although they heard the shot, the Atshuara men did not dare leave their stockade to see what had happened. Guns in hand, they waited until dark. When they found the woman's body, they needed no witch doctor to tell them who had done the killing.

A month later, Tsantiacu set out to get his revenge on Catani. Once more he lay in ambush along the trail that led to the witch doctor's house. After a while, Catani and his family came up the path. This time Tsantiacu did not miss. He took aim carefully and fired many times. One bullet passed through the body of Catani's favorite wife and through a young child she carried on her back. The baby died instantly, the wife before daylight next morning. Four of Tsantiacu's bullets entered Catani's body. He fell to the ground. After the Atshuara left Cantani's friends found him there. Amazingly, he was still alive. A long time later a couple of Cantani's Indians showed me the gun he had been holding at the moment Tsantiacu shot him. Catani was holding his carbine across his chest with one finger on the trigger. Tsantiacu's bullet cut off two of Cantani's fingers and glanced off the side of the gun. The dent made by the bullet that almost got him was plain to see. I bought that gun to keep and show others how God had once saved a witch doctor from instant death.

Word of the shooting spread like wildfire from house to house. Catani lay dying from his wounds. Shuara from around Makuma went to see him, and urged that he let himself be brought to us for treatment, saying, 'Panchu and his woman have powerful medicines that will make you well.'

But the stubborn old warrior shook his head.

'Was it not Panchu who warned Tsantiacu? Is it not Panchu on the side of my enemies the Atshuara? Then why should he want to help me?' he asked.

Believers from the Makuma church tried to tell him that the love of Christ was a free gift to all men, that it applied equally to Atshuara and Shuara. But their words fell on deaf ears.

Catani held out for five days. Then, failing fast and with no other hope, he consented to come. Indian runners hurried ahead to tell us he was on his way. As we questioned them about his condition so that we would be better prepared to treat him, it appeared that his case was too grave for us to handle by ourselves. We put in an emergency call for Dr. Fuller at Shell Mera.

Our yard filled with Indians who had come from miles around. They stood there recounting Catani's feats as a warrior and a witch doctor.

The slow jungle ambulance moved through the clearing, up to our porch. Lying there, wrapped in a blanket, Catani looked at us with pleading, suffering eyes. Here was no longer the arrogant chief, the witch doctor with magic powers. He was another helpless soul, lost without Christ, terrified by the thought of death.

I knelt beside him, explaining that God had not spared him for nothing, that he had been given another chance to hear and believe God's true words. He listened without reaction as I prayed that God would save both his body and his soul.

The plane came and bore him off to Shell Mera. As its motor faded into silence above the trees, the air was rent with the piteous wailing of the women who believed they would never again see the sick one alive. To die away from home, especially among white men, is greatly dreaded by all Indians.

Catani was on the operating table for eight hours while the doctors probed for bullets and cleaned the neglected infections. He did not quickly respond to the anesthesia, as his system was too used to jungle narcotics. It took a very strong dose to put him under. Doctors and nurses said he made that hospital room a fearsome place as he fought and struggled and moaned the weird chants he was accustomed to singing as a witch doctor in a subconscious state.

A week later, he was back home almost as strong as ever. Our neighboring Christian Indians came and offered, as a gesture of love for this wicked man, to pay what they could toward the expense of Catani's hospital care. Then they visited him in his home. They hoped they would find him chastened and grateful, and interested in the Lord who had saved his life. Not at all. Catani's heart remained unchanged. He shunned the church members and avoided me. He had no intention of giving up his witch doctoring, his warfare, or his hatred of Tsantiacu.

Tsantiacu was sure to find out that Catani was still alive, and we wondered how he would react. Would he think we were now enemies of the Atshuara? Would our efforts to reach them with the gospel come to an end? I prayed, 'May You, Lord, help Tsantiacu to understand that Your ways are higher than men's ways, and that we, as Your people, could not possibly take sides in jungle warfare.'

With Catani well again, fear reigned once more in the stockade of the Atshuara. They kept watch through many long nights, determined not to be taken by surprise again. Word reached me that Tsantiacu had said to his Indians, 'Have you heard what Panchu has done? After I shot Catani and left him to die, Panchu gave him medicine and sent him to the big doctor in Shell Mera who made him well. If Panchu hadn't helped him, Catani would be dead. Besides, the Wampimi Shuara are now saying that Panchu plans to bring soldiers here to catch us. He is Catani's friend, not ours.'

This was discouraging. The outlook for establishing a church among the Atshuara looked darker than ever. But I was not ready to abandon hope. Somehow, in God's good time, our chance would come.

# CHAPTER THIRTEEN
## THE OPEN DOOR

A great door for effective work has opened ... and there are many who oppose me (1 Corinthians 16:9).

There was not much that went on in Ecuador's Oriente (eastern jungles) which we didn't know about. But now I was hearing only hints and indications of a bold, imaginative operation being initiated in the northern jungles. My good friends Nate and Roj were busy with mysterious activities. When I asked Nate directly what was going on, he answered me just as directly that he could not tell me. He was engaged in a project that called for the utmost secrecy.

I was occupied in trying to follow up our first contact with the Atshuara. In the fall of 1955, the job in hand was to finish the airstrip so that we could more easily visit Tsantiacu.

Roj was working in Shell Mera, helping to build the HCJB mission hospital. When he returned to Makuma, Nate flew us over Tsantiacu's house to check on how the airfield was coming along. We saw the Indians working down below. But we were unhappy to notice that they were extending the strip in the wrong direction so that it pointed toward the house.

Roj insisted on going in and directing them. We landed at Wampimi and had one of the Indians walk the trail with him. Others were to follow with his bedroll, food, and radio. Several days went by without any word from Roj; although we called him on schedule, he never answered. I thought something must have gone wrong. Nate came to Makuma with his plane; we rigged up the aerial telephone and flew the half-hour to Tsantiacu's place.

There were a few low clouds, but through them we glimpsed Roj working with the Indians. That made us feel better. We let the phone over the side and began to fly in a tight circle. Half the time we were in the clouds and half the time in the clear.

'It's like fly casting,' Nate said. We had to make several tries before the phone landed on the ground.

Roj came on and explained that the other Indians hadn't followed him, so he had no radio. He faced a bad situation: influenza had broken out and the Indians were in need of medicines. He asked us to come back three days later, assuring us the strip would be ready then for the first landing.

Nate went back as agreed. Although he found the strip still quite rough, it was good enough to land. He flew Roj out and took me back there the following week to take some more medicines and to do more Bible teaching. Nate seemed to enjoy the challenge of landing on the short rough strip. When he remarked that this was good practice for him, I knew he must be thinking of landing somewhere on an even rougher, shorter strip.

I had heard that three missionaries in the north jungles had been doing some flying that wasn't talked about. Putting two and two together, I figured they might be trying to make contact with the isolated Auca Indians. The Auca people were one of the fiercest and most dreaded of all of Ecuador's tribes; they lived cut off not only from white men but from their own kind

The Makuma Shuar were proud of their first church building. 'This is not a shelter for travelers to sleep in,' they said. 'We come peacefully together here to sing God's songs and listen to all He says to us. This is God's House!'

Missionary pilots landing on the short airstrip at Pakientsa ('Pig River') in the southern Ecuadorian jungle barely miss the roof of Chief Tsantiacu's palm-pole house. Because the strong, warrior-chief had many enemies, he built the stockade around his house for protection from attack.

The path from the Makuma airstrip (right corner) leads past the church, shop and some missionary dwellings to end at the small medical dispensary. Other buildings include the radio studio and school houses. The path in the left foreground leads downhill toward the river.

Shuar warriors near Makuma demonstrate the traditional 'Call to War'. In bold, loud, staccato terms accompanied by stomping dance steps, they challenge each other to fearlessly gain the victory over their enemies.

Shuunta, Chief Tsantiacu's nephew, holds a large piranha caught near the Peruvian border. The fish's teeth were sharp enough to make deep dents in Frank's fishing lure. With gusto, the men ate these so-called 'man-eating' fish for dinner!

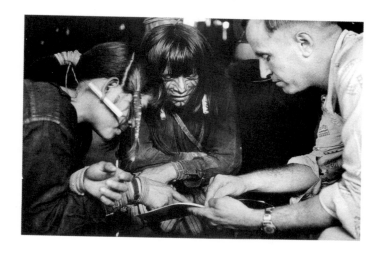

**Above:** As curious and intent as children, Chief Tsantiacu and one of his warriors study paper drawings of characters in Biblical history.

**Below:** Atshuar Chief Tsantiacu and his men fill the canoes and direct our party down the unpredictable waters of the wide Pastaza River.

**Above:** As Frank sings Gospel songs and speaks about God's plan for peaceful happy living, the Atshuar men relax their grip on their muzzle-loaders and the women wistfully hope these wonderful words are true for them.

**Left:** The oldest Atshuar relative of Chief Tsantiacu that Frank met was the gray and wrinkled Aiju, the trader.

**Above:** On the last trip with Chief Tsantiacu Frank and his friends mounted outboard motors at the back of the two canoes. Only on the calm waters of smaller streams did they enjoy smooth travelling. They made friendly contacts with many of the chief's friends and were able to tell the Gospel to Atshuar people who had never heard it before.

**Below:** Frank and Marie built their first jungle home of the same materials used by the Shuar Indians: palm-leaf thatch for the roof and split palm or bamboo walls. Everything was tied and braced together without nails. Their family of five children grew up in the same environment as the Indians expect that the Drown family home life was centered around God, love and worship of Him instead of suspicion and fear of enemies and evil spirits.

**Above:** Born-again Shuar believers publicly express their faith in Christ as Frank Drown baptizes them 'in the name of the Father and the Son and the Holy Spirit'.

**Right:** Marie Drown (foreground) and Barbara Youderian check a Gospel lesson hand-lettered in Shuar. Before missionaries came, the entirely oral Shuar language had never been written.

**Above:** Makuma Shuar believers Chingasu and Chumpi often accompanied Frank and Marie on evangelistic trips to other communities. Though neither of the two knew how to read, they could listen. After hearing a selection from God's Word several times, they could repeat and explain it to others in their own dramatic and personal way.

and other Indians. Each warring group carried long spears with which they attacked anyone who tried to come near them. They had even been known to throw their spears at planes flying overhead.

Other hints were dropped. During one of Nate's regular visits to Makuma, an Indian returned a borrowed trap of mine. When Nate saw it, he asked if he could have it, saying cryptically, 'It's just what I'll be needing one of these days.'

I asked him how the project was coming.

'I'm sorry, I can't tell you a thing about it,' he said. 'All I can say right now is that it looks encouraging. Pray for us.'

Roj brought his family to Makuma to spend Christmas. He informed us that after the holidays they were going to stay a while with the Ed McCulleys, who had charge of an outstation far to the north. This was close to Auca territory. I knew then that Roj was in on the operation too.

Just before they left, Roj, with Nate's approval, told me about their plans and why it had to be kept secret. It was such a dangerous undertaking, one that others before them had tried and failed, that if word leaked out in advance, it might be misunderstood or exploited by the outside world, or ruined by too much publicity.

When Nate came to get Roj he asked if he could borrow the transceiver we had used on our trip to the Atshuara. He said they were going to establish themselves on a beach in Auca territory and needed the radio to maintain contacts with Shell Mera. But he didn't tell me what day they would be there or any other details.

I shall never forget our farewells. We all went out to the strip to say goodbye. When they were strapped in and ready to go, I said to them, 'May the Lord bless you. Come back soon.' Nate looked at me and said, 'Yah.'

All through the next week I tried to get news of their activities. But nothing was said on the regular contacts. I had no success. Then one day a message was sent out for Jim Elliot to get over to the 'conference.' That must mean they were ready to start their plans very soon. After that, no one said anything.

A couple of days went by, then curiosity got the better of me. I wanted to know what was happening. They were using the plane; therefore I surmised, they must be using the radio. They must be having secret contacts on another frequency. Then I remembered something: Nate had a crystal that he once used to call the Shell Oil Company tower. I tried listening the next morning on that wave length; Roj was talking from some unknown point in Auca territory with Nate at Arajuno and Marj at Shell Mera.

They were using a kind of code language. Roj was telling Nate, 'We took on a little water on the football field last night. If the sun comes out in an hour or so, everything will be okay.' To me this meant that the sandstrip along the edge of the Curaray River, where Roj had told me they were going to land to make contact with the Auca, was usable. Roj told Marj that they had a good 'conference' the day before, and that 'three had come.' To me this meant that three Indians had appeared in friendship.

On Sunday I was busy getting ready for the services and did not have time to listen. Monday morning nothing was yet revealed. When I turned on the radio at contact time Tuesday, I heard Marj's voice calling me. It was steady as usual, but strained. By this time Operation Auca was being made known to everyone. But I had not yet heard the news. She said, 'The fellows are missing. The last contact we had with them was Sunday noon. Johnny (a newer MAF pilot) flew yesterday morning over Palm Beach, the landing place in Auca territory. He saw the plane. It had been stripped of all its fabric. Not one person was in sight. We don't know what has happened to them. Would you come and lead a rescue party to the site?'

My quick reaction was that of course I would. Roj would have gone anywhere to help me.

'I'll ask Marie if it's all right with her. If she says "yes" I'll be right back with the answer.'

I ran across the yard to the house and told Marie the sad news. 'They must all be dead. If the plane's gone, they're gone,' I said.

'Of course you must go,' she replied. 'That's the only thing for you to do.'

I ran back to the radio.

'Makuma calling. Yes, Marj, I'll come.'

Pilot Johnny Keenan, who had joined Nate in Shell Mera eight months before, came for me in the one remaining MAF plane and took me to Shell Mera. People were coming from everywhere, from Quito, by bus and car, from Panama, by plane.

On Wednesday we started for Arajuno. This place near Aucaland had been headquarters for Operation Auca. There our ground party made its final plans. We had a good group, among them seven missionaries. Any one of them could have directed the search as well as I.

We went on foot straight through the jungle to the Oglan River (a tributary of the Curaray River). From the few Quichua Indians living there, we obtained some dugout canoes and started down the river.

My heart was sad. I had never expected to find myself in a situation like this.

We were paddling along when we saw overhead the helicopter that had been sent from Panama. It landed on a nearby beach, kicking up a great storm of sand. The occupants stepped out. They had worse news for us. They had just returned from a trip over Palm Beach. The bodies of three men were lying there in the water, with spears in them. One of them was wearing blue jeans.

I didn't say anything. Who, of that group, always wore blue jeans but Roj? I couldn't bear the thought of Roj being dead. We had walked hundreds and hundreds of miles through the jungle together; we had built houses at Makuma together; we had opened outstations, built airstrips together. In my mind I could see him lying there in the water, a little way ahead of us downstream. Would I be equal to picking him out of the water and giving him a burial?

And there was Nate. He had become as dear to me as my own brother. He had always been there to pull us out when we were in a tight hole. He had been unfailing in his faithfulness, ingenuity, and good nature. There would be other pilots, but there was only one Nate Saint. The other three missing men I didn't know so well as they had been working in the northern jungle. But Roj and Nate had been my pals.

As our canoe slid over the rapids following the helicopter I prayed, 'Lord give me strength.'

We were approaching Palm Beach. I was weak with a double fear – the fear of seeing the bodies of the ones I had loved, and the fear of being killed by Auca spears. But the experiences of the next few minutes – looking at the skeleton of the plane on the beach, climbing the ladder to the tree house where my friends had slept, bringing the bodies of my dead companions up from the river – were good for me. I felt the Lord calming my heart and giving me a new determination to serve Him, regardless of what might happen to this body of mine.

We laid the men on that sandy shore. The fact of death could not have been more real; but so was the truth that our dear friends were 'absent from the body and present with the Lord.'

We said to one another, 'They are not here. This is only the house they left behind.'

Their burial ground was under the tree house. How close were the forces of evil in that dark and dismal hour! Black clouds cut off the sun and a fierce wind and rain beat upon us.

I had a Bible with me in my rubber pack. But neither time nor weather allowed me to get it out. I conducted the burial service from memory, while the rain poured down and mingled with our tears. I bowed my head in prayer, commending the bodies of our loved ones to God's care until they should rise again on the Day of Resurrection.

The aftermath of that killing – the Christian forgiveness

shown by the widows and relatives – is one of the most inspiring chapters in Christian missionary history.

Barb soon returned to Makuma with her children Bethy and Jerry. As they climbed out of the plane, four-year-old Bethy looked expectantly toward us.

Barb greeted us with a smile and explained, 'Bethy thought her daddy would be here to meet her. Although I've told her many times all that has happened, she was sure she would find Roj in Makuma.'

During the several weeks the three of them stayed in our house, we never heard a word of complaint or self-pity, although we knew Barb felt her loss greatly. We praised the Lord for the wonderful privilege of having her back with us and the Shuara.

She was truly happy to continue in the work that she and Roj had begun, and soon moved with Dorothy to spend several months at the Cangaimi outstation.*

At Makuma, the outlook for continuing contact with Atshuara was disheartening. Almost every day, visiting Indians brought fresh reports that Tsantiacu and his people had turned against us. Every Shuara had a different story: Tsantiacu had rolled logs onto the airstrip; his women had planted the field to cassava plants; or the chief said I was coming back with soldiers to take him away. Worst of all was the rumor that since Auca Indians had killed Roj and Nate and suffered no consequences, Tsantiacu now felt no compunctions about killing me. The trouble was, we had no way of knowing how many of these tales were true and how many were merely the product of the fevered Shuara imagination.

---

* The story of the martyrdom of Nate Saint, Jim Elliot, Pete Fleming, Roger Youderian, and Ed McCully is told in detail in *Through Gates of Splendor* by Elizabeth Elliot (Harper, 1957). See also *Shadow of the Almighty* by Elizabeth Elliot (Harper, 1958), *Jungle Pilot: The Life and Witness of Nate Saint* by Russell T. Hitt (Harper, 1959), The *Dayuma* Story by Ethel Emily Wallis (Harper, 1960), and *The Savage My Kinsman* by Elizabeth Elliot (Harper, 1961).

There were physical difficulties, too. The only plane we could count on to make a safe landing on that tricky Atshuara airfield – Nate Saint's – was lying on Palm Beach, stripped by the Auca killers.

Johnny Keenan was still on the job with the other MAF plane and was always eager to lend us a hand. But his little Pacer was much too fast to land on Tsantiacu's small clearing. With the big house at one end of the strip and the tall trees at the other, there was no margin for tail winds or any slight miscalculation.

Another thought lay heavy on my conscience. I could see, after having helped to pull the bodies of Nate Saint, Jim Elliot, Pete Fleming, and Roj Youderian from the cold waters of the Curaray, that my life might go in the same way. Besides my own life, the reputation of those five martyrs who had died for Christ at Palm Beach was at stake. I reasoned this way: their sacrifice had electrified the entire Christian world. From all continents had gone up the spontaneous cry: 'Wonderful! Great courage!' But if, within a few months, there was to be another violent death in that same part of the world, the cry could very easily change to, 'Those fool missionaries have done it again! Why do they take such risks?'

Yet I could not put from me the need to bring more of the Word of God to the Atshuara. When I thought of how much preaching and teaching we in our homeland receive and how long it takes us to understand the necessity of salvation through faith in Christ alone, I realized how much greater was the need of the Atshuara. I felt the urgency of the situation. The wars were still going on. Besides the Atshuara, the Shuara, too, would soon be wiped out. Only personal relationships with Jesus Christ could save them from their self-annihilation.

I made up my mind to go. It was God's will. But I would take every precaution to make sure that I wasn't killed.

A few months later, my chance came unexpectedly. The Wycliffe Bible Translators had brought a new plane into the country, a slow-landing, fast-lifting Helio Courier, ideal for a short airstrip. With it had come a newly arrived pilot, Bob Griffin.

In March I had to go to Shell Mera, then on to Quito. This gave me the opportunity to get the expedition organized. Johnny Keenan introduced me to Bob. When I asked Bob if he thought he could fly us in, he replied promptly, 'Sure thing! When do we start?'

Mindful of my promise to Tsantiacu to bring a missionary doctor, I told of the need to Dr. Ev Fuller in Shell Mera. He also readily accepted. Faithful Mike Ficke eagerly joined our team.

I had one other thought. I recalled that on that sad day at Palm Beach, as I walked away from the newly-dug grave, Major Malcolm Nurnberg of the United States Air Force had asked if he could go with us whenever we went to visit another tribe of Indians. A warm friendship had grown between us. I wrote to him now, inviting him to come. To my pleasure and surprise, he replied promptly, saying he had just returned from a trip to the States and would soon be able to join us.

Since we had learned that it is never wise to venture into the jungle without an Indian companion, we decided to take one who was also a believer. He could then help with the preaching.

Icam, son of Big Saantu, offered to go. Icam had grown up in our school and had become a Christian. He would be able to make Tsantiacu understand why we wished to be friends. Also, I wanted the chief to hear of the love of Christ from the lips of a jungle Indian like himself.

On 16 April, 1956, we all gathered at Makuma, ready to start. First, Bob and I made a reconnaissance flight with Johnny Keenan in his little Pacer. We wanted to see if the airstrip had really been planted with cassava and strewn with logs.

As we drew near the clearing, Johnny kept a fair altitude. We could not be sure that rumors that the Atshuara would shoot at us were untrue. We were pleased to see that, contrary to what we had been told, the airstrip was bare both of vegetation and of logs. A minute later, Tsantiacu himself came running out of the house, followed by a swarm of men, women, and children. They waved to us in a friendly way. Johnny banked, circled the field, and cut the throttle so that I could make myself heard. I called out to the Indians below: 'We'll be back later!' They waved and nodded as though they understood me. We dropped a length of cloth before Johnny turned the plane and headed back to Makuma.

That night we talked over our plans. The Atshuara had convinced me by their actions that they would welcome us as before. Bob Griffin thought the Helio plane could get in and out okay. My doubts looked foolish now. After all, what was there to fear?

We flew both planes next morning to Wampimi, about halfway from Makuma to Tsantiacu's airstrip. There we repacked our cargo, and planned to make the final lap in several shuttle flights.

This was my first visit to Wampimi, where Roj and Barbara had once been stationed, since Roj was killed. The sight of it made me sad. No Indians came running to greet us. There was no sound, save the screech of the katydids and the humming of myriad insects. The trail so grass-grown, and the crazy-quilt house that Roj had so energetically pounded together, were sorrowful reminders of happy times gone by. Wampimi had served its purpose as a stepping-stone to the Atshuara, but for lack of personnel it was abandoned.

I put aside these mournful thoughts and we set about repacking our gear. Johnny Keenan and Mike Ficke would go ahead in the Pacer; Major Nurnberg and I would follow in the Helio plane. Icam and the doctor and baggage would remain behind at Wampimi, until the last flight.

The plan was that Johnny and Mike would keep circling the sky in the Pacer above us, while the major and I landed. They would be in constant radio contact with Shell Mera, reporting on all our movements, in case the Atshuara turned hostile. Also, we reasoned that the presence of the second plane overhead would discourage them from attacking us, since they wouldn't know the Pacer could not land there.

We watched Johnny and Mike step into the Pacer and take off. We shoved the Helio back onto the strip; the major and I took our places beside Bob Griffin. As we fastened our seat belts I had a last twinge of misgiving. I looked at the major.

'Remember, Major,' I said, 'the same thing could happen to us that happened to the five. Do you still want to go?'

'I wouldn't miss this for anything,' he replied. Bob revved up the motor and we were off. As we climbed into the sky, we waved back to the tiny figures of Dr. Fuller and Icam, who were bidding us Godspeed from the ground.

Everything seemed to be made to order for this day and hour. The sky above was blue; the jungle below a gentle, friendly carpet of green. From time to time we were reassured by the sight of Johnny and Mike in the Pacer alongside, not far off our wing tip.

Looking down on the familiar terrain brought memories of wearying experiences hiking over those jungle trails. Now we passed the place where Taisha's house once stood. It called to mind that first attempt to reach the Atshuara Keith Austin and I had made long ago, and of how we had been threatened and driven off.

A scattering of cumulus clouds began to veil our vision of the jungle floor. But then I saw drifting lazily upward in the cool morning air, a thin column of smoke. I knew we were coming over Tsantiacu's house and the tiny clearing as we lost altitude.

I fixed my eyes on the yard within the stockade, watching for any sign that might give a clue to the Indians' reaction. Ant-sized figures began to pour out of the *tangamash*. But I saw no cause for alarm.

Captain Griffin circled the clearing several times, then he made a wide circle a little to the east to see at what speed he would need to be landing on that short airstrip. He lowered his flaps and throttled back the engine. For some reason it backfired a little and Bob was ready to head right over the top of the house. He was watching the roof top and the field ahead. I was watching the Indians who had gathered.

What Indians? As we cleared the roof I could not see a single Indian. 'What is going on? We're in trouble,' I shouted as the wheels hit the ground. It was a one-way strip. There were too many trees to go around at the last minute.

'What should I do?' Bob quickly asked as we rolled to the farther end of the strip.

I jumped out and looked around. Then I stopped in my tracks. A cold sweat broke out all over me. I could feel the prickles go up my spine. There was not an Indian in sight.

I turned back to the plane.

'Something's wrong,' I called. Then I shouted, 'Turn the plane around and stay in the plane. Be ready to leave any second.'

The major was already on the ground. He was pulling his army rifle from the luggage compartment.

'Put that back,' I yelled. 'The sight of it will only make them more suspicious. You stay right here. But don't use that gun unless they start to shoot. Then don't shoot to kill – only to scare.'

I faced about and started toward the house. There was no sound. I had not taken twenty steps when three Indians moved out silently from the garden in front of the house.

In the middle was Tsantiacu, flanked on either side by a warrior. The chief was waving a gun at me with one hand, and with the other, motioning me to go away. As he did so, he would take a few steps forward, then a few steps back, then a few steps forward again. His warriors weaved back and forth in unison with their chief. The way they brandished their guns and the meanness of their looks left me no doubt as to their message. They were telling me to get out of there quickly. Nevertheless, I faced those Indians and kept on walking toward them. They still motioned me back.

Then I remembered I was wearing a hat they had never seen before, a big white one with a wide brim. Perhaps they did not recognize me as Panchu. I took the hat off and threw it on the ground. It didn't change things a bit. They still brandished their guns and danced and threatened. I kept on walking very slowly.

From the corner of each eye, I checked the sides of the strip for the stirring of a leaf that would betray an ambush. I saw none.

By now I was fearful. But I had worked and waited and hoped and planned for this moment. If I were to turn and run, the door to the Atshuara would be closed to me forever.

The nearer I crept, the more Tsantiacu and his men danced and shouted. My thoughts flashed back to the Curaray River. The picture of those bodies of my friends lying in the sand came again into my mind. But this time it gave me courage. Those men faced death and had not drawn back. They had not counted their lives dear to themselves. Was I any different from them? Did I have any more right to live than they? I thought: 'Our lives belong to God. May He be glorified in me – "whether by life or by death"' (Phil. 1:20)!

As I continued to inch forward, Tsantiacu and his men kept edging toward me uncertainly. Then I remembered the gun in my own hand. I always carried it when visiting Indians. I never intended to kill one. They always wanted me to kill the game high in the trees. It occurred to me that the sight of it might be one cause of their fear and suspicion. I laid my gun on the ground, hoping they would take this as a sign of friendly intent. But it brought no change in their attitude. They kept on shouting and threatening.

Cold sweat poured from my body. I was right on the point of turning back. Instead I prayed, 'Lord, give me strength to take a few more steps. Then, if they don't change, I'll have to get back in the plane.'

I took those steps. I called out as I did so. 'I am Panchu. You know I am your friend. You do not have to be afraid of me. I have come to tell you more about God. I am bringing you the doctor as I promised long ago.'

At the sound of the word 'doctor' Tsantiacu changed in one instant the motion of his hand from 'go' to 'come.' Thus encouraged, I moved closer to him. The hand went up again, this time with wide palm out. His meaning was clear, in universal sign language: 'STOP! Right where you are.'

Now we were less than twenty paces apart. I was conscious of three pairs of sharp black eyes fastened intently on mine. Then I understood that they were less concerned with my words than with trying to read my expression. Indians can always tell more by the look on one's face than by the word spoken. They had been deceived too many times. I, in turn, tried to read their faces. I thought I saw expressions that were less distrustful, more puzzled, if not friendly. I stepped forward as I repeated my plea. Finally, I went all the way and stretched out my hand to Tsantiacu. He reached his hand out to me. He gripped me in a bear hug and we danced around, patting each other on the back. Suddenly he held me off and fixed me with a piercing gaze.

'Why did you shoot at us from the plane?' he demanded.

Now I understood. When the plane backfired he thought I was shooting at them.

The tension eased. I looked up at the sky and signaled to Johnny in the Pacer that all was well. He waggled his wings, then streaked off for Wampimi.

But Tsantiacu's suspicions were not entirely dispelled.

'Why do you come this time in a different plane?' he demanded. I explained that the one he knew had been destroyed by Auca spears and that the Helio was the only missionary plane left that could land on such a short strip as his.

The major had made his way up to us by then. As he and Tsantiacu shook hands rather stiffly I explained that the major was the one who had gone with me in search of Roj.

Linking my arm to the chief's, I said, 'Come with me and have a look at the new plane.' He shook his head and refused to move.

'No,' he said suspiciously. 'It's a trap. You have soldiers in there.'

Rumors spread by the Makuma Shuara had definitely reached him. He had believed the story that I would come one day with soldiers to take him away. Another good reason for his hostility...

Tsantiacu thawed a little when I asked his permission to send the plane back to Wampimi for Dr. Fuller. But he grew wary again when I told him the pilot would also bring a young Christian Shuara from Makuma.

'Is this young man a witch doctor like Catani?' he asked. I assured him that Icam was no witch doctor, but a true Yus Shuara. I hoped I was making the distinction clear to him, because his knowledge of God's power was still very limited.

A little later, when Icam arrived, a situation arose which I had not anticipated. As the two men were greeting each other in the formal Indian fashion, Tsantiacu stopped in mid-sentence.

'Are you not the son of Big Saantu, the old witch doctor who killed my cousin Chiriapa?'

'Yes,' replied Icam without hesitation.

'And was it not Big Saantu who at the same time captured and married my niece?'

'Yes, you say the truth,' Icam answered calmly.

'And where is the girl, now that the Big One is dead?' Tsantiacu wanted to know. 'Tell me, does she still live?'

'She lives,' nodded Icam. 'She has since married my uncle. She now has children by him.'

Tsantiacu's troubled gaze wandered out over the jungle. In his eyes I could see two forces striving for mastery – the memory of tribal injury calling for personal revenge, and Christian forgiveness with which he had so little experience. If the former were to win out, our work among the Atshuara would again be threatened.

The chief turned back to Icam.

'But you are different,' he said very slowly. 'You are not like your father, Big Saantu. You are a Yus Shuara. And Yus

Shuara do not send curses, or carry on wars.'

His next statement was conclusive: 'You are welcome here.'

The warrior's face broke into smiles. The two members of enemy tribes put their arms around each other's shoulders in token of fellowship. I praised the Lord that the few lessons in the love of Christ we had been able to give the Atshuara had found their mark far beyond anything hoped for at the time. This gave me fresh courage.

We spent four days with Tsantiacu and his people. Three times daily we sat down together for singing and teaching, and as before, the Atshuara could never get enough. They loved to sing, and we were pleased to find that they had learned several of the hymns from the phonograph records Roj and I left behind on our previous trip. Even in the night or while eating, Indians would ask us to sing a song about Jesus just once more.

On this trip, we found we had a new and powerful spiritual weapon. That was Icam's moving personal witness as to how the Lord had saved him from a life of cruelty and terror, of witchcraft and warfare. This held the Atshuara spellbound.

They also wanted to know in great detail everything that had happened since our last visit. When I told of the tragedy at Palm Beach on the banks of the Curaray, the chief's eyes flashed with anger. He interrupted me.

'When I first heard that the Tawi Shuara (Auca people) had killed Uruchu (his name for Roj Youderian),' he said, 'I was so angry I wanted to call all my men together and go kill them. Wasn't Uruchu like a brother to me? I still have in my house the box of things he left for me to take care of. Didn't Uruchu suffer in the hot sun to help us build this airstrip? I tell you, if I knew the way to Tawi Shuara territory I would go there with my men and kill them with guns. They with only spears wouldn't have a chance. They should suffer and die for what they did to Uruchu and the *pirutu* (pilot).'

I was both moved by this demonstration of loyalty and affection for Roj and disappointed that he should still believe so firmly in 'an eye for an eye.'

Meanwhile, Dr. Fuller had arrived and gone right to work. Some of his first cases were minor: he extracted a thorn from the foot of a man named Tucupe and an infected tooth from the jaw of one of Tsantiacu's women. He dispensed worm medicine wholesale, giving it to all the children and many adults. He also gave shots of penicillin to many who suffered from tropical ulcers. Upon examining the men, he found there was hardly an Atshuara in that household who did not have a scar from a bullet or lead lodged in his flesh. As he won their confidence, the married adults began coming to him and complaining that they were unable to have babies. Dr. Fuller quickly diagnosed their trouble as gonorrhea and administered the proper treatment. This was to earn their lasting gratitude. Many of them later were able to have children; and for years afterward they still remembered affectionately the kind doctor who had made this possible.

In our few minutes of free time when we weren't teaching Bible truths or assisting Dr. Fuller, we went hunting or fishing. One afternoon while Tsantiacu, the major, and I were out together, a rain squall caught us by surprise. Tsantiacu began gathering a few leaves to make a shelter. The wind was blowing hard. Suddenly Tsantiacu straightened up, faced the wind, and gave a strange whistle. This aroused Major Nurnberg's curiosity. He asked me to find out why he did this.

'I am communicating with the spirit of my dead father,' the chief replied. 'When the wind blows, my father's spirit often comes very near me.'

As I interpreted these words for the major, I noticed him shudder a little. 'What a creepy feeling that gives me!' he said.

I understood that the chief's contact with spirits was a real part of his daily life. The chief and I began to speak about it.

'You pray to God whom you can't see, don't you?' he said. 'We talk to the spirits of our ancestors whom we can't see. Tell me, is there any difference?'

I tried to make clear to him the difference. But he seemed unimpressed.

'When we drink *tsaangu* and *natema* we can see the spirits of our ancestors, and hear what they have to say to us. Do you have any such medicine that will help you see God?'

I answered him emphatically that we did not. Then I explained, 'God has revealed Himself to us in the person of His Son. He has written in His Book all He wants us to know of Him. But we will see Him someday in Heaven. And there we will be like Him forever. He has done much more for us than the spirits of dead men can do.'

I could see that in spite of the hunger with which they received the gospel and the gusto with which they sang hymns, there would have to be many, many more such conversations before Tsantiacu and his people really grasped what we were trying to tell them.

Throughout the visit, and underlying the spirit of friendship and good feeling, I was burdened with a growing uneasiness. I could not dismiss it. Tsantiacu and I had never discussed Catani, so I did not know if he still held a grudge against me for having helped save the life of his bitter enemy. The answer came on the last day of our visit.

The chief and I were talking. Suddenly and without warning, he said to me bluntly, 'This Catani, does he still live?'

I nodded. Tsantiacu scowled.

'I thought I had finished him for good.'

'You killed his favorite wife and child,' I told him. 'As for Catani, you wounded him in the hand, leg, and chest. His Indians brought him to me. I sent him on to the hospital at Shell Mera where the doctor took out all those bullets you put into him. Yes, Catani still lives. He is back home once more and getting well.'

Tsantiacu gave an outcry as of one betrayed. 'What did you do that for? Why did you not let him die? Are you not my friend?'

I decided we might as well have it out.

'What's more,' I told him, 'the doctor who is here now, helping free your family from sickness and pain, is the very same doctor who took the bullets from Catani and saved his life.'

Again the question, 'Why? Why?' I faced Tsantiacu.

'We wanted Catani to live. Only if he lived could he hear God's Word and become God's child.'

The chief appeared to be struggling to understand this new thought.

'Do you mean that if he becomes God's child, then he will have a new heart and will not want to kill any more?'

'Yes, you say the truth.'

'Then preach to him plenty!' he said as he walked away.

Had I made an impression on this tough old warrior? Could he see that God's compassion was great enough to give me love for both him and Catani? Had the strain between us been resolved? I could not tell.

The plane came. I was to fly out on the last shuttle to Wampimi.

As Tsantiacu walked with me to the plane, he put his arm around my shoulders and said, 'Panchu – I will never threaten you again so long as I live. Come back and tell us more about God's Book as soon as you can.'

As always, I praised the Lord. After all our struggles, setbacks, and disappointments, the door to the hearts of the Atshuara was open. There was every reason, too, to hope that it would stay open so that Christ's Church could someday be established here. This experience was a lesson in God's power to us missionaries – as well as to these Indians.

# CHAPTER FOURTEEN
# SHUARTICA BEGINS TO SHAKE

The weapons we fight with are not the weapons of the world. On the contrary, they have divine power to demolish strongholds (2 Corinthians 10:4).

Roj was gone but the impact of his testimony was strongly felt in Makuma. When I had first returned from Palm Beach I told the Shuara believers the story of Operation Auca. Their hearts, too, were touched.

'He was our brother,' said one, 'and now he is dead.'

'Oh, but we will see him again,' said another. 'He has gone to heaven just a little while ahead of the rest of us. We will soon catch up to him.'

And they all agreed that because he had died for the sake of reaching wild men for Christ, they would be willing to do the same. Their zeal to spread the gospel increased. Attendance in the church services rose. Back-slidden members repented and prayed to God, seeking forgiveness and promising to live righteously.

I encouraged the leading believers to take more responsibility in conducting the services and business meetings. Within a few weeks, during one of the monthly business sessions, the baptized believers, who by this time numbered twenty, elected six of their number as elders. These became the main preachers, manual work directors, treasurers, and evangelists. They also enlisted other members to help them. There was no paid pastor. But the organization of the church was no longer only my responsibility. We worked together. Although I continued teaching the Wednesday Bible studies, I would not preach on Sundays unless they asked me. When the church needed repairing, or land had to be cleared for new school gardens, they accepted these duties as a part of their job.

In January 1958, a group of the elders came to me with a new proposition. 'Panchu,' they said, 'we think you are right when you tell us we should hold school for nine months of the year. With only short sessions, such as you have held up till now, the children forget what they have learned from one term to the next. How can we help?'

'You will have to help a great deal,' I told them. 'This is not my school; it is yours – for your boys and girls. You will have to take much of the responsibility. You will have to see that the children come and that they stay in school. I will find the teachers. We are in need of a new dining hall and kitchen. These you must build. Someone must be found to cook for the children. Above all, you will have to plant bigger gardens if we are to have enough food throughout the whole nine months.'

After further discussion, they were satisfied and I was delighted with their long hoped for co-operation. *Shuartica* was loosening its hold. By this time many parents wanted to send their children to school, and were persuading some unbelievers to do the same. I was no longer alone in my battle. When problems came up about the cooks, food supply, new buildings, teachers, clothing, medicines, or runaway boys, I took them to the Shuara church leaders and together we prayed and worked out solutions. The Indians began to respect these joint decisions

– changes that were being made, not by a white man alone, but by their own people as well.

The following October we launched our first nine-month school term. The Indians had built a big new dining hall. Chingasu and Chumpi did the cooking, with half their salaries paid by church offerings, half by us. The school enrollment had reached nearly a hundred, so we employed two Christian Ecuadorians as teachers.

But now that we had to feed all these children for a full nine months, the gardens weren't nearly big enough. The Indians themselves helped by bringing basket loads of cassava, plantain, and smoked tapir, mostly to sell, and occasionally to give to the school kitchen. This supply at best, however, was spasmodic.

I gave much thought to this problem and kept encouraging the Indians to plant bigger gardens. By improving my own jungle farming methods I could show the Indians how to get more out of the poor clay-type soil. As I studied the way the Shuara farmed, I knew that here, too, *shuartica* would have to change.

Since the planting as well as the cultivating and harvesting is done by the women, I would have to talk with one of them about it. Who better than wise old Chingasu? She was always at hand, cooking for the school children.

One afternoon, as she stood in the kitchen watching a huge kettle of soup bubbling over an open fire, she seemed in a talkative mood. I asked her a few questions to draw her out, then sat on a stump stool and listened as she related the Shuara women's age-old way of insuring a good crop.

This is Chingasu's story:

I think of a time when we had just finished planting a new, big garden. Our whole family had suffered much trying to get established in a new place. I was only a little girl then, but I remember it well. We had made a big clearing and built part of our house. We had to carry our food from so far away, that even while we worked we were always weak with hunger. None of us wanted to go through this again. We wanted to make sure we had plenty to eat in the future.

At last our new garden was planted. True to *shuartica,* we had to perform a secret ceremony. My mother got me up early one morning. We left the house quietly.

Mother carried in her hands a small clay bowl. Within it was a little stone with mysterious powers – a little stone we called *nantar.* We had painted our faces and our arms bright red with a dye from the *annotto* tree; without this protection, my mother told me, the spirit in the stone would draw the blood from our bodies. Mother looked to the right and to the left to make sure no one was watching. I carried some more of the *annotto* dye to paint the *nantar* when we reached the garden.

My great-grandmother had used this very stone in her gardens; and so had my grandmother; and so had my mother after her. Only now I was learning its true meaning. The *nantar* is always passed from the mother to oldest daughter in the family. Being the oldest girl, the *nantar* was to come to me as soon as I married. When I was younger, I knew my mother had often gone out to see the *nantar.* But we children were never allowed to go near the spot where it was hidden. Mother told us that if we touched it we would become sick and might even die. I don't think this was really so. I think she was afraid we might show other people where it was, because there were lots of women who did not have a *nantar* to hide in their gardens. They wanted one, because it would make their food grow well and they would even steal a *nantar* so they could have a good crop.

Now, out in the far end of the garden, just as the sun was coming up, my mother made a pile of sticks. She set the bowl on them and took the clear flint-like stone gently in her hands. I handed her the dye, and as she applied the fresh covering of pretty red, she sang a strange song.

She told me that in this stone was the spirit of her great-grandmother. Her own grandmother, whom she remembered, had been a great woman, too. She never lacked for food. Everything she planted grew wonderfully well; her cassava was of tremendous size, her sweet potatoes the largest and sweetest anywhere around. She was a hard worker and had lots of children.

'So now, dear child,' my mother told me, 'we must treat this stone with much care and secrecy. If we do, our gardens will grow and grow and we shall not know hunger. I am the best loved of my husband's wives because I feed him the most. Learn, my child, and you, too, will be loved by your husband and your name will be well known throughout the jungle. Just look at our neighbor's family. Are they fat? If their mother had a *nantar*, maybe she would have a bit more energy and would work a little harder and more of her children would live. As it is, her husband looks like a snake and a hungry one at that. No wonder they are always coming here to beg food. What a shame to be so lazy! My dear daughter, don't you ever be like that!'

Placing the *nantar* back in the bowl, my mother covered it with some wide leaves so that the rain would not wet it. 'The spirit must not suffer,' she said. 'If it does, you will be awakened in the night by its cries: "I am suffering, oh, I am suffering so. Come see me, come see me. I need you." When you hear the voice of the spirit you must obey, and the next morning before it gets light you must come and see the *nantar*. You'll find that it has become moldy or wet. Then it must be repainted with the *annotto* dye. But before you touch it, be sure you have plenty of the red dye on your face and hands. I don't want you to lose all your blood.'

Having finished her instructions, my mother stretched her hands out over the garden. Then she sang a song to *Nungui*, the earth goddess. She sang as feelingly as you do when you pray. The sacred stone was well covered and hidden, and we returned home.

So the *nantar* is handed down from mother to daughter and moved from garden to garden to make things grow. We thought it would help; we knew no better. If I had known the true God before, I would have prayed to Him. But how were we to find out about Him if you missionaries hadn't come? God is the one who can help us grow more food, not the earth mother.

I agreed with her. She turned to her soup. I thanked her and went about my chores.

We needed to clear more jungle to plant more gardens, so I bought a section of land from the Ecuadorian government. This made us the owners on paper; but the real owner was the stubborn, tangled, snake-infested ancient growth. We now began our attack.

Cutting down trees anywhere calls for skill; but the Shuara are the best ax men I have ever seen. Since the vines are so thick, there is no room for the horizontal swing we use. Instead, they bring the ax up after the stroke and around their heads in a smooth continuous motion, flashing it down to the cut again and again.

First the smaller trees in the area to be cleared are cut about halfway through the trunk. Then the middle-sized trees are hacked until they begin to weave. Finally the ax-man singles out a big tree in a key position that can be made to fall on the smaller ones. He chops away until a creaking sound warns him to run clear. As the giant falls it starts a chain reaction like a tenpin in a bowling alley. With leaves and branches flying, it carries all the smaller, weakened trees in its path, laying the whole space open to the light and warmth of the sun.

This could be a dangerous moment for the ax man. If he had to re-enter the area now, he might run afoul of poisonous snakes angered by having their hiding-place in the branches disturbed. But long before the trees are cut down, the underbrush has been cleared away and the corn sowed broadcast. No one need enter the patch till harvest time. Their method, though shocking to an Iowa farmer, is no doubt best for these sons of the jungle.

Planting cassava requires a different procedure. Every inch of the ground must be grubbed of its vegetation and small bushes which are piled around the field literally by the ton. The trees are then chopped down one at a time, and the leaves and limbs trimmed away before the next is felled.

A man and his wife will work from one to three months to clear a patch one hundred yards square. If the weather is bad it may take much longer. When the space is what the Indians call cleared – although it may be littered with hundreds of trees large and small – the women loosen the ground with a pointed stick and put in place the six-inch cuttings of the cassava plant. Within two months the weeds start to grow and the women must spend more hours slashing away with machetes to keep them down. Since it takes a year for this crop to mature, the long tuber becomes expensive in terms of labor. For lack of food the Indians are likely to start eating the cassava tubers before they are full-sized, thus further reducing the harvest.

Hunger, an ever-present phantom, stalks the Shuara. He looks upon it as an inevitable fact of life. Nor does a good harvest insure the Indian of having enough for his household, for visiting relatives may descend upon him at any time like locusts.

I learned more of this from Wampiu, when he complained that so many relatives had been staying with him for so long that he was about to run out of food. I asked if *shuartica* demanded he carry hospitality to such extremes. He replied that it did, explaining that if a Shuara didn't feed his relatives when he had enough himself, he was considered selfish. For this reason, many Shuara planted their small gardens close to the house, and had big ones off in the bush where they could not be seen.

The Indians would farm their hard-cleared patches for a couple of years; then, upon finding the weeds too thick to fight, they would move away and start the process all over again elsewhere. To have an Indian here today and gone tomorrow was not very healthy for the church. He might have become a Christian while with us; but for him to move too far to come to services or send his children to school was not good. He would have no Bible instruction and no fellowship with other Christians. His children, finding no other believers with whom to marry, could not found Christian homes. No indigenous church could well develop among a roving population.

More food for our school children, a different way of life for our church members – these were some of the goals before us. To achieve them, we would have to make basic changes in our missionary methods for these primitive people. The gospel was saving their souls. But if the church did not have a better climate in which to grow, it would never be able to stand on its own feet without missionaries. More food, and a more stable way of life, could result only from better ways of farming. But we could not learn, nor could the Indians learn, overnight. We would have to proceed by trial and error. It would be a long undertaking.

Perhaps one of the most significant things we had already accomplished was to help the Indians get cattle. When they had harvested most of the food and weeds were taking over, we encouraged them not to abandon the land but to plant it to pasture grass. For several years we had had our own small herd of cattle to supply milk for our children. We had bought some calves over in the Upano Valley and while they were still young, Nate and Hobey had flown them to Makuma.

We worked out a program whereby we gave heifer calves from our herd to the Indians. Since they had so little money, and we did not believe in outright gifts, we kept a half-interest. When the animals were sold, our half went toward educating their children. In this way they got a start for nothing and helped themselves at the same time.

Ramon, the chief Shuara elder in the church, was our first customer. He bought his heifer outright with money he had earned sawing boards for the missionary dwellings. Ramon treated his heifer like a pet and did such a good job of raising it that he set an example for the others.

This encouraged us. We saw that the cattle program could be a stabilizing influence. As Marie pointed out, 'It would be hard for an Indian with a cow and a pasture to put his possessions in a basket and move away.'

Our mission farm was becoming an agricultural experiment station as well as a source of food. Rice was introduced and proved very successful. Lima beans did remarkably well. A new strain of corn produced three times as much as the scraggly Indian maize. But for the first five or six years we had done all our farming with no other tools than machetes, shovels, and axes.

Then new help came to us in the form of a small tractor, a gift from a friend, Mr. Leonard Reimer, a Canadian Christian businessman. With this equipment we could expand our program. One of our time-consuming chores was to keep the airstrip clear. Where ten Indians were needed for a week every two months to cut the grass with machetes, now with the tractor and sickle bar we could do it in a matter of hours.

The Indians were greatly impressed with the new machine. On one occasion I heard a Shuara say to a visitor, 'Does not that beast do much work? Does it ever get tired? Does it ever feel the heat of the sun?'

But the Indian babies cried at the sight of it whenever their mothers took them past the place where we were working.

I began to experiment with methods of planting cassava. Having read in a magazine that cassava cuttings in the Far East were planted in the ground vertically, rather than horizontally, I decided to try it. Opposition arose immediately.

I plowed a piece of land near the house and asked the schoolboys to bring some cassava sticks. They protested: only women planted cassava. I told them we were going to try a new way.

A serious old Shuara mother watched me, and shaking her

head, assured me that cassava planted in that way would produce nothing.

Contrary to all expectations, the plants grew very well. Then everyone said, 'But will they yield any fruit?' When the cassava roots were ready to dig up, the Indians were surprised and very pleased. The tuber was almost half again as large as their former ones. No doubt plowing the land had as much to do with it as anything. But I had a lot of fun letting them think my new way of planting might have helped.

Now that we had food in plenty, we could watch the growing number of children coming to school with happiness and confidence. We were especially pleased that more than a third were girls.

We hoped their lives would be better from now on, for we were making progress in teaching the Indians many new customs, all of which would affect the future of these children. Among these customs were: postponing marriage until the girls had at least reached their teens; replacing polygamy with marriage between one man and one woman; learning to call on God for help, instead of on the witch doctor; learning to accept death as from God, rather than as a curse from an enemy.

At this time help came to us from an unexpected source. Representatives of the Ecuadorian government in Macas co-operated with us in helping to stop tribal wars and polygamy.

But these destructive customs, a part of *shuartica,* so long entrenched, were not to be quickly or easily routed. Heartbreaking situations arose to plague this generation in the years of changing from the old to the new. There was ten-year-old Tsapacu, for example. Although her father, Jeencham, had heard the gospel since Ernest Johnson first came to Makuma in 1945, he still adhered to all the old customs of *shuartica.* He let his daughter come to school only because her mother had died and there was no one to care for her. But to obtain a new wife for himself, he planned to sell Tsapacu. She was just the age of our own Irene, which impressed on us how unready the child was for marriage. But not so Jeencham. He was going to take her out of school and give her to a young man named Jua, the son of an old Cangaimi witch doctor. In return, Jeencham would receive the witch doctor's desirably plump teenage daughter as his own wife.

I heard about this and, knowing that Tsapacu didn't want to be married, sent word to Jeencham that either the child would come to school or I'd call the government soldiers. Tsapacu came – but so did Jua.

Although they lived in separate dormitories, the others looked on them as man and wife. Jua kept track of everything Tsapacu did and sent her little presents of soap and bobby-pins. As she soared on the swing, or played tag, she looked like any other carefree child. But when we asked her if Jua was really her husband, she ducked her head in shy assent. In spite of the fact that the bargain had been struck and the old custom not completely changed, the young couple were attending school. This showed that *shuartica* was giving way, even among the unbelievers.

Besides helping with the outstations, school, and farm, the believers often worked together with us on the language. Although it was not *shuartica*, they wanted to learn to read the Bible for themselves and were vitally interested in solving translation and literacy problems.

Even some of the women could give Bible lessons and help Marie express Bible history and truths. Old Chingasu, though she could not read, often taught the weekly women's Bible class. Her first attempt years before was one that Marie would never forget. A group of nearly forty women had gathered to sing, pray, and learn more of the Word of God. At that time most of them were still unbelievers. Chingasu stood before them, her dark eyes flashing to the challenge. Impatiently, she flung a lock of unruly hair out of her eyes and spread her open hands for all to see.

'I do not hold any paper,' she admitted simply. 'I am one

who cannot read to you from God's Book. Only what I have heard and know in my heart to be true, can I tell to you. Listen well, and you will learn, too.'

She then proceeded to tell with amazing accuracy the story of creation and man's fall into sin, and of his redemption through the death and resurrection of Jesus Christ. She spoke with such vividness and eloquence that she held her audience enthralled. No one scratched or turned a head to look outside. She made the way of salvation clearer than we foreigners could do.

As Marie listened to Chingasu's presentation, she was more convinced than ever of the importance of teaching the Indians to read as well as of encouraging them to help translate the Bible.

'If we should have to leave them without the written Word, they could not last long in the battle against their old evil customs,' she said. 'The Shuara church needs the Bible in the language of its people.'

Marie was not alone in her conviction. She was only one of several missionaries who were working toward this goal.

While Roger Youderian was still with us he had worked long hours with the Indians to develop reading materials in Shuara. Just before he went on his mission to the Aucas, he handed Marie a big oatmeal box.

'You probably won't have time to look at this before I get back,' he said, 'but in case you do, here it is.' He smiled and left the room.

When she opened the box she found it filled with hundreds of illustrations of animals, birds, reptiles, insects, plants, trees, and other visual objects of the Shuara world. Some he had traced; some were original sketches. All were accompanied by the Shuara names he had learned from the Indians. We were awed to think how many hours he had devoted, without our knowing it, to that monumental work. We hoped to carry on what he had begun.

His was one more contribution to the missionary effort. Mr.

and Mrs. Charles Olson had begun the job of reducing Shuara to writing. At that time Shuara had no written alphabet. The Olsons based their proposed grammar on the structure of their own language and Spanish. An Italian priest, Padre Juan Ghinnassi, who worked most of his life among the Shuara in the southern Upano Valley, put together a grammar which he had printed in the early thirties. This was a help to all of us. The priest and the Olsons had also compiled dictionaries. Ernest Johnson added simplified grammatical forms and illustrative sentences. Dorothy Walker further revised the grammar and taught it in lesson form to the Youderians and other new missionaries.

While Dorothy and Barb lived and taught in Cangaimi, we were joined in Makuma by Mr. and Mrs. Glen Turner, of the Wycliffe Bible Translators. Glen, a linguistic scholar, further analyzed the grammar and shortened the alphabet to twenty-three letters, thus making it phonetically scientific. Then we and the Turners incorporated everyone's contributions and produced the first five simple Shuara reading primers. Marie taught them to the school children and to classes of adults. Believers like Wampiu, Chingasu, and Tsamaraing were delighted to discover that their own language could speak to them from marks on paper. Some of them took copies home to teach other members of their families. They began to hope they could learn to read God's Word.

In all the world there were less than twenty thousand people using the Shuara language. With its limited alphabet, its nasalized and voiceless vowels which changed the meaning of words, it was one of the most difficult of languages to learn, and particularly to set down in written form. Yet if these Indians were ever to understand the true meaning of the gospel in the only way it could be brought home to them, namely, in their own tongue, the job had to be done by someone. Dorothy Walker of GMU and Glen and Jean Turner of Wycliffe focused their energies on this task.

Then they enlisted the aid of the Christian Indians in translating passages of Scripture from Spanish to Shuara. The Indians had already helped us coin words and phrases needed in preaching Scriptural truths – words for God, Jesus Christ, devil, prayer, peace, and others.

Even 'Yus Shuara' had been their own choice for 'Christian.' We foreigners knew we could not produce accurate translations without their co-operation.

When the leading believers, who by now were growing rapidly in knowledge of the Word and Christian responsibility, first sat down to write God's Word, they thought it would be a simple task. Some of the very ones who years before had ridiculed our preoccupation with paper and pencil, began to understand that this was hard work. A new door of intellectual accomplishments was opening before them. Day after day they improved translations of already familiar verses and worked on new ones.

When the translators dealt with John 1:11, 12 – 'He came to that which was his own, but his own did not receive him. Yet to all who received him, to those who believed in his name, he gave the right to become the children of God' – we were puzzled by the word 'receive.' Although we considered using the Shuara words for 'buy' and 'take,' neither of these fitted this situation. We explained to the Indians that we needed a word that meant 'to take or bring into one's heart' as they would a visitor in their homes.

'I know a word,' said Wampiu. 'Once when Tsantiacu came to visit an Indian in Wampimi they wouldn't open the door to let him in. The door was barred. Tsantiacu called "I am Tsantiacu, Tsantiacu, Tsantiacu," but they would not *"itaacharrniayi,"* accept him.'

'That is the word I want,' we said immediately. The finished translation read thus: 'He came to the things that He had made but His own people did not bring Him in. But to any person who does bring Him in, God makes to become His own – to all those who say "yes" to His Son.'

When through our joint efforts such verses as these became clearly understandable to them, they gained a new appreciation of the translation task and of the important contribution they themselves had to make.

But greater victories over *shuartica* were still ahead. *Shuartica* refuses to accept death as a natural end of life – but attributes it to an enemy's curse. Our Makuma Indians had to learn from experience how faith in Christ could triumph over their most dreaded enemy, death.

It was a quiet morning, something unusual at the mission station. The silence was broken by the shrill voices of our little school girls calling, *'Shuara winawai! Shuara winawai!'* This warned us we were about to have Indian visitors.

Marie and I stepped out to greet Uyungara, a powerfully-built warrior from the headwaters of the Makuma who had the reputation of an evil killer. His skin was hideously mottled from the ravages of *pinta*, a blue skin disease.

But he appeared gentle and soft-spoken. By his side stood a tiny Shuara woman, who was plainly very ill. Uyungara's small restless eyes shifted from the woman to us and back again before he could find words to speak. Then they poured out, the gaps filled in by the other Indians who had come with them. The woman was Masuinga, Uyungara's favorite wife. Sick as she was, she had walked the long trail from her home on the other side of the Cutucú Mountains in the hope that we could help her.

As Marie and I looked at her, our first impression was that she must be not only pregnant, but past due by at least a month. Her relatives, however, hastened to assure us to the contrary. Just three months ago, they said, she had been normal and it was only since that time that her abdomen had swollen to its present enormous size. Here was something baffling. She did not seem to be suffering a great deal of pain, but she was very tired and had difficulty breathing.

We took Masuinga to the dispensary for an examination, and Marie wrote down her symptoms on one of our cards: 'Huge swollen abdomen. No fever. Bowel movements normal. Urination normal. No swelling of feet, hands, or face. No engorgement of breasts. Respiration, 36; heartbeat, 105. Abdominal cavity appears to be filled with liquid.'

We lost no time in communicating these symptoms by radio to Dr. Fuller at Shell Mera. He offered to come, and arrived next day by MAF plane, bringing with him the instruments necessary to perform a minor operation. He went directly to our dispensary where Marie was waiting with Masuinga.

Marie now continues with the story, since she was the one most closely concerned:

Masuinga sat on the edge of the operating table, her feet swinging freely. Uyungara stood behind her, holding her little hands in his rough, mottled paws. He showed as much concern for her as Frank would have for me in a similar situation. Watching the tenderness with which he comforted his wife, it was hard for me to think of him as having taken part in many murders and head-shrinkings.

Dr. Fuller gave Masuinga a local anesthetic. Then he skillfully made a small incision and inserted the trocar. With this instrument he passed through the abdominal wall, allowing the liquid to flow out slowly into a pail. We measured six gallons before the liquid stopped running. When Dr. Fuller had finished stitching the incision, Uyungara turned to me with tears in his eyes and said pleadingly, 'Now give her one of your injections so her stomach won't fill up again.'

I interpreted for him. Dr. Fuller solemnly shook his head. 'There isn't any cure. Tell him there isn't any hope of her ever getting completely well. She appears to have either cirrhosis of the liver or cancer. All that can be done is to remove the fluid again when it fills up, which we'll be glad to do.'

I repeated to Uyungara in Shuara what the doctor had said.

He was heartbroken at the news. He begged us to fly Masuinga to the hospital for treatment. 'If only you will make my wife well,' he said, 'I will work for you for the rest of my life.'

I talked to him all that afternoon. Knowing how hopeless it was, I could only comfort him by telling him of the beautiful heavenly home that waited for Masuinga if she would become a Christian. Once he interrupted: 'Oh, as for me, yes, I'm a wicked Shuara, I know. I have killed many Shuara. But my wife is not bad. She does not kill. She only prepares good food and serves it to me. Why should she have to suffer and die?'

This I was unable to explain to him; he was not yet ready to understand.

For several days they stayed with us near the mission station. Our Shuara believers did their best to give her an understanding of eternal life as they visited with her. After gaining strength she walked to her relatives' home. Christians from our church took her a portable phonograph and the gospel records she had first heard and enjoyed in Makuma.

Six weeks later Uyungara brought Masuinga back again in the same unwieldy condition as before. This time we did not have to send for Dr. Fuller. Fellow missionaries Bill and Gladis Gibson had just returned from furlough. Gladis, who had had medical training, was able to drain off the liquid with a borrowed trocar. Once more Masuinga thanked us; but it made us sad to know we could offer only temporary relief. We wondered how much longer she would live.

She heartened us one day by saying in a firm, confident voice that she was no longer afraid to die. She now had sure hope of everlasting life with the Lord; therefore it no longer mattered to her what happened to her earthly body.

Uyungara worked faithfully every day to help pay for Masuinga's medical care. Once he disappeared and we learned he had gone fishing in a nearby stream. In the Shuara way, he built a dam, then rinsed a basket of pulverized rotenone roots in the water just above it.

The milk-like fluid, mixed with water, suffocated any fish unlucky enough to be there. Uyungara could then wade in and pick them up with his hands.

Late in the afternoon he appeared at our door, offering his basket of fish. The largest were not so big as his fist, the smallest not so large as his little finger. There was hardly a meal there for Masuinga and him, let alone for us. Yet to have refused would have hurt Uyungara, so I gladly accepted the tidbits which we found were delicious.

The next day I returned the favor by taking Masuinga some ripe plantains as a gift from us. This led to a long talk with Masuinga, which brought us much closer together.

It was late in the afternoon, a beautiful hour. We sat together in her doorway, watching the sun go down behind the Cutucús. The familiar saddle hump and the lower ridges stood out black against the brilliant pink and orange of the sunset sky. Masuinga looked at me inquiringly.

'Is the country where you used to live anything like this one?' she asked. Then, before I had a chance to answer her first question, she went on, 'Do you have a living mother and father? Or any brothers and sisters?'

As I groped for words in Shuara to picture sights she had never seen, I described our large cities, farms, the highways, and the factory where my parents worked in the United States. I told her about my only sister and her family.

She seemed surprised that I had living parents and a sister. She couldn't understand why I had left them, why I had chosen to live so far away.

'Don't you love them?' she asked.

This viewpoint was not unfamiliar to me. I had found that most of the Indians – not unlike many people in the States – thought we could only have come here for reasons of personal gain, or because we lacked the intelligence to make a living at home.

I told Masuinga why we were here. I explained to her in

terms she could grasp that the Creator God who had made the sunset and the mountains had called us to come and give His Word to her Shuara.

'We have found so much joy and so much satisfaction in serving Him,' I said, 'that we would not change places with anyone in the world.' A warm smile of understanding lit up her face.

She wondered why, since my parents were still living, I had no other sisters or brothers. She wanted to know if people in my country killed one another like the Shuara. This led her to tell me a moving account of her life as a Shuara.

Long ago when my dear mother was very young and I was just a child, my father was killed. We lived then, far away, on the other side of the hills near the big volcano, Sangay.

One night the rain was beating hard on our roof. The wind was blowing – 'Ooo-ooo-ajamai.' Suddenly many enemy Shuara rushed upon our house. We could not see them until they were among us, shouting and shooting. They killed all the men, among them my father. Mother tied my baby sister to her back and we ran out into the rainy night. Never did we go back to live in that country. Never have I had any more brothers or sisters.

The sun had gone down behind the Cutucús. As I looked out over the beautiful landscape and thought of what Masuinga had just told me, I recalled the words of the old hymn: 'Where every prospect pleases and only man is vile.'

We sat for a few minutes longer and prayed together. Several days later, Masuinga went back to her relatives' house with her husband.

A month passed. Then we received word on the radio that Uyungara and Masuinga had appeared at the hospital in Shell Mera. That tireless strong-willed Indian had carried his wife on his back over the two-day trail from his home to Macas. With money earned by working for white colonists, he had paid for their passage on a small commercial airline to Shell Mera. Uyungara stubbornly refused to give up hope that his wife would yet improve, if only she could get better treatment.

At the hospital, he encountered Dr. Fuller again. But Masuinga now had malaria as well.

Throughout the night she lay unconscious while Uyungara watched at her side and the missionary nurse despaired of her life.

At this time I left Frank in Makuma in order to visit our children in school at Quito. I went by way of Shell Mera. But since my schedule was tight, I hadn't thought of stopping in to see the Indian couple. Masuinga was in good hands and there was nothing, really, that I could do for her.

When I reached Shell Mera, the pilots told me to eat a quick lunch as they would be ready to take off for Quito by 1:00 p.m. Our flight, however, was postponed again and again owing to heavy clouds over the mountains. After the first delay, I lay down to rest and fell fast asleep.

I was awakened with a message from Uyungara who had heard I was in Shell Mera. Masuinga had regained consciousness and wanted me to go to her. I felt rebuked. How could I have gone to sleep after lunch when these people were so in need of my encouragement and friendship?

I was distressed to see Masuinga lying there, her face drawn with pain, her eyeballs yellowed with the disease, her lips and eyelids puffy from the high fever.

All afternoon we talked and sang hymns, repeated Scripture, and prayed in Shuara. Again Masuinga gave sweet testimony of her trust in the Lord. Again she declared she was not afraid to die, now that she was God's child. The radiant smile on her face, the light in her eyes, the sound of her high thin voice as she joyously sang the new and wonderful words of the hymns, made me feel she was already closer to heaven than to earth.

Now that I was assured Masuinga knew the Lord, I wanted

Uyungara to know Him too. Turning to the strong man, I asked, 'When do you expect to become a Yus Shuara? What are you waiting for?'

His face broke into the most beautiful smile – yes, in spite of his blackened teeth and his mottled skin, his expression made it beautiful – and said, 'I am already God's child.'

I could hardly wait to tell this to Frank and the Shuara believers back in Makuma.

When I asked Uyungara to pray, he addressed the Lord God in heaven who had given him a new heart and began describing his present situation.

Halfway through, he started talking to me instead of to the Lord. I opened my eyes and looked at him. His eyes were still closed and his black brows knit in the conscious effort of pretending to talk to someone he could not see. He seemed totally unconscious of the fact that he was using 'Señora' where he should have used 'God'. He had not yet learned to close with 'In Jesus' name, let it be so,' so when he came to the end he merely declared, 'That's all I have to say right now,' and opened his eyes.

I really believed that this sinful old Shuara had accepted Christ.

I left Shell Mera feeling very humble. I thought to myself, 'What reason have I ever to complain? Why should I waste time and effort on non-essentials when there are people so hungry for the knowledge of the Lord?'

After my visit in Quito, I returned to Makuma where Frank told me that Masuinga and Uyungara had come from Shell Mera and were now staying again with their relatives in the neighborhood.

I asked Frank if Uyungara had said anything about having become a Christian. Frank told me that he had asked Uyungara point-blank whether he were God's child. The old warrior had turned away his head, muttering only that he was thinking about it.

My high hopes were dashed. Uyungara must have purposely deceived me then, hoping that if he professed Christianity, he would get better care for his wife. Then I thought of his faithfulness to Masuinga. Could I blame him? All I could do was to pray for him.

Another month went by. One night, while I was on my knees in our bedroom, I felt I had an urgent message from the Lord. He was trying to impress on me that I ought to go visit Masuinga. I would not have had such an impulse by myself, because she was already beyond my help.

Before I could get ready to go, word came to us by way of the jungle grapevine that Masuinga had died. I found this very puzzling. I could not understand why the Lord had asked me to go to her, knowing that she was already dead.

The next day came the explanation; the rumor was false. Masuinga, though still living, was so emaciated and distorted that she could hardly sit up or move. To the Shuara mind, weakness is the same as death, so the mistake was a natural one. However, it confirmed my faith to know that the still, small voice, which had spoken to my innermost being, had not come from my imagination.

Almost immediately thereafter, Masuinga's brother-in-law came to say that she wanted me. She needed badly to be tapped again. Unhappily, Bill and Gladis Gibson were away. But another friend and I decided that we would go. Chumpi and Chingasu volunteered to come along.

The room in which we found Masuinga seemed cluttered and full. Several dogs were tied to the bed poles. Little children sat or stood about eyeing us shyly. Women were busy nursing babies, tending their fires, and preparing the food for cooking.

On a rack at one side lay Masuinga. The eyes she turned on us were clear and bright as she welcomed us with a smile of recognition. She remained cheerful and talkative for the three hours of our visit.

She told us how much it meant to her to have another

Christian in the house. She was referring to the eleven-year-old girl from our school, with whom she prayed and sang hymns.

About twenty-five Indians gathered around as Chingasu and Chumpi each gave testimony of what God had done for them and recited truths they had learned from the Bible. When it came to Masuinga's turn and she began to pray in her weak, yet unfaltering voice, no one stirred or whispered. Even the dogs were hushed and still. She prayed for everyone in the room, repeating their names and asking that all would be changed in heart, as she had been, in order that one day they would be unafraid of dying.

Masuinga proudly but sadly showed me a dress she had been making out of some material that Uyungara had bought for her. This was most unusual, for among Shuara, it is *shuartica* for the men to do the sewing. She was sad because she had almost finished the dress and now she would have nothing to do with her hands, no way to fill the long, empty hours.

This made me think of all the dresses for the schoolgirls that would have to be sewed before the beginning of the next term. I asked Masuinga if she would not like to do some of this sewing. She responded with delight, so I promised to send her material, scissors, and thread. Her face brightened as she said she would make the first one for her little Christian friend who had been such a comfort to her.

I noticed that Uyungara was conspicuous by his absence. Masuinga told me quite frankly that he was searching for another witch doctor, one who would be powerful enough to effect her cure. I reminded her then of the scene at Shell Mera and of how I had been convinced of Uyungara's conversion. She shook her head slowly.

'He has not really become God's child,' she said. 'He told you that so you would think well of him and give me more help. But he has not changed his old ways one bit.'

She asked me to pray for him. But even more, she wanted me to pray for her one young son, Wachapa, who would soon be left without her care. 'I want Wachapa to learn God's way. He is old enough now to be in your school. But his father will not let him go. He is bent on teaching him *shuartica* in order that he will grow to be a strong warrior – one who will kill, and drink, and have many wives. But that is not what I want. I want him to learn God's Word and be a Yus Shuara.' As I sat listening to this Shuara woman lying on the bamboo rack in the dimness of that smoky room, I realized I had never been in the presence of anyone closer to the Lord. Heaven was real to her – and she was almost there!

But I was sorry I had neither the skill nor the instruments to relieve her of the burden of liquid that had again stretched her abdomen to such unbelievable limits. Before I left, Masuinga made me promise that I would be back in a week – the following Wednesday – to help her. I gave the promise readily. At the moment I could see no reason why I couldn't fulfill it. Gladis and Bill were due back in Makuma in five days. I was certain that Gladis would go with me to perform the simple operation.

A day or so after my return, I was dismayed to hear over the radio that the Gibsons would be detained for several days more. How could I keep my promise now? I pictured Masuinga lying there on her bamboo rack, with her perfect faith in the Lord and in me, waiting in vain – hour after hour – for me to come. She might die before Gladis could get there to help her.

Prayer was all I had left. 'O God,' I prayed, 'send someone before the week is over – someone who will be able to relieve Masuinga before it is too late.'

My answer came in an unexpected way.

Two days before the week was over, on the regular morning radio contact Dr. Fuller sent me a message from Quito that he had a good friend from the States to whom he wanted to show some of the medical work being done among the jungle Indians. He asked if it would be convenient for them to come to Makuma at this time, and if there were any Indians particularly in need of a doctor's care. We sent back a quick affirmative to both questions, with a prayer of thanksgiving in our hearts.

We trusted the Lord for good weather. Wednesday dawned clear and cloudless, and we soon saw the yellow MAF plane over the trees, bringing in Dr. Fuller and his friend, Mr. John Copley, from Oley, Pennsylvania. Dr. Fuller had the trocar in his pocket and tennis shoes on his feet ready for the jungle hike. Mr. Copley insisted on going along in spite of his sixty years and lack of experience with jungle mud. His special interest in herbs and running comments on jungle plants enlivened our journey.

We found Masuinga even larger than when I last saw her. As she smiled her welcome and reached for my hand, she seemed to know that God had enabled us to keep our promise.

Dr. Fuller sat cross-legged on the bamboo rack and opened his black bag. The usual audience of naked children and longhaired Indians gathered round to watch. The incision was made and the trocar inserted without difficulty. Mr. Copley held a large clay pot while it was filled three times before the liquid would stop flowing. Then after a short service and visiting a while with Masuinga, we started homeward. Mission accomplished. Hearts contented. Promise fulfilled.

Three weeks later, just after Christmas, Gladis and I were planning to visit Masuinga again.

'We'll go next Tuesday,' I said, 'as soon as our children have returned to school in Quito.'

But on Friday an Indian runner came to Makuma. He brought word that Masuinga had died. This time it was true.

'Did she die like the rest of your people?' Frank asked the young man, who looked frightened at the very mention of the word 'death.'

'No,' the Indian said at last. 'It was very strange. Masuinga died differently. She wasn't afraid. When we heard her say "I'm dying," we all gathered around her bed to watch. But she did not scream or cry as others have done. She shut her eyes and smiled. She only said, *"Shiir jeajai"* ('I have arrived beautifully'). That was all.'

We could not be sorry that Masuinga had been released from her distorted body. She had helped her people to know God is real and it was a comfort to us that we would see her again.

It would make Masuinga happy to know that little Wachapa left Uyungara's house with his grandmother soon afterward, and never returned to live with his father. He and his grandmother live now with their relatives near the mission. Wachapa, who became a Christian, has been in our school every term since then.

From Masuinga's testimony on her deathbed, several Shuara men, women, and children have come to know Christ and have been freed from the fear of death that oppressed them for so long. This was a great triumph.

# CHAPTER FIFTEEN
# EVIDENCE OF THE HOLY SPIRIT
**But now in Christ Jesus you who once were far away have been brought near through the blood of Christ (Ephesians 2:13).**

The time had come for the Christian Shuara believers at Makuma to take the gospel to the Atshuara. But they could not go on foot because Catani was at large again. And we had no plane with which to fly them there.

Early in May 1956, we received word that the replacement plane had arrived. Johnny Keenan and Hobey Lowrence were both available to us as pilots; both wanted the experience of flying to all the outstations and landing on the short rough strips. Now we could proceed with our mission.

One Sunday morning at the close of the service I stood before the Indians and asked that everyone interested in teaching God's Word to the Atshuara remain seated. Most of them stayed.

'Since a new plane and pilot have arrived, I made a trip with them last week to visit the Atshuara,' I began. 'Tsantiacu and his people were happy to see us. They told me they would like us to come often so that they, too, may learn about God. But I cannot speak as clearly to them in their language as you can. Therefore it is up to you as Christians to go teach the Atshuara what you have learned and experienced of Jesus Christ's love and power.'

A hush fell over the room. Then came an outburst of excited voices.

'Will you go with us, Panchu, or do we go by ourselves?'

'There are no Yus Shuara among them. They may kill us.'

'Catani lives between us and Atshuara territory. He has said he intends to kill Tsantiacu. If Catani finds we are going to the chief's house, he may attack us, too.'

I raised my hand for quiet.

'Listen,' I said. 'I will tell you what Tsantiacu and I talked about. Perhaps that will quiet your fears. I told him, "Don't think that only foreigners like me know God. Do you remember Icam, who came to visit you? I want you to hear more of God's Word from other Yus Shuara. If I sent some to visit you, you would not feel like killing them, would you, because they were once your enemies?"'

'Tsantiacu looked at me solemnly and said without hesitating, "Oh, they aren't our enemies now. They are God's people. We wouldn't kill them."

'I asked if he would let you stay in his house, if he would feed you and take good care of you. He assured me he would. He only cautioned that you not go hunting or visiting, as other Atshuara who do not know you might shoot at you.

'The plane will take you to Tsantiacu's place. I will go with you but I won't stay long. Now – who will say to me "I will go"?'

There was a buzz of uneasy conversation. Some were afraid of flying, others of what might happen to them. At last Naicta – the one who had accompanied Keith and me on our first trip – and Ramon volunteered to go.

A few days later I flew with them to the Atshuara and

introduced them to their one-time enemies. Both Ramon and Naicta were Mura Shuara from the Upano Valley, whose people had never been friendly with the Atshuara. I bluntly told Tsantiacu that Naicta had been one of the war party who, years ago, killed his relative Chiriapa.

The two men and the chief greeted each other with no trace of fear or distrust. The change in Ramon and Naicta was plain to Tsantiacu. Instead of guns they came bringing mimeographed copies of Christian hymns and Scripture. I returned to Makuma, leaving the men happily counting off on their fingers those who had heard of Christ and those who had not.

Five days passed before the plane went back to bring them home. As Johnny flew over the landing strip he told us by radio he could see Ramon, Naicta, and the Atshuara walking with their arms around one another's shoulders. An hour later the Shuara stepped from the plane at Makuma loaded with gifts – beautiful feather ornaments, a live parrot, and some roast pig. They smiled at us, exclaiming, 'Already many of them want to become Christians.'

But we knew with what ease Indians can say 'Yes – I want to become God's child,' so we were not persuaded. However, we rejoiced with the two faithful witnesses while following in our hearts a policy of 'wait and see.'

Some days later I went to visit Tsantiacu again. He awkwardly tried to tell me that he was becoming like God's people. But he admitted he had gone with his warriors on a killing raid.

'We did not kill anybody,' he told me proudly. 'You and the believers from Makuma have taught us that God's Word says "Do not kill." So all we did was capture some of their women and bring them back in our canoes and turn them over to our own people.'

I felt like crying and laughing at the same time. How absurd that he should think that capturing and selling women would be acceptable Christian practice – even though it was somewhat better than killing. But at least it indicated that he was beginning to understand, in his own strange way, that sin separates people from God.

On another occasion Tsantiacu, greatly agitated, asked me if I'd help him learn to pray. 'I know God is powerful,' he said, 'and I need His help.' I asked why. 'I am getting threats from my enemies,' he replied. 'I hear they are planning a raid to kill us. I have my gun ready. But you tell us that God's people do not kill. If I am to defend myself, I must have God's help. I want to learn to pray.'

I couldn't tell whether Tsantiacu wanted to obey God no matter what happened, or whether he just wanted God's power to help him out of a tight situation. But I prayed with him, asking God to prevent the killers from reaching Tsantiacu's house. I told him to keep on praying, that I would return after two moons, and that, in the meantime, God would make it unnecessary for him to use that gun.

Two months later, Tsantiacu told me triumphantly that his enemies, the Copataza River Atshuara, had never reached his stockade. Word had come that they started out, then suddenly turned back when they were halfway over the four-day trail. This seemed to convince Tsantiacu that God could answer prayer.

I once asked Tsantiacu point-blank if he had become a Yus Shuara. This I rarely do with Indians, because they are inclined to answer in the affirmative, just for the sake of pleasing. I have learned that it is better to wait patiently for them to take the initiative in expressing a change of heart. But I put the question to him now because I wanted to know how much understanding of the gospel he had obtained from the believers. He looked at me a moment, then answered, 'Yes, I asked God's Son to come into my heart. But he hasn't done it.'

Then I knew that he did not yet understand the way of salvation.

After that first courageous visit of Naicta and Ramon, other

Indians from Makuma went to stay with the Atshuara, to teach them to know Christ. Among them were Chumpi and Chingasu who remained on different occasions for weeks at a time.

It is usual among the Indians for the men to become converted first. But in this instance most of the women became Christians before the men, largely due to the wonderful testimony and teaching of Chingasu.

She would gather a group of the women around her and begin her lesson as follows:

I am a Shuara woman who never heard about God when I was young. I never went to school and I do not know how to read. But I know God loves me – He has forgiven me for breaking His law and given me eternal life. Because Christ took my punishment on the cross and overcame death He now lives in my heart and that is why I am happy. Even those of you who are old like me and have never been to school can learn that Jesus died for your sins so you can be forgiven, too.

Chingasu's clear, sympathetic presentation won many converts. Tsantiacu's niece, Mamatu, was the first to be saved. When I visited there later, others in the household told me with awe that Mamatu had become a *Tikishmamtaicawaru* (one who has bowed the knee). 'She kneels and prays by herself every day,' they told me. 'The rest of us would like to do it. But we don't know how.'

One by one, through successive visits from the Christians from Makuma, many of them were converted.

I had long tried to persuade Chief Tsantiacu to come to Makuma to see the Christians and their church for himself. We discussed this possibility many times. But there was Catani to be reckoned with. Tsantiacu pointed out that the walk over the five-day trail would give his old enemy too many chances to do away with him.

When I promised to send the plane for him, he seemed to

lose his fear. Since I could not go myself, I recorded a message which Hobey could play to Tsantiacu upon landing: 'This is Panchu. Don't be afraid. Just sit quietly in the plane, and soon you will be in Makuma listening to God's Word with many of God's people. They are not your enemies. They love you and want to help you know God. Without fearing, you come.'

But Tsantiacu's reaction was unexpected. His old Indian superstition took hold of him. He was mystified by the voice coming from Hobey's little battery-powered tape recorder. He thought this was some piece of deceit on the part of his enemies to lure him away from his home so they could kill him.

There was poor Hobey on the ground with nothing but sign language to encourage the stubborn Tsantiacu who was refusing to come. Hobey called me at Makuma by radio and asked me what to do. I told him to put his earphones on the chief and let me talk to him. Hobey complied. Tsantiacu had worn the phones before and they did not frighten him. After much persuasion, I convinced him that this was really Panchu talking, and that he would be in no danger if he took the trip.

The chief took off the earphones and disappeared into his house. He was gone for forty-five minutes, leaving the pilot fidgeting and wondering what was going on. When at last he came out, here was a different Tsantiacu. His face was startlingly painted with alternate straight and wiggly lines. His long hair had been done up and decorated with brilliant multi colored toucan and parrot feathers. He had discarded his drab and shapeless garment for a clean, new black-and-white striped *itipi*. Across his chest were rows of small, round, flashing mirrors, held in place by narrow belting. He was an impressive figure.

With Tsantiacu were his favorite wife and his only son, equally decked out in their best ceremonial paint and finery, and obviously expecting to climb into the plane with him. Hobey radioed me for further instructions. I thought a minute and then told him to bring them all, if he could do it within the weight limit.

In the next few minutes, Tsantiacu spanned the centuries.

He stepped proudly into the plane and submitted to the safety belt with the self-assurance of a much-traveled diplomat. As the plane soared into the skies he laughed loudly and kept up a constant stream of talk. Then he began to sing 'Jesus Loves Me,' one of the hymns he had learned, as though practicing for the meeting with the Yus Shuara. As he looked out the window, he pointed at every river and ridge they passed, recognizing them all.

When the plane circled Makuma for a landing, he shouted down to the people in the houses below in the expectation of being heard as he had heard my voice at times from the plane.

The first few hours of his weekend in Makuma were happy ones for the chief. He listened to testimonies, and prayed and sang with Shuara who, but for the teachings of Christ, would have still been his enemies. I was reminded of this when I saw him sitting side by side with Mangash, whose chest still bore the scars of bullets from Tsantiacu's gun.

Then, some time on Saturday, came a disturbing rumor that Catani had entered the jungle across the river from our settlement and was threatening to kill the Atshuara chief.

When this word reached Tsantiacu he went wild. He shouted and stamped and waved his gun. He recited instances where members of his household had either been shot by Catani, or died from the curse he had put upon them. The chief upbraided us for bringing him here and exposing him to danger.

We had scheduled a baptismal service at the river for that afternoon and looked forward to showing Tsantiacu how Christians were baptized. But to reach the spot he would have to walk down a short jungle trail. If there were any truth in the rumor, this would provide too good an opportunity for Catani or his men. So, regretfully, we left the chief behind, while the rest of us went to the river.

By the next morning the rumors of Catani's presence had been proven false. Tsantiacu relaxed and began to enjoy himself once more.

He was especially impressed by the Shuara church. He had heard, he told us, of this building used solely for thinking about God and learning more of His Word – a house where no one slept or ate. But he had not believed there could be such a place until he now saw it with his own eyes. Just before stepping aboard the plane to take the Atshuara family home, Tsantiacu said earnestly, 'Some day we will build a church among our people.'

We saw more fruits of the missionary work of our Indians among the Atshuara the following fall when seven of their boys, including Tsantiacu's own son, appeared to attend our school at Makuma. At first we were worried. Would the Shuara students accept the Atshuara newcomers or would they make fun of their long hair, bare-chested bodies, and queer-sounding dialect?

Our fears were foolish. Most of the boys treated the Atshuara as their special friends. They helped them learn the rules of school life, taught them to play their games, and were quick to take their part against any who mistreated them. Only one Mura Shuara, who reflected the attitude of his father, persisted in bullying the new boys until I had to send him home. The Atshuara boys proved apt at learning. By the time their year was out, most of them had become Christians and learned many hymns and passages of Scripture. They went home well-equipped to help their people know the Lord.

Some months later – in February 1957 – when Ernest Johnson was visiting the Atshuara with me, came a moment I had long prayed for. We had just finished conducting a service at Tsantiacu's house. As we were getting ready to lie down for the night, I felt a touch on my arm. Turning, I saw the chief standing beside me.

'Panchu,' he said softly, 'I need to bow the knee. I want God to forgive me the many evil things I have done. I want Him to give me power to overcome the devil.'

Then and there, we knelt together. He talked directly to God as he had talked to me, asking His forgiveness and help. While

I prayed I heard two other male voices raised to God. I knew that two more Atshuara had become Christians that evening.

When we arose, we found ourselves surrounded by women of the household. 'Now Tsantiacu has become a *Tikishmamtaicawaru,*' they cried happily. 'He and his men have bowed the knee.'

On one of my trips nearly a year later Marie went with me to the Atshuara and wrote of her experiences to our four oldest children in school at Quito:

Dearest children,

I am writing to you while sitting on a bamboo rack in Tsantiacu's big house. A little Indian boy wearing a pair of baggy shorts big enough to fit his father is standing beside me, open-mouthed, watching me. My arms are stinging and itching from the bites of tiny gnats. In fact, I itch all over – even inside my clothes – from chigger bites. My eyes burn and feel tired because of the constant smoke in the air.

I just changed my blouse for one with slightly longer sleeves to protect my arms from the gnats. None of the women and children paid any attention while I took my blouse off and revealed my slip. But when I opened a tin can that we brought with a few cookies in it, they all gathered around to see what I was going to eat.

This is the biggest jungle house I have ever seen – almost as big as a circus tent. There must be fifteen beds around the outside wall, and one in the middle full of snarling, mangy dogs, and a big, ugly monkey. About eleven women, a dozen children, and three men are here now.

Daddy and I arrived at noon yesterday. Tsantiacu is not at home. They told us he had gone visiting with his two younger wives and they do not know when he will return. After the plane left, we walked slowly to the house. Daddy visited with two men. Staring, giggling women crowded around me, touching my hair and clothing.

I singled out the oldest woman in the group and learned what her name was from a little one standing beside me. Then I got the oldest one to tell me the names of the others. Indians never like to tell you their own names. You must always learn them from someone else. After repeating their odd names until I had learned them thoroughly, I asked about their husbands and children.

Six of them are wives of living husbands; four are widows; and one of them is *ajapamu*. That means 'thrown away' – or maybe it is like being divorced. Her husband is still living with his three other wives, but the women gave me the impression that he would probably kill the new husband if she tried to remarry. She looks like a very young girl to have had such troubles. They told me she has lost a baby, too. Her name is Antri.

The widows' husbands have all been killed by their enemies; none died a natural death. One of the men told me these women had come to Tsantiacu's house to hear more of God's Word. But I think they said that just to please me. I believe he brought them here to protect them.

One has a baby boy. She must have shaved her head as a sign of widowhood and grief when her husband was killed, because now it is about an inch long, sticking out in all directions like an overgrown 'butch' cut. Another has a baby girl who looks exactly like her – shy eyes above puffy cheeks, framed by ragged, tangled hair. Their faces are even dirty in the same spots.

When I asked a third widow if she had always lived in this house, she laughed and said, 'Oh no. I am only the dung of the Atshuara. They threw me away.'

'They? Who are "they?"' I asked.

'The ones downstream. My husband gave my daughters in marriage to Chiipa. After my husband was killed I thought I would go live with my daughters, but they did not want me. They feared that their husband would love and marry me, too. My husband's friends would not let me stay with them either. They were afraid that if I did those who had killed my husband would kill them, too. Everyone was afraid. I was all alone, I had no place to go, no one wanted me. Then my uncle, Tsantiacu, brought me here.' These Indians often use the word 'uncle' just as you do for your missionary uncles – to express endearment, rather than exact relationship. 'Come learn a new way of life,' he said to me. 'Take God's way and you will be happy.'

The fourth widow is a deaf-and-dumb woman whose husband was killed two years ago. It is inspiring to watch her; she takes part in all the household activities just as though she had no handicap. She talks with her hands and seems to understand those who talk to her in sign language. She made friendly signs at me. I tried to guess what she was saying, and when I answered with a smile and some made-up motions, everyone laughed.

The women told me that all the adults in this house have now become Christians. They sing and pray and apparently have quit making war plans and calling on witches.

Two men have just arrived. The little boy who is watching me write tells me they have been hunting for seven days and have brought back two wild pigs to skin and roast. One of them is Shuunta, a relative of Tsantiacu's. Shuunta used to be a witch doctor, but he says he is a Christian now. One of the women told me that when Shuunta was a witch doctor he drank the *natema* and called up evil spirits. But he does not do so any more. He still has the powerful witch's arrows in his body, she said. But the last time her baby was sick he put his hands on the child and prayed to God. He did not drink *tsaangu or natema* or call up the evil spirits. And the baby got well.

Now Daddy and the other men have come into the house and the women are bringing us all some food, so I will put this letter away until later. Wish you could be here with us to know and love these strange people.

*Makuma – a week later.*
I want to tell you about the rest of our visit with the Atshuara. When the Indian hunters came into the house, each man sat on his own *cutanga*, making a circle around the food the women served them. They all bowed their heads and, in a loud voice, a man named Tucupe thanked the Lord for His goodness. They didn't so much as look at us before or after praying, so we don't think they were just trying to impress us. When I commented about it to one of the women, she said, 'Oh, they always thank the Lord before they eat.'

On Friday morning nearly all of the men and women went to work with Daddy to lengthen the airstrip. I stayed in the house with Tayujinta's attractive bride to watch her dye some shirts and blouses. I knew the Indians dyed their clothes when they got stained but I had never seen them do it. I supposed they boiled them as we do. But she just used cold water, mixed with the leaves of a certain plant which turned it the color of grape juice. After dipping the garments in the dye several times, she squeezed them as much as she could and then spread them on the roofs of chicken houses to dry. From a distance they looked like people lying there.

As we walked out to the airstrip she showed me the plant she used. She crushed some of the leaves between her teeth to make the juice run out. It was green at first, but soon turned dark purple. 'We use this as you use soap,' she said, 'so all the ugly dirt stains won't show.' How would you like to change places with her?

The sun was so hot on the airstrip I wished I had some lemonade to give to Daddy. But I thought of something almost as good. Borrowing his jackknife and calling a couple of little boys to help me, I picked several papaya and peeled them. A leaf spread on the log was the table; the juicy fruit was sweet and thirst-quenching. I thought the Indians might enjoy it too and Daddy said I should offer them some. I served the most important men first, just as the Indian women do, and then all the others. They laughed and laughed. Guess they thought it was a big joke that the 'white mother,' as they called me, should be serving them. The men teased the women, telling them they, too, should learn to feed them while they worked. Some of the women were too embarrassed to eat in front of the men.

Maybe it was while I was picking the papaya that I got more chiggers. Anyway, I still have their bites here in Makuma to keep reminding me that I really visited the Atshuara.

You, Timmy, would have loved their pets. They had dogs, monkeys, birds, and one little wild pig. He had a longer nose than pigs we know, and longer legs, and stiff, bristly hair. The women fed him from their mouths and he followed them everywhere. The boys had tamed a young tapir and then set him free. Every evening he'd show up in one of the gardens to be fed and petted.

The most exciting thing of all was the amazing evidence of God's power at work in the lives of these people. We held services for them morning, afternoon, and evening, but they couldn't seem to get enough. After dark, when all the beds were full of sleepy Atshuara, we could hear different ones praying and then Tucupe's voice singing until we fell asleep.

Friday afternoon Chiip came to visit, bringing his two short, fat wives and six dogs. When they came into the house, Shuunta's wife stirred up a choking dust as she tried to sweep the floor clear of its dirt and garbage. I was longing to go outside, but didn't want to miss anything, so I stayed and watched.

Tucupe started preaching to Chiip, who is not a Christian. Tucupe told him that since he had become one, the Lord gave him a heart of love for everyone – even his enemies. 'We don't make war any more,' he told Chiip, 'and you wouldn't either if you had a new heart.'

'Would you kill your own brother or sister?' he went on. 'Of course you wouldn't, because you love them. Well, that's the way it is when you become a Christian. Every other Christian is your brother and sister and every unbeliever can become your brother and sister too.

'But we ourselves are newborn ones as yet. We have learned just a little about God. Others, like Panchu, know a lot more. He is like our older brother because he was the first one to bring God's Word to us.'

Then the women came and sat down on the dirt floor and the men drew up their *cutangas*. Tucupe quit talking and sat down too. Now we could begin the service. I had my flute and so I played some of the hymns before we started to sing. Daddy taught them the song about the thief on the cross who asked Christ to forgive him. They sang it several times, but they were afraid they would forget it, so they wanted to sing it over and over. After a short message, we all bowed our heads and everyone, except the deaf woman and the visitors, prayed aloud.

The women wanted me to play the flute some more so they could sing. When I had first arrived I wore long cotton hose for protection against insects. But after supper I went to the spring and took them off and washed my feet and legs before returning to the house for the service.

Now when someone noticed I did not have any stockings on they became curious. They pinched and felt my legs and one of them said, 'Take her shoes off. I want to see what her feet are like.' So I took off my tennis shoe and bared one big foot for all to examine. They pinched and rubbed it until I began to think I must be a freak. And what remarks!

'Look how white it is.'

'And it is so soft – just like a newborn baby's flesh.'

'Poor thing, that's because she always wears shoes. If she stepped on a sharp stone it would cut her foot wide open.'

'See how close her toes are. It must hurt to have to have them all squeezed together in shoes like that.'

They laughed, and so did I, at my poor, tender, strange feet. But how glad I was that even though there were many differences between me and these ladies, they still accepted me as their friend and sister.

When the women returned to their fires and babies, Daddy suggested that we go for a walk on the airstrip. The night scene was perfectly beautiful and seemed especially so by the light of the full moon, in contrast to the drabness of daytime. Earlier that evening we had watched the flaming and fading of a gorgeous sunset. It thrilled us to think how lavishly the Lord spreads out His beauty, even in this faraway corner of the jungle. There is no place where one is shut off from the presence and power of God. As we lifted our eyes to the beauties around us, we had the warm feeling of being right at home and close to the Lord.

But we were not to enjoy our walk alone. As we started out, Tucupe and several of the young boys came running up. They wanted us to sing some more about the dying thief. So we walked back and forth along the airstrip in the moonlight, lifting our voices in harmony with those who, only a few short years ago, did not know anything about the Lord.

On the way back to the house we came to the garden where cassava plants stood shoulder high and sweet potato vines covered most of the ground. A little way beyond me, I saw a woman, and walked toward her while Daddy went on with the men. As I drew nearer I saw clearly that she was kneeling in prayer. So I knelt in the dirt beside her and prayed with her. An old woman, she was lifting her heart in praise to the Lord who had saved her, and in petition for His help and protection over her son. At this time he had gone on a long trip through the jungle to visit relatives and she was afraid for his safety. 'But even if my son should die on the trail from a bite of a snake, which is what I always fear,' she said, 'I will love and trust You, knowing I will see Mayapruwa again in heaven.'

Tears filled my eyes as I listened, and I wondered if I had ever heard a more trustful prayer. As she continued, this primitive jungle garden became to me holy ground – a place where fellowship with God had brought beauty of soul to this Indian woman in her haggard, stooped old body.

When she finished she took my hand and told me that she knelt to talk with the Lord in this place every evening when it wasn't raining. As we walked to the house, I asked her when she had become a Christian. 'A long time ago – when Chingasu was here,' she answered. 'She's old like me but she taught me to kneel and pray to God.'

Back in the house with Daddy, I told him I felt these Atshuara Christians, though they knew so little, had helped and encouraged me more than I had them. Our visit with them was a wonderful experience and we were sorry when it ended. They begged us to stay longer and teach them more of the Bible, but we could not. Knowing the Lord cares for the Atshuara, we pray for them and want you to pray for them, too.

We love you much and pray for you each day.

Mom

# CHAPTER SIXTEEN
# THE TESTING OF TSANTIACU
You cannot serve both God and money
(Matthew 6:24).

A few weeks later in April 1959, I received an urgent message that Tsantiacu wanted to see me. This was good news, for we had been concerned about the Atshuara chief. Some of the women had expressed their anxiety to me on former visits. He was far from being steadfast and growing in his new belief.

'Tsantiacu is not always happy,' one of them said. 'When there is no Yus Shuara here to remind us of God, it is easy to forget. More of the devil's Indians come here than Christians from Makuma. Do Indians who do not know God talk beautiful words? No, they talk only of witch doctors and wars. When Tsantiacu goes visiting he tries to tell of God's Word. But nobody listens.

'Lately men have come from downstream to tell Tsantiacu about the wars to the south. His favorite nephew has been killed, they say, and they want Tsantiacu to go and avenge his death. They also try to stir him up to kill his enemies nearby – Timas and his brother, Cashijintu, who have threatened him. When Tsantiacu listens to the devil's Indians, he goes wild and wants to kill. Then he remembers he is *Tikishmamtaicawaru* and does not want to do wrong.'

From what the women told us, the chief might already have gone to war had not the Lord put a series of obstacles in his way. First, his warrior, Tucupe, whose Christian faith was stronger than the chief's, refused to go with him. Then he hurt his leg. By the time it healed, a trader came for pigskins. Tsantiacu went hunting and put aside his plans for war.

Now I hoped I could revive his faith before he reverted to his old ways.

Tsantiacu was waiting for me.

'Panchu,' he said, 'I am going to visit some of my kinfolk who live far to the south. These people have never heard the wonderful words from God's Book. If they die without knowing Jesus Christ, they are sure to go to the big fire that burns and burns. Also, I wish to bring back with me the widows and orphans of my nephew who was murdered. I wish you to go on this journey with me, to tell the gospel to these, my relatives. Be ready after two moons – at the time the moon is straight up.'

His words filled me with joy. I had long wanted to reach those Indians living farther away who had never heard of Jesus Christ. But it would have been too dangerous to go by myself. I needed a Shuara to go with me, one who was known to them. I had intended to suggest such a trip to Tsantiacu. But this was better; it came as his own idea, in fact, his command.

After returning to Makuma, I wrote to Ralph Stuck, a fellow missionary, who had once said he'd like to go with me on a trip like this. He replied that he was still interested. Wampiu said he'd go along to help preach and teach.

When the moon was straight up, we flew to Tsantiacu's house. Since we would take no equipment with us for radio communication, we and the pilot had to decide when he would come back to pick us up. Upon questioning Tsantiacu and his men, we learned that the farthest group of relatives whom they wanted to visit lived not along the Huasaga River as I had supposed, but two days' walk inland. I had recently injured my foot in Makuma, and I could not possibly walk that far. After much discussion with the Indians, we said we would go with them only as far as the first settlement of Atshuara, three days downstream. Ralph and I would stay at the house of an old chief named Aiju, while Tsantiacu and his men walked inland. We made an appointment to meet the pilot at Tsantiacu's house after eleven days.

We went to work repacking the clothing, thread, knives, and other trade goods into rubber packs for stowing in the canoe. The Atshuara women were busy getting things ready. The men rolled up the pigskins for trading. Tsantiacu still seemed troubled in his mind.

'Many moons have passed since they murdered my nephew,' he said. 'How can we forget about it? Are not his women and children still crying?'

'My gun is clean and ready,' put in the warrior, Shuunta. 'But can I use it on the dirty killers? Have I not learned that Christians do not kill?'

'Must we not then bring the widows and orphans back with us?' said Tsantiacu, changing his mind again. 'Will they not be safe here from their enemies? Will we not teach them God's Word and so save them from burning in hell?'

Both men nodded. They now appeared satisfied that the plan for the expedition was a wise one.

I had brought my outboard motor, which, to the Atshuara, was a wonderful new toy. Women and children followed along to watch us try it out. We took them on test runs down to the rapids and back. Those aboard clapped their hands and shouted; those ashore clamored for a turn like children at a pony ride. It looked as though our journey would begin in a light-hearted spirit.

Then a remark from Shuunta, who had been looking at the motor, cast a shadow on things.

'It may be that this engine will make too much noise.' He frowned. 'Can we forget that between here and where we are going, we pass through the territory of our enemies? Do not Timas and his brother, who have sworn to kill us, live close to the river? If they hear the big noise going down will they not be waiting in ambush for us when we come back?'

In the silence that followed, Tucupe spoke up. 'God has told us to go; we must obey. With His power, we will return safely.'

Wampiu pursued this theme when he preached that evening.

'God does not promise His children any easy road to heaven,' he told the Atshuara. 'But He does give them courage to sing and pray even in the face of danger.'

In the morning there was murmuring among the women:

'Tsantiacu should not go ... Haven't we heard that Timas is saying, "Will not my enemy be an easy shot? Is he not weak as a woman since he has become a Yus Shuara?' No, Tsantiacu should not go.'

At the riverbank, the Indians were already waiting with their loads. Standing silently, they looked at one another apprehensively. I quickly called them together to pray. After the final 'Amen' I gave them no chance to say any more, but stepped into one canoe, while Ralph eased himself into the other. The Indians followed. In spite of the women's worries, Tsantiacu also stepped into the canoe. One of them, Wajare, gave us a push with his pole and we were off.

In the first few hours of travel the pools of smooth water were too short to use the motor. We had to rely on the pole. But soon we lashed the two canoes together with vines and drove them with the outboard motor.

The Indians forgot their fears. We all had a good time, singing hymns together, talking and laughing.

Later a smaller river emptied into the Huasaga, making it considerably wider and deeper.

'The river will be like this for a long way,' Tucupe assured us.

'Yes,' agreed Shuunta, 'until we get to a certain point near where Timas and Cashijintu live.' At the mention of the two names, dark eyes flashed signals of alarm.

If I encouraged them to talk freely about this man Timas, I thought, it might relieve the tension. So I asked the Indians just how far he lived from the river. Unfortunately, Shuara have no accurate way of measuring distances. Long distances are reckoned by the number of nights spent sleeping on the trail, while short distances are calculated according to opinion or circumstance.

Some of the Atshuara seemed to think that Timas' house was quite a long way off, while others didn't think it far at all. Some tried to describe, by pointing their fingers to imaginary positions of the sun, how long it would take them to walk it. Since they didn't move their fingers very far, I judged that Timas' house might be a mile or two from the river. This was reassuring; for from that distance Timas' Indians would not be likely to hear the sound of our five-and-a-half horsepower motor – especially since we would be passing in a deep river canyon bordered by high banks and heavy vegetation. I said so to the Indians. But their fears were not easily quieted.

'But what if they happen to be hunting on a trail near the river?' one of them asked. This idea seemed to frighten them anew.

I tried another approach.

'Are they not also Atshuara? Why should you fear them? And Timas – did I not meet him a couple of years ago at your own house?'

'Timas has long hated us very much. When you saw him, he had set it aside for a while. Since then, has all not changed?'

'How?' I asked.

'A child in his house died. He thinks Shuunta sent the curse. Oh, would not Timas kill us quickly if he could!' 'Don't forget,' he went on, 'we hate Timas, too. He cursed a child of ours and made him die. We are Yus Shuara now,' he added hastily. 'We would not kill. But Timas is different. Once we sent word to Timas and his brother that we wanted no more war. They would not listen.'

'Timas' full sister is Shuunta's wife,' Tucupe put in. 'Will that stop him from killing Shuunta? I myself am brother to Cashijintu. We have different mothers but the same father. Does that mean anything? Is his anger at me not like a dog's?'

I let the subject drop.

The poor Atshuara! He can trust nobody. A relative – or supposed friend – may turn on him any time. From illness or accident comes suspicion that the unfortunate one has been cursed. Suspicion grows to hatred and hatred breeds killing. Nothing can end this vicious circle except the love of Jesus Christ.

Such were my thoughts as the motor hummed and the water slapped rhythmically between the two canoes. The scene looked so peaceful. Behind us the waves spread in a rippling V from the propeller to the banks where tangled vines made a solid wall.

About 5:00, Tsantiacu ordered a stop. High up on a bank was a shelter he had built on a former trip. There we spent the night.

At noon the next day, as we were purring along, the Indians suddenly fell silent. They fixed their attention on a spot high up the far bank. Ralph and I looked at each other. We couldn't see anything unusual. Tsantiacu, sensing our bewilderment, said, 'Cut the motor. This is the place. It is from here that the trail leads back to the house of Timas.'

All eyes remained fastened to it as we poled by. There were no canoes, no clearing, no life. It looked the same as the rest of the bank to me. But it told its story to the Indians.

Shuunta stood up and put his gun to his shoulder. I thought he saw something. Then, as he spoke, I realized he was acting out a drama.

'This is how they will be waiting for us when we return. They will be ready to shoot from ambush,' he predicted darkly.

'Would they shoot, knowing white men are with you?' asked Wampiu.

'They would shoot,' nodded Tucupe. 'They fear no one.'

'But we can trust in the Lord,' Wampiu tried to assure them. 'Remember, we pray to Him for protection and He promises to take care of His children.'

The Indians grunted and nodded their agreement. We had passed the trail. As abruptly as it had ended, the busy conversation began again. 'Start the motor.'

We were now in deep, smooth water. Turning the motor over to Ralph, I began to cast toward inviting fish holes. Something grabbed; a splash and a swish left my line limp and minus the hook. Where there is one hungry fish there must be another. Putting on a new lure, I cast again. Another one bit. This one was smaller; I hauled him in without any trouble.

'Paani! Paani!' yelled the Indians, looking down at my catch which was flopping about in the bottom of the canoe. It had a big ugly mouth full of sharp-pointed teeth. I had never heard the name before, nor had I ever seen such a fish in the waters of the upper Makuma. Wampiu recognized it and explained to me that this was the dreaded man-eating piranha fish. Although it was smaller than my arm, I could easily see how a school of them could tear the flesh from a man's body. Later in the day I couldn't help being impressed by the ferocity with which a piranha snapped in two a hard plastic lure and then some stout twigs. A man's finger would present no problem at all.

Shortly after, while I was casting, the canoe bumped into a log and threw me overboard. Visions of those sharp piranha teeth kept me from enjoying what might otherwise have been a pleasant swim. Ralph, shaking with laughter, said, 'You came out of there so fast you hardly got wet.'

Although the Indians claimed that piranha would attack a

man only if he were bleeding, I had no desire to put their theory to the test. We were surprised, however, to find the fish tender and succulent when we roasted the white meat over the coals that night.

By mid-afternoon we had gone as far down river as we intended. We set up headquarters in an abandoned hut. Aiju's house was two and a half hours inland. Tsantiacu sent some of his Indians to tell him we had come and to bring him the next day to barter for hides.

While we waited, I showed the chief one of the wordless booklets and taught him the meaning of the colored pages. He made me repeat it many times. He asked if he could take the book along with him. 'It will help me explain God's way of forgiveness to my relatives.'

'You may have it,' I said. 'But first tell me what it means to you so I will know you have learned it well.'

He took the book tenderly in his big, dirty hands. Page by page, he told the meaning of the colors to me – accurately and in much better Atshuara than I could have done.

That evening we gathered around the fire to sing hymns and talk of Jesus' teachings to His disciples. Long before Tsantiacu and Shuunta tired of singing and listening, Ralph and I were yawning and shifting our legs from one uncomfortable position to another on the hard bamboo racks.

Our Indian brothers weren't even aware of our weariness as they listened to our teaching of the Scriptures. When we stopped they begged us for more. There were times when I wondered if their interest was not pretended to gain our favor. But if pretense it were, it was certainly consistent.

As Ralph and I moved away from the fire and stretched out for the night, I heard a sound which brought surprise, joy, and thanksgiving to my heart. It was the voice of Tsantiacu praying, as a son talking with his father. He reviewed the events of the day; then he prayed for the women and children left at home, for Aiju and his household, and for his people that he was going to visit. It had been well worth coming all this way just to hear Tsantiacu's spontaneous prayer.

Morning dawned on a scene of bustle and impatience. Tsantiacu was fidgety. He was anxious to meet with Aiju, sell his pigskins, and be off down river. While we waited, we planned the return journey.

'Today,' I began, 'is Wednesday.'

'Today,' Tsantiacu repeated, turning down the little finger of his left hand, 'we will go downstream to where the trail takes off to the right. Then, after walking all afternoon, we will be caught by the night. Next day we will walk all day without meeting anyone.' He turned down the fourth finger. Touching the third finger, he continued, 'From there we will walk fast and come to the place of my people before the sun is straight up over our heads.' He turned down the middle finger and index finger. 'These two days we will spend searching for the widows and children of the murdered one.' He turned down his thumb. 'The next day we will leave very early and start back with them.' Switching to his right hand, he turned down the little finger and looked at me. 'You sleep here and we will meet you before the next day. I will come upriver at night, so that if my enemies are watching they will never see me.' He turned down his fourth finger. 'On the following day we will start back together to my house.'

I reminded him that we had already arranged for the plane to come for us on the eleventh day, which would be a Thursday. Tsantiacu assured me we would be back by then – if all went well.

Voices outside told us Aiju's men were approaching. They marched in with quiet assurance, holding their big Winchester .44's proudly over their shoulders. They were wearing striped skirts; fresh black and blue designs were painted across their bare chests and stomachs. Ralph and I moved quietly to one side as they sat down possessively on our bamboo racks. We were very conscious of our drabness in this colorful Atshuara world.

No one spoke. Then all four began to talk at once, so rapidly and with so many unfamiliar expressions that we could barely catch the gist of what they were saying. Suddenly a remark of one of Aiju's men seemed to cause Tsantiacu great agitation. His dark face flushed; his heavy brows knit together in a worried frown. He turned on me angrily.

'They are saying that Timas and Cashijintu have sworn to kill me if I ever come into their territory,' he said excitedly. 'Now they tell me we have already passed very near their main trails. This means they know I am here. Will they not be lying in wait for me on the return trip?'

He began to talk angrily to me.

'I never should have come on this trip!' he shouted. 'Why did you make me?'

It took all my patience to keep from reminding him that the trip had been his idea. Quietly I said to him, 'Have you forgotten how God answered our prayer years ago when the Copatasa Atshuara started out to kill you and your family. Have you forgotten how, after we prayed, they went back home without ever coming near your house? I ask you, have there been any attacks on your place since you built the airstrip? God will never forsake you, Tsantiacu, no matter what happens. Trust in Him!'

Tsantiacu did not answer. He began to open his rolls of stinking, bristling pigskins. We heard the calls of Indians outside. The rest of Aiju's men were approaching from across the river. They were waiting for us to come and get them in the canoe.

One of the last to come gingerly down the bank was a short, stooped old man. His wizened face peered out at me from under a brown and yellow plastic cap and a thick mat of graying hair.

'Are you not the old and respected Aiju?' I asked.

'I am,' he answered, straightening up proudly. 'And are you not perhaps Panchu?'

'I am he,' I said. 'I have come to be your friend and to tell you about God.'

'That is fine,' he nodded approvingly. 'I want to hear those beautiful words. Now let us cross to the other side.'

The hut quickly overflowed with Indians, all bartering noisily for hides. Aiju, Tsantiacu, and Tucupe measured and counted and haggled. They might have gone on all day. But Tsantiacu, noticing the straight-up position of the sun, ordered his Indians to be on their way.

Tsantiacu and his men stepped into their canoe. With the other canoe and motor we towed them an hour's travel farther downstream.

'From here the river becomes too rocky for your motor,' the chief said. 'We go on by ourselves. Then we will hide our canoe and walk as far as we can before nightfall.'

We were ready to say goodbye. As we sat in the two canoes, we all bowed our heads.

'Lord, give these men strength for their journey, and bring them back soon,' I prayed. 'May they help their relatives to know You and turn away from their terrible wars.'

Tsantiacu, Shuunta, Tucupe, and the others poled away downstream. We waved to them until they were lost to sight. We turned our canoe back upstream.

Until Tsantiacu's return, we would stay in Aiju's house. But we arrived at the trail too late to walk there before nightfall; so we had to pass the night again in the hut along the river.

In the morning we took the greatest care to leave no sign. After hiding our motor and gasoline cans in the brush, we looked for a place to conceal the canoe.

'I can show you where I always hide my own canoe,' said one of Aiju's Indians.

He took us to a stream well-hidden between high banks. No canoe was there.

'Where is yours now?' I demanded.

'Oh,' said the Indian, 'someone helped himself to it a few days ago without so much as asking. It was one of Timas' men.'

This cast a chill over everybody.

'But what if he comes to return it and finds Tsantiacu's

canoe? Won't he then go tell Timas and Cashijintu that Tsantiacu is nearby?'

The Indian had to admit that this was not impossible. All we could do was pray that Timas' Indian would not return the borrowed canoe until after Tsantiacu had made his way back upstream.

Our welcome at Aiju's house was quite different from that which we had received in other Indian houses. These people did not crowd around us like curious children, eager to handle our clothes and our belongings. Foreign visitors were no rarity, for Aiju's house was a key trading post. He gathered hides from widely scattered Indians. In the rainy season when the river was deep, traders came from far downstream to exchange their white man's goods for his wild pigskins.

That explained their indifference toward us. The few goods we had brought for trading were hardly worth their attention. They brightened up when they learned we had medicines, but lost interest when we told them medicines cost money.

Their trading visitors had never mentioned Jesus Christ. If He meant so much to the foreigners, why had none of them ever spoken of Him? They could not grasp this as the real reason why we had come.

It did not seem likely that we would make much impact on this smug, materialistic household in our four-day visit.

An Indian with a hoary head such as Aiju's is rare among either the Atshuara or the Shuara. Most of them die of disease or in war long before their hair turns white. But Aiju, as a valued middle man, had achieved a kind of neutrality. He boasted, though, that in his prime he had killed his four fists of enemies.

Aiju's house was not attractive. The thatched roof was alive with cockroaches. They ate our bananas and cassava and crawled over us when we tried to sleep. Aiju spent most of his time hunched on his low *cutanga*, scratching or combing lice from his straggly hair. Seated at his feet were two plump, comely young women. Now and then one helped pick a thorn from the old man's leathery foot, while the other helped him comb, occasionally killing a louse between her teeth. A third, older woman served him his food from a steaming clay pot. Although the young women looked contented with their job of making the patriarch's last years as pleasant as possible, we knew they served Aiju because there was no other choice.

One afternoon I asked Aiju to name me as many of his Atshuara neighbors as he could, and to tell me where they lived. As I wrote down their names I judged that including the children they must number nearly four hundred. All were persons for whom Christ had died; but they were cut off by geography, language, and custom from knowing Him. I felt ashamed for the weakness of our missionary effort that had not made any headway in this area. The thought made me determined to do all I could now to win these people for Jesus Christ and to pray that someone would be able to live and work among them soon.

We got the household together morning and evening for singing and telling of God's love. The first morning I asked Wampiu to speak to them. He began with John 3:16: 'For God so loved the world,' he repeated in Shuara, 'that He gave His one and only Son, that whoever believe in Him shall not perish, but have eternal life.'

I smiled to myself. Wampiu was beginning at the wrong place, making the same mistake I had made the first times I tried to tell how to become God's child to an animistic tribal people.

The result was discouraging. He was not holding their attention. Some of the women who had sat obediently at their husbands' feet during the singing got up and went to the other end of the room to tend their fires. The sound of little children quarreling distracted them. The men yawned, swatted flies, or looked listlessly into the jungle through the open walls.

Then came bored, cynical questions, along with a weary shaking of heads: 'Just who is this God?' 'Is he a man like I am, with many wives?' 'How could He have a Son?' 'These are unknowable words. We have never heard them before. Therefore we cannot understand.'

Then Wampiu behaved like a true Christian. Laughing at himself, he folded the little pieces of paper on which he had painstakingly written out some Scripture verses in Shuara and put them away. He faced the crowd with humility.

'I am sorry,' he said. 'It is so long since I first heard these wonderful words that I have quite forgotten how little meaning they had for me. If you will listen again, I will try to help you understand.'

He began this time with 'In the beginning God created the heavens and the earth' (Gen. 1:1). 'You all know that God made everything – you and me, right?' He had their attention. He went on to the account of our first ancestors. Here they also listened intently, as ancestry is a subject of great importance to all Indians. He held them until he tried to explain the present-day existence of sin. Once more he lost them. They began to get up, stretch, and walk about – that meeting was over.

Undaunted, Wampiu tried again that night. He began where he had left off, with sin. His audience couldn't go out, since it was raining. They just sat there dully. Wampiu went on to the subject of eternal life. All of a sudden they sat up. They were taking it in. They asked questions. Here was something they really wanted to know – how they could live forever.

At every meeting after that, they asked to hear the same message again. We were also heartened when the men came to our bed racks often and asked us to tell them more about God. But this was only a first step: we did not press them to become Christians before they fully understood.

During our visit we saw all around us the turmoil and misery common to polygamous households. If I only had the time to stay with these people – if I could teach them patiently, then I would see Christ change their lives as He had mine and those of so many believers around Makuma.

THE TESTING OF TSANTIACU

But we were due to meet Tsantiacu by the river to start the journey home. Aiju, with most of his men, insisted on going with us as far as the hut by the riverside. Tsantiacu was uppermost in our minds. We hoped that he would be there waiting for us.

But he wasn't.

When we went to get our canoe, we saw another floating alongside. But it was not the one Tsantiacu had taken downstream.

'That's the canoe Timas' Indian borrowed a few days ago!' said one of Aiju's men. 'Now he has brought it back!'

This was not good. Timas' Indian had no doubt recognized the canoe as Tsantiacu's.

'The plot thickens,' Ralph smiled wanly.

All that day we waited anxiously. As afternoon wore on, we kept telling each other the chief must be hiding through the day to travel upstream in the hours of darkness. We stayed the night in the hut, sharing the cramped sleeping quarters with old Aiju and one of his wives. I awoke at 3:00 a.m. No Tsantiacu. Rousing again at 4:30, I saw no one had arrived. Our lone canoe rocked gently on the waves nearby.

Dawn came. We expected Tsantiacu to show up any minute. After breakfast, we busied ourselves reloading the canoe. By mid-morning, we decided to go downstream to the point where he had said goodbye. Though we reached the place, we found no signs of Tsantiacu and his Indians there, either.

On the way back upstream, I tried without success to think of some plan. Then, at the moment of my despair, God's words came to me: 'Do not fret because of evil men... Trust in the Lord and do good; dwell in the land and enjoy safe pasture... Commit your way to the Lord; trust in him and he will do this' (Ps. 37:1, 3, 5).

Peace came to me. Here was a situation I could not control; this was the Lord's doing; He would find a way to bring Tsantiacu back safely.

Time was running out. We could stay here no longer if we were to keep our date with the plane. Wampiu shoved a long pole into a sandbar opposite the place where we had left the chief. The end of the pole pointed upstream. This was his way of letting Tsantiacu know we had gone on.

Reluctantly, we buzzed the motor and started back. Swift currents slowed our progress. We wondered if we'd make it in time to meet the plane. We had been traveling quite a few hours when Wampiu again pointed out the trail that led to Timas' house. I could not cut the motor without drifting back downstream in the swift current; we kept on; but our speed past that point seemed agonizingly slow.

One more day on the river and we reached the landing at Tsantiacu's where we had started. We only wished we had Tsantiacu with us instead of having to speculate on what had happened to him.

We pulled the tarpaulin over motor and gas cans, shouldered our other gear, and went off to the house. As we labored up the last rise, we saw the women come running out to meet us. Their faces were expectant; but when they saw we were alone, their expressions changed.

They set up a shrill, mournful wailing. It was a terrible sound to hear, but we could not quiet them. When they did not see their men, they believed the worst: they had surely been killed by enemies.

Then they accused me.

'Why did you leave them?'

'Why didn't you wait and bring them back with you?'

'If they have not already been killed, they surely will be.'

'Now we are helpless. How we will suffer without our men!'

I had to wait until we were back at the house before I could persuade them to listen quietly. I asked them to trust in the Lord.

'Your men have many times returned safely from long trips even before they were Christians,' I said. 'Why should they not this time? Remember, God is with them. He has promised never to leave or forsake them. Even if they should die, they would go to be with Him forever. Now stop your crying and think about God and His power.'

The wailing gave way to subdued sobbing. The women began to busy themselves with their children and their fires. I promised that after supper we would hold a prayer meeting for their husbands.

That night in the big, smoky Atshuara house, we sang and prayed together. The light from the fires flickered on moving lips and strained, intense faces. Their voices rose and fell. Formerly, it had been easy for them to say they trusted in God, but now they were in trouble. They were praying for something very dear – the safe return of their men. Only by such a trial as this could they really learn to trust God. It was a test of their faith. I could not believe God for them. They had to learn for themselves.

Next day the MAF plane, with pilot, Dan Derr, came to pick us up at the appointed time. I hated to leave without knowing what had happened to Tsantiacu.

Wonderful as it was to be back home in Makuma once more with Marie and the children, I could not get the chief out of my mind. After a week had gone by, Dan came to Makuma on his regular bimonthly vegetable run. I asked him if he could spare the time to fly me back to Tsantiacu's to learn what had happened and pick up the equipment we had left there. Happily he could.

As we flew again over the little clearing, I could hardly bear the suspense. I looked out of the plane, straining my eyes. Surely those figures streaming out of the house were men!

Tsantiacu himself stepped forward to meet me before the propeller had stopped turning. Foregoing the usual greetings, he put a hand upon my shoulder and said reproachfully, 'Why did you go away and leave us, Panchu? Why did you not wait a little longer?'

'I did wait longer than we promised,' I answered. 'When you did not appear, we had no way of knowing how much longer you would be delayed; and we had to be back to meet the plane. But,' I added, 'before we left, we went back downstream to try to find you. Did you not see the pole we planted in the sandbar?'

The fact that we had made this extra effort seemed to satisfy him.

'We missed you only by a little passing of the sun,' the chief said, indicating the time by bending his finger.

He went on to describe the journey home. 'Not having any motor the trip was slow. There were many in the canoe and it was hard poling against the strong current. When we came to enemy territory' – his voice became matter-of-fact – 'we –'

'Tell me!' I interrupted.

'Coming around a bend in the river, I saw a canoe, far ahead coming downstream. Two men were in it. As they came closer, I saw who they were – Timas and Cashijintu. They gave no sign they had seen us. We stopped, climbed quickly up the bank, and pulled our canoe after us. From behind jungle leaves we watched. Timas and Cashijintu passed quite close by. We had our guns cocked. We could have shot them. But remembering God's Word, we didn't. We are Yus Shuara; we do not kill.

'We did not want to return by the river. They might have seen us. They are not Christians and would kill us. We fled through the jungle. There was no trail. The widows of my nephew we were bringing back with us ran ahead. They carried the children on their backs. We did not eat. At night we ran. We did not sleep. We suffered much. But now we are here!'

'Praise the Lord!' I exclaimed. 'Praise the Lord!'

The dignified chief looked at me in puzzlement.

'Why do you say that, Panchu? Did we not suffer much? Were we not in great danger? Did we not almost die?'

'I praise the Lord,' I told him, 'because now I know why He let me come up the river without you. He planned everything to work out just the way He wanted it. You see, He does not want you to put your trust only in me. He wanted to show you that He could take care of you without my help. Do you not understand?

God kept your enemies from finding you. He brought you home safely. I cannot always be with you. God wants you to remember that He is always with you.'

Slowly his grim expression relaxed in a smile. He put his arm around my shoulders and led me toward the house.

'So that is what God wants,' the chief said, nodding his head as we walked along. 'So that is what God wants. Well... Fine. Fine. Fine.'

# CHAPTER SEVENTEEN
# STRENGTHENING JUNGLE CHURCHES

To him be glory in the church and in Christ Jesus
throughout all generations... (Ephesians 3:21).

At the beginning of every year in Ecuador's jungles, we
watched for the ripening of the chonta palm fruit. For the Shuar
Indians this annual occurrence was the marker, the calendar by
which they reckoned their age and the passage of years. Their
New Year celebration occurred in January or February when
the fruit was ripe. After the drinking and dancing, some of the
older ones would throw their spears into the door of the house,
as their ancestors used to do. This, they believed, would kill the
spirit of the old chonta and so insure better fortune for the chonta
to come.

For us, too, each New Year was a time of fresh beginning.
We reviewed the events of the previous years and planned for
progress toward our goals in the future. We wanted to do as the
Apostle Paul expressed in Philippians 3:13, 14: '...Forgetting

what is behind and straining toward what is ahead, I press on toward the goal to win the prize for which God has called me heavenward in Christ Jesus.'

Our immediate goals for this new beginning in 1960 were to broadcast the gospel by radio and to strengthen and multiply the jungle churches. We applied this also to the territory of the Atshuar where there was not yet even one small group of believers gathering together regularly for worship of God and the preaching of how to live for Him.

As we reflected on the past year, we could see that training the young people to read and write and to obey Christ's teachings had brought us farther along toward our goals. The second year of the full nine-month school session had ended with a striking program. We had watched with admiration as the yellow, blue, and red striped Ecuadorian flag was carried proudly by the first Shuar boy in a long line of sprucely-uniformed school children. Together, boys and girls had taken their places; together they had sung the stirring national anthem of this Latin American Republic.

The sound of their young voices rising on the quiet jungle air, as they gave back to us with assurance the difficult Spanish phrases, had stirred our hearts. These were Shuar Indians, but they were also Ecuadorian. They were beginning to comprehend a culture of which they were a rightful part, and to feel a sense of belonging. We foreigners from a far northern land were thankful we could help them become Christians, and thus better citizens of their country.

The singing over, we had entered the girls' hand-sawed board school building which had long since replaced the crude, open thatch-and-palm-pole structure where the first handful of youngsters began their lessons. The girls at their desks had squirmed nervously, while teachers and parents, seated on hard benches around the walls, also squirmed in sympathy. These round-faced, intelligent, healthy children were proud of their neat white blouses and blue jumpers. But they had grown self-conscious on finding themselves the objects of admiring eyes, pointing fingers, giggles, and whispered remarks. Even the familiar squeaks of their pets – tiny agouti, marmoset monkeys, toy-sized green-and-blue parrots, failed to reassure them.

One Indian girl had stood to answer the questions put to her by the Señorita Profesora. She tried hard to concentrate on what the teacher was saying. But her mind was on the people watching her. She was so afraid of making a mistake that her face reddened, her head drooped, and her fingers became as stiff as the chalk she held. But in spite of her shyness she had read from primers in Spanish and Shuar, recited the alphabet, and, with the others, counted in singsong fashion from one to a hundred.

When the girls had finished we went to the boys' school. For these sons of the jungle, who were used to being the center of attention and were pleased to perform, examination day was a treat. As I watched the sixty-four young Indian boys, I realized how much not only they, but I also, had changed since first coming to Makuma. I noted afresh that, though ranging in age from six to sixteen, they all had the same warm brown complexions, round faces, and high cheekbones. Here were sixty-four identical black 'butch' cuts in various stages of growth; sixty-four pairs of black eyes, fixed intently on their Ecuadorian teacher or wandering restlessly over the walls and windows in hope of finding some interesting distraction; sixty-four pairs of bare feet shuffling on the board floor in a vain attempt to elude the stinging gnats and flies.

Thirteen years before, when we had first come to work among the Shuar, I couldn't tell one boy from another. They all looked alike to me. It was a long time before I could distinguish Wampiu's jet-black eyes from Tsamaraing's or Jimpicti's shaggy head from Icam's. Today, each one was a distinct personality. I knew well their family groups, their backgrounds. Some were sons of witch doctors or warriors; some were orphans of men killed in battle or taken by disease; others were children of Christian Shuar. Five were sons of former schoolboys now grown to manhood and eager for their children to learn the Christian way of life.

As they finished their program we prayed once more that they would grow to establish Christian homes and that some would be future preachers and leaders of their churches.

There were treats of hard candies for all the boys and girls and then began the noisy goodbyes and the scramble to gather belongings. Family members grouped together and took the trails to their homes. It was hard for us to see them leave. Some we would see again at Sunday services, some, not until the next school term, and some – never again. A number were relieved to be free and ran happily away. Others cried and did not want to go. We understood their fears now and felt personally involved with each one. We knew that some must return not only to unhealthful living situations but to the witchcraft and immoral practices of their parents and relatives.

Such a child was Tatsemai, small daughter of Catani. That vicious sly warrior, having killed his last wife in a drunken brawl, had been taken away by the authorities and was now locked up in a white man's jail. Tatsemai was being brought up by an aunt who sent her to our school. She learned very slowly, but loved being with us. We had never been able to win Catani, who remained a man of violence. But 'no-man's-land', now bordered by Christian homes, was at last clear of his shadow so that both Shuar and Atshuar could go freely back and forth. And we found joy and satisfaction in teaching Catani's daughter to know Christ.

Then there was Casent, oldest son of Uyungara, whose favorite wife, Masuing, had died. Casent, like his half-brother, Wachapa, would not be in school at all were it not for a freakish accident. This was one in a series of tragedies that befell Uyungara, but which failed to move him to repent and allow Christ to change his life.

One night a loaded gun had fallen from the rafters in Uyungara's house. When it hit the ground shots rang and a bullet lodged in Casent's abdomen. For months he was in the hospital at Shell, where he underwent three major operations. There was little hope for his life. But he recovered and came to us. His treatment had been very costly and Uyungara looked at allowing Casent and Wachapa to go to our school as his way of making payment. We knew God had used these strong measures to give these boys a chance to learn that Christ had died for their sins. Casent was not yet a Christian; but he had no wish to follow in the footsteps of his warrior father. We had faith that one day he would accept Jesus Christ as his Lord and Savior.

Another sad case was that of Ayuy, Pitur's son. Ayuy was the boy who had been badly burned when as a baby he rolled into the fire . He wore a cap at all times to cover his scarred head. A solitary introvert, he dreaded the jibes of other boys and often ran away from school. We knew God had saved Ayuy's life for His own purpose, and it hurt us to see the boy so rebellious. We prayed that he would respond to God's love and mercy and find the strength to live at peace with his disfigurement.

Tungui, a son of Big Saantu the witch doctor, flashed us a confident smile as he departed. Although only recently a Christian, he delighted in leading chapel services. In spite of his changing, hoarse, and squeaky voice, he inspired listeners to sing and listen well. Tungui went home with his Christian mother and brothers. Ridicule from their neighbors did not stop the young men from explaining the gospel to the many visitors in their house.

As with our own children, we had played games with these kids, worked beside them in the gardens, cared for their medical needs, walked to the river to swim with them. How rewarding to watch them grow taller and more healthy. Every school day we presented and discussed Bible lessons with them. We could see they were learning to know God and wanting to please Him. Their attitudes were more respectful and actions kinder. Now many would face a hard struggle to keep from falling back into witchcraft, polygamy, suspicion, and killing. Since we knew they would need God's power to keep them strong in faith, our prayers went with them. We didn't want them to become imitators of white people but to become Christian Indians expressing God's love and power in their own language and culturally fitting ways. We believed they would be the ones who in the future would spread the good news of salvation in Christ throughout the jungle.

No longer were the Shuar fearful of coming to us for help in times of sickness or accident. Almost every morning long lines of Indians by the dispensary door meant long hours of work for some of our missionary group. Caring for the sick softened our own hearts as well as the Indians'. They learned to trust us as friends and to listen as we talked about God who had created them and sent his Son to die for their sins. And as they experienced relief from suffering, many were more willing to come to church to learn more about Jesus Christ.

One day an Indian mother with a baby on a sling around her shoulders came running up the path to our new, freshly painted dispensary. Marie was startled by the anguished look on her face. The baby was burning with fever.

'Help me!' the mother implored. 'My child can't get her breath. Oh, she is going to die! She will die the same way my last baby did. Don't you have some medicines that will make her well?'

We diagnosed her illness as near-pneumonia and administered antibiotics. The child lived — one of many saved from respiratory infections.

When the older Indians count on their fingers they bend down the little finger toward the palm for 'one,' the fourth for 'two' and so forth. We often watched Indian mothers as they counted the children they had birthed. They usually turned down all the fingers of one hand plus several of the other as well. Then when they indicated the number still living, it was unlikely that they would turn down even half as many fingers. But the younger mothers, by contrast, would have lost at the most only one or two children. As we looked into our patients' files of nearly a thousand names, we found that the infant mortality rate had been reduced from nearly fifty per cent to less than ten. We knew that the medical ministry was worthwhile. One needs only to have heard the heartbreaking death wail of a mother holding the lifeless body of her child to be motivated to do everything possible to eliminate this sorrow from their lives.

Many of the babies saved by medicine had grown up to know Christ, just as many adults after having first come for treatment for their bodies, had also found forgiveness for their sins and healing for their souls.

We had begun training some of our leading Christian Shuar to give shots and simple remedies to the people in their own communities. As a result, they learned to treat tubercular patients, among others, thus helping many who were unable to come to us. All of this was adding to the growth and influence of the Christian churches among the Shuar. We were also praying for a full-time missionary nurse to come to better help and train these people.

As a part of our missionary calling we found we needed to help the growing communities improve their standard of living. This meant helping them find ways to increase their food supply and to earn money. Since the first year we started schools I knew I had to find better ways of increasing food production from the poor jungle soil. I obtained different kinds of seeds from an organization run jointly by the Ecuadorian and United States governments called the Co-operative on Agriculture.

As I had some success in increasing our food supply for the schools, I began to see that the benefits of better farming should be made available to all the Indians. It was clear to me that they needed not only new spiritual values, but also practical help in improving their economy. They could never establish a lasting Christian community in the jungle without changing their methods of gaining a livelihood.

When we first came to Makuma, the Shuar were warriors

and hunters. They still lived as they had for centuries. But by this time, their world was changing. Because of the increase in population the game was diminishing. Wars were becoming a thing of the past. The day of the valiant Shuar, whose prowess was measured by the number of enemies he had killed, was gone. The day of the big raiding parties in search of the head of a distant foe for a *tsantsa* feast was gone. With it was gone the need for a big house in which to hold the victory feast.

But stripped now of the incentive to become great warriors, the people could easily sink into a purposeless existence. If nothing was done, I feared they would soon vanish as a people. Christianity provided new motivation. Zeal to win their one-time enemies for Christ was replacing the goal of destroying them. Because they were becoming more peaceable and less nomadic, it was more possible for them to live in communities centered around their churches and schools.

Now faced with a diminishing jungle food supply, they could not support community life unless they changed their primitive methods of farming. They needed all the agricultural help we could give them.

If I could help the Indian become a better farmer, he would not only win the respect of others but would be on the road to becoming self-supporting. In the early days he could earn money for his medicines and clothing only by working for someone outside the tribe. The Indians often worked for us but that was not enough to support a growing community. We wanted them to support not only their families, but their churches and schools. Agriculture would help the Indian reach that goal. Later, Don Caswell, a trained agronomist, would come from Arizona to help with this, along with his wife, Maxine. He helped the Indians to become more self-supporting by teaching them how to raise cattle and plant different foods. We were teaching them, as Paul the apostle told the early believers in Thessalonica: 'to mind your own business ... work with your hands, ... win the respect of outsiders ... so that you will not be dependent on anybody' (1 Thess. 4:11, 12).

On the edges of the jungle, the white man's civilization was steadily coming closer. The Shuar were suspicious and distrustful, and not without reason. The benefits modern civilization offered were not always good. Unless the Indian could be shown a Christian way to preserve his own pride and culture, then the only destiny for him was to become a shabby imitator of the white man's poorest ways. One story in particular, among many that I heard, spurred my efforts to help the Indians raise their living standards in their own environment.

Some Indians from a different tribe in the northern jungles, having learned Spanish in mission schools, were going to the coast to work on banana plantations. It seemed to them like a good way to make more money. I had heard many accounts of homes broken because only the man went out, never to return or perhaps to come back to die of white man's diseases.

Would the same thing happen to the Shuar we were training in our schools? Would the very help we were giving turn out to be a curse? I was shaken when I heard that just such an experience had befallen one of our schoolboys. His name was Cajecai.

Cajecai was a jungle boy who loved to hunt and fish. He was an orphan and lived with his grandfather across the river. He came to our school when he was about ten years old. He had already learned some Spanish from oil company employees near where he lived, so schooling in that language was not hard for him. After a while he married and seemed happy with his young wife. But he had not become a Christian and was restless.

Then one day a party of Indians came visiting from far away. They told Cajecai that he could make a lot of money working on the coastal plantations run by Ecuadorians. With no language handicap, he could not resist. He left his wife and went.

At first he found that what he had been told was true; he

made five times the money he might have made back in his jungle home. He worked hard and saved to buy tools, blankets, and other things for his family. But loneliness soon became too much for him. He spent his savings carousing. Why worry, when more could be earned so easily?

It wasn't long before he fell sick. He packed his few belongings and hopped on a bus for home. His faithful wife, who was still waiting for him, surprised him with a son born during his absence.

He stayed at home for a while. But the taste of high living left him dissatisfied with the humdrum jungle. Again he left his wife and boy and went back to the white man's country. He was full of good resolves; but a recurrence of his illness made him too weak to work. There was no one to extend a helping hand. His money gone, his health gone, in despair he headed back once more to the jungle. This time he went to other relatives and took a different wife. But he was no happier. He became an outcast, a wanderer, drifting helplessly back and forth between two worlds until all trace of him was lost. I wondered what more I could have done for Cajecai and what we needed yet to do to prevent families and communities from disintegrating.

This led me to think about the value to the Indian of legally owning his own land. Many of the Shuar settled along the Makuma River had moved here from the Upano River Valley. They and others they knew had lost their land there to Ecuadorian settlers. These colonists had papers from the government entitling them to the land. So many Indians were continuing to do more to less desirable areas where they could live independent of the white people. Those who stayed among the colonists earned their living mostly by working for the land owners. Now in Makuma I was hearing talk about white men taking over this area.

'I've seen it happen before,' one said. 'Sooner or later the white man will come and take this land away from us. So why work hard clearing the jungle for them? Why not do as little as necessary, get drunk, and live for today?'

When I became aware of that attitude, I encouraged several Shuar community leaders to go with me to Quito. In the government offices we began the process of getting titles to their land. This involved a lot of paper work. The great distance between capital city offices and jungle land further complicated the process. I had to spend long hours not only with the authorities but also with the Makuma Shuar. At first they were suspicious even of me. A hundred acres didn't seem very much to them when they had been using many times that much for nomadic hunting and farming. They felt they were being fenced in.

But gradually they came to understand that the hundred acres allowed by the government would be theirs for years to come, and that they would be assured of liberty and security for themselves and their children. We firmly believed that agriculture wasn't just a waste of time for missionaries, but a necessary foundation for continuing church development.

Problems faced by the Indians have changed through the years. We have always spent many of our days just sitting and listening to their troubles and counseling them. Murders and plots for revenge are no longer the chief subjects of their talk. Rarely do they come seeking our help in their wars as in years gone by. Now, when they turn down their fingers, they are not counting the members of their families who have been killed since we last met, but rather those who have become Yus Shuar. And they tell us of their victories and their defeats in trying to live for Christ. Although they are no longer likely to be overcome by the temptation to kill, they still fear the witch doctor.

One of Washicta's sons, Canusa, often came to talk. My heart went out to him as I listened to his story, typical of many others:

Long ago when Turuti (Dorothy Walker) was here, my wife

became a Yus Shuar. After that my little boy gave himself to God and talked to me about doing the same. I had known for a long time that I should become a Christian too, but I couldn't do it. Is my father a Christian? Did he teach us about God when we were young? Did he send me to school? I was already married and too old when you missionaries started the first schools. How could I become God's child? But after listening to God's Word from the preachers, as well as from my own wife and son, I finally became a Christian.

Canusa stopped, overcome with emotion at what he was about to tell me. I knew he had wanted to be baptized but had not been. Now perhaps I would learn why. He continued:

There is a powerful witch doctor that used to treat our family. Before I became a Christian I went to him but he didn't help me. Then I went to your woman. She gave me injections and I got some better. But after I became a Christian I got worse instead of well. I couldn't understand why. So I didn't pray to God; I went back to the witch doctor.

'Why have you cursed me rather than helped me?' I asked angrily.

'It was not I who cursed you, but another witch, a young one living on the lower Makuma. He has done it,' the old one said.

Since the old witch told me those things, I cannot pray, I cannot trust in God. Am I not getting sicker all the time?

The evil spirits follow me and are always talking to me. When I go hunting partridges in the evening I hear them in the voice of the owl . They speak through the pangu bird when I walk through the forest in the daytime. Even in my sleep the demons come to me and tell me I am going to die. Then I lie awake on my bed and think about how to get rid of that witch. And my head aches all the time.

Lately I dreamed a herd of angry bulls was after me. They

were going to kill me. Then a man came and said, 'I am Christ. Give me your hand and believe in me.'

I know God was talking to me, but I cannot talk to Him so long as that witch is cursing me. If I were really God's child I would not be cursed. But because I am still sick, I wonder if God has really come into my life. Maybe He has forgotten me. My wife prays for me, but I cannot pray. When I try to trust in God then I get sicker and I know I am cursed.

He looked at me appealingly as he continued.

We must get rid of that witch doctor who is cursing me. Is not Catani in jail? Can you not put my enemy witch doctor there too?

'You don't need to do anything to that witch doctor,' I told him. 'Lots of Yus Shuar get sick like anyone else; sometimes I get sick, too. But that doesn't mean the witch doctors are more powerful than God. God can heal you, but He wants you to love and trust Him even while you are sick. That is a better way to overcome the evil spirits and all the bad words they are sending you than even getting well would be.'

Canusa's eyes rested on mine.

'Pray for me, Panchu,' he pleaded.

Canusa went home, still wavering between faith in God and fear of the witch doctor. We felt sorry for him in his misery, but proud for him that he was waging the struggle. Before the gospel came to these people, shuartica always won. Now we could see evidence of God's power at work. We prayed that He would win the battle in this man.

One of the exciting times each year for all of us was when Shuar believers from all seven churches in the Makuma-Cangaimi-Cumai area gathered together for a Bible conference. Among them were Indians from far places, once separated not only by distance but fierce family hatred. Now they came together, some out of curiosity and others for the love of God.

They come, not to indulge in the drunken orgy of the tsantsa feast, nor to recount to one another all the horrible details and frightful experiences of their latest killing raids, but to attend what they called 'a great feast of the Lord' – the regional Bible Conference.

To us these conferences were always amazing – the fulfillment of our dreams during the years when we were struggling to learn the language and working in the jungle in the face of open hostility and threats of bodily harm.

The 1960 conference was held in the long bamboo church at the outstation of Cumai on the banks of the wide upper Pastaza River. More than a hundred and twenty Shuaras had trudged from their homes many long weary hours over muddy jungle trails to get there. Marie, Barb, and I had walked to Cumai ahead of time and were on hand for the thrilling moment when the Indians began to arrive.

Marie later wrote to her friends about two interesting people she noticed:

I was standing on the riverbank with several Cumai Shuar, watching Frank shuttle the Indians across in his outboard-driven canoe. Wichur, the leading believer at Cumai, was helping him. A toothless Shuar grandmother at my side was shaking her head in disbelief.

'Are all of those crossing the river truly God's Indians?' she asked me. I nodded.

'When I was a girl,' she said, 'so many Indians would only have crossed this river for war or a tsantsa feast. Nothing else would have brought them.'

She laughed hoarsely and spit on the rocks. Later that evening as she was entering the building I caught her eye. We both smiled and she came unhesitatingly to sit beside me.

In the big Shuar-style church, more than two hundred Indians, including the hosts from Cumai, overflowed the crude log benches and aisles and filled the open space around the platform.

On the wall behind the pulpit hung a large sign written in the Shuar language: 'WILL I RETURN THE SAME?'

Just before the service one proud old Shuar warrior stalked in, glared at the sign, and asked a young man standing near what it meant. Laughing derisively, the old one turned around, addressed those just beginning to fill the benches and announced: 'Are not many of these arriving Indians old enemies of mine? If Tsantiacu comes, could I stand the sight of him? No. We have tried to kill each other too many times. Would we sit peaceably together now? No. I cannot change. I go, I shall return the same.'

Shouldering his gun, he stamped off into the night. Everyone listening looked after him unbelievingly, yet wishing he would change his mind. But no one tried to restrain him and no one cared to follow him. He had made his choice.

These were two of the many who represented the older cultural mindset. The differences between them and the younger adults and school children really proved to us that the Shuar culture was in transition.

Just as their fathers had worked for a year to have plenty of food for a tsantsa feast, so these Christian Shuar at Cumai had enlarged their gardens to grow quantities of cassava, plantain, rice, and beans. They had also raised many pigs which were to be the supreme delicacy.

It gladdened our hearts, therefore, to hear the Indians declare during the period of testimony:

We did not come here to fill our stomachs with the Cumai Shuaras' good pig meat. Since we are 'born-again-ones' we have come to feed our minds on God's Word so we can return home better Christians.

Each morning as the rising sun turned the blackness of the

jungle to green gold, Wichur blew a blast on his cow horn to summon all to prayer. We praised God in song, then divided into four groups for the morning prayer hour – one group sitting together on the steep rocky bank of the Pastaza, one in the church, one in the yard, and another in the nearby cook shack. Afterward, everyone came together for Bible studies and reports from the various churches.

This year there were reports not only from Makuma, Cangaimi, and Cumai, where we missionaries had concentrated our efforts, but from four other groups of believers that had sprung up mainly as a result of the Indians' own evangelistic efforts. News of the changed lives of the Yus Shuar had spread through the jungle.

'These Christians don't kill any more,' the other Indians were saying. 'They don't get drunk and they don't talk bad. They are living happy, peaceful lives. It would be good to be like them.'

My heart skipped a beat as I listened. Seeing how God had changed these people's lives was better to me than having a great job in the States and earning big money. I didn't need better pay than what I was seeing and hearing.

One of the school boys who had come to Makuma from along the Cusutca River had returned home and repeated the gospel until, one by one, his relatives, including 'Big Eyes'' mother, Tsetsempu, became Christians. They were willing to forgive their enemies and stop warring. Soon they built their own church and began holding regular services.

One of the boy's uncles learned to do some preaching, too. Wherever he visited, he told how God had changed him and that He could change anyone who chose to follow Christ. One day, while calling on some of his relatives who lived far downstream on a tributary of the Cusutca called the Yuwientsa, he found that they, too, wanted to become Christians. Another former Makuma school boy who lived there had already told them about the Bible. The uncle led them to become Christians and to build a church of their own. Two other churches sprang up at about the same time, also through the efforts of school boys – one between Makuma and Cumai, and the other between Makuma and Cangaimi.

We were impressed during these report sessions by the calmness and reason with which the Shuar discussed problems. They respected one another's opinions without becoming angry or trying to out-talk each other.

One thing that saddened us was the absence of any Atshuar Christians. None had yet come to any conference. There was no Christian church among them. We listened hopefully to Wampiu as he gave a report on one of his recent visits to Chief Tsantiacu's group. He had spent most of his time at Tucupe's house.

'Tucupe is my friend,' he smiled. 'Although he has killed more than twenty men, including some of my relatives, he has become like a brother to me. Christ has changed his heart just as He has changed mine.'

His report on Tsantiacu was not so favorable. 'Tsantiacu and Shuunta are not following God as Tucupe is. They are not happy because they sent other Atshuar warriors to avenge the death of their nephew. They told me that they themselves did not kill anyone but I knew they had ordered others to do it. They have disobeyed God and they know it. Many in Tsantiacu's house prayed and confessed their sins, but those two men sat on their cutangas and said nothing. They looked at the ground. We did not talk angrily with them; we only felt sorry for them. You must remember they are weak because they have no church where they can hear God's Word like we do.'

Affirmative nods and exclamations came from the audience. Marie and I agreed with them that, without regular Bible teaching and constant church fellowship, it is very hard for illiterate converts to become strong Christians.

We regretted that we had been unable so far to establish a church among the Atshuar. Then I thought back to that night around the campfire when Keith and I had made our first exploratory trip into Atshuar territory. How unlikely it had seemed then that Shuar evangelists would ever be visiting Atshuar people as friends. And yet it had happened, as Wampiu just described. Was the establishment of a strong Atshuar church in the future any more impossible? With God's help, we reaffirmed our purpose and set our hearts on this goal with new resolve.

In the course of the conference we also made plans. The greatest need in all churches was for fuller knowledge of the Bible and ability to read it. Slowly, painstakingly, this work was going forward. Dorothy Walker would continue giving her time to the translation of the New Testament. Together with Bill and Gladis Gibson, she would also continue teaching adults the concentrated two-week Bible classes they had organized.

We were very excited to disclose to the Indians our most thrilling plan. This was to establish a radio station in Makuma and to place transistor radios in Shuar homes. For several years we had been praying about this and contacting other knowledgeable people to help. We were still awaiting government permission to use a medium wave frequency.

The crowning blessing of the conference came as we, with our Indian brothers and sisters, celebrated the Lord's Supper. A hush fell over the congregation as leaders from the various churches stepped to the platform. Ramon, head elder of the Makuma church, took his place behind the small communion table. It did not matter that there was neither bread nor grape juice. The elements in this jungle setting were simply tomato juice and pieces of steamed cassava. Their humble representation of the broken body and shed blood of our Lord Jesus Christ was clear and precious to all of us who knew Him. Here was evidence that the Holy Spirit of God could lead even illiterate jungle savages to know Him and to preach His truths.

Ramon had lived through all the changes. As a boy he had seen the first gleam of the gospel penetrate the jungle darkness and spread out over the towering hills and across raging rivers to change the lives of many of his people. He had gone to Mr.

and Mrs. Olson's school when that courageous couple was living in a simple, Indian-style hut in the Upano Valley. As guide and carrier, he had tramped the trail with Ernest Johnson while he ministered ceaselessly, unmindful of danger and hardship, to spread the Word. He had helped Ernest clear the land for the Makuma airstrip and hew the first timbers for the mission buildings. Ramon knew from his own experience what it was to carve a station out of solid jungle, and how a missionary must face the hostility and ridicule of those who do not know the Lord. Later, when Christ had changed his own heart and given him eternal life, he understood why those early missionaries had kept on through the seemingly unrewarding years in which no churches were established.

As we watched Ramon pour the red juice into the crude pottery cups and listened to his prayer of thanksgiving for Christ's shed blood, we were moved by the consciousness of God's immediate presence. It was He who was changing the hearts and lives of these former headhunters, and was establishing His Church among them. It was He who had brought us to take part in this work.

We were encouraged by all we had seen and heard during the conference. Much had been accomplished in our area, but it was only a small beginning compared to the task still remaining. Far out beyond the few thousand who had been brought within reach of the gospel – far down the rivers and tangled forest, beyond the most distant points reached by the Shuar believers, countless fearful, death-doomed Shuar and Atshuar tribesmen still lived in the evil grip of the devil. These, too, must be set free. We felt that our work was just beginning.

# CHAPTER EIGHTEEN
# A WILD TRIP WITH TSANTIACU

We are therefore Christ's ambassadors, as though God were making his appeal through us. We implore you on Christ's behalf: Be reconciled to God (2 Corinthians 5:20).

While I was rolling up my sleeping bag in preparation for leaving, I heard my friend, Chief Tsantiacu, calling my name. He strode to my side and looked me in the eye. 'Now what?' I wondered. My Shuar friend, Jimpikti, and I had been with the chief and his people for several days. The MAF plane would soon be on the airstrip to take us home. Our good visit was almost over. We had spent three emotion-filled days in this big house crowded with Tsantiacu's family and relatives. During the Bible-teaching sessions, many had 'bowed the knee' and committed their lives to God. Tsantiacu himself had confessed his sin before them all and asked God to forgive him for hating those who had killed his nephew and for inciting others to avenge his death. I was really sorry that our time here was over.

Now the chief was watching my every move. I had the feeling he was reading my thoughts. He didn't want to see me leave without giving me good reason to come again.

'Panchu, I need you to come with me on another trip to visit more of my relatives.'

'Where to? To whom do you want to go this time?' I asked. Again he fixed his dark eyes on mine.

'God is telling me to help more of my relatives understand how God has forgiven my sins of hating and killing so many people. God wants all Atshuar to stop warring and ask Him to forgive them. They need new hearts so they can live happily as we do here.'

To hear him talk like this thrilled me. Not only was he desirous of obeying God but was offering me a chance to contact more Atshuar. The longer I knew these people, the more I admired and loved them. They had been untouched and not so exploited and spoiled by white colonists. They worked harder and had larger gardens and houses and wider trails than the Shuar. Their hearty laughter and boisterous commanding talk always aroused my admiration. Like the Shuar, they tried to give the impression they were strong and invincible and could overcome any opposition. But I knew their jovial manner was only a desperate attempt to cover the fears that dominated their lives. With every contact I longed for them to know and obey God instead of their witch doctors and their own insistent desires to do away with their enemies.

On previous trips together, Tsantiacu had always told everyone what God had done for him. Then, after answering questions, he would give my Christian Shuar companions and me chances to teach the truth about freedom from guilt and fear. This proposed trip would be another opportunity for the chief and me to serve God together. I was almost ready to agree to his plan.

As we walked to the airstrip he told me more of the situations we would encounter. One man named Etsa lived downstream from Chiriboga. I knew this was an Ecuadorian military outpost on the Pastaza River. Feeling a little fearful, I thought, 'The Pastaza is larger than any river I have traveled and Chiriboga must be the farthest from Makuma that I have been. It is also on the disputed border between Ecuador and Peru and is guarded by soldiers.'

To Tsantiacu I said, 'You know I have no official permit to cross the border, so if Etsa and his people don't live in Ecuador, I cannot reach them.' He assured me that Etsa lived on this side of the border. We talked of other details until I climbed into the airplane. Smiling, he added, 'Be sure to bring gun for hunting game and your noisy motors so we can cover the distance more quickly!'

Back in Makuma I began making arrangements for the proposed trip with Tsantiacu. I challenged the Christian Shuar, Jimpikti, to go with me and also invited some American friends to join us: Dr. Wally Swanson, photographer Ken Gosney, and adventuresome Mike Chutuk. They were all excited about being part of a mission to contact unknown jungle Indians and to help them know God.

On the appointed day we five were ready to leave for Pakientsa. We had already filled a previous flight with the heavier items like the motors and cans of gas. Tsantiacu's men had agreed to carry them to the small Cashpa River where we would begin our trip. This stream that flowed into the mighty Pastaza was about a four-hour walk from Tsantiacu's house.

It took two more flights to move the five of us and the rest of our personal necessities to the Atshuar airstrip. As soon as we stepped out of the plane I knew by their boisterous welcome that Tsantiacu's people were as excited about this venture as we were. Even the chief's teenaged son, Yuu, wanted to join the party. Tsantiacu had also chosen two other men, Shuunta and Wajare, to go along because they were experienced river travelers. After all the farewell talks we nine lifted to our backs the stuff we had brought, plus heads of bananas and rolls of wild boar skins, and took off for the Cashpa. We hiked through dense undergrowth for nearly five hours before spotting the small leaf-roof hut where we would spend the night.

'This must be the chief's hunting lodge,' remarked photographer Ken dryly.

'All we need for a good night's sleep,' I smiled back, while setting my rubber sack of blankets on the bare, dirt floor.

The motors and gas cans were there waiting for us. Finding tools we had brought and hoisting the motors to our shoulders, we soon covered the short distance to the stream. It was good to see the two canoes tied and resting partially on the bank. It didn't take us long to fasten a motor on each canoe. Mike, Ken, and Wally were really impressed with the canoes' twenty-foot length and over two-foot width.

'What must it have been like to fell the trees and shape these dugouts from solid logs!' exclaimed Mike. His respect for the Atshuar was increasing.

The Indians were as eager as children with new toys. They could hardly wait to try out the motors. Everyone took turns riding as we made trial runs. All agreed that with the heavy motors the canoes were too tippy. We had to somehow fasten them together. Tsantiacu and his men knew what to do. They felled and skinned some balsa trees to make outriggers to steady the canoes.

'We've done this before,' the chief reassured me as he produced some vines to tie one pole in between the two canoes and the others on the outer sides. By nightfall our craft was ready.

At dawn after a quick, cold snack, we happily loaded the canoes. Surprisingly, there was still plenty of room for all nine of us. When we found the stream too shallow to use the motors, the Indians poled smoothly along. Shortly, we could hear the roar of fast moving water and pounding waves. We hugged the bank, stopped poling, tied the canoes, and walked toward the junction of the two rivers. Just one look was enough for me to feel like calling off the trip.

Wajare, seeing the fear in my expression, shouted above the roar, 'Don't worry, Panchu, even though you think the high waves would swamp us, we Atshuar aren't afraid. We've traveled when it was like this many times. Besides the river won't stay flooded long. Soon it will recede so we can go safely. Don't we Atshuar know this river well? Don't be afraid!'

He and Shuunta said that they would stand in the front of the canoes while I steered from the back. They would tell me which of the many forks in the swollen river to take. Often, after killing one of their enemies, they had traveled this wild river even at night on flimsy rafts to get away from possible counter-attack. Tsantiacu talked of his wars with Tariri, the chief of the group of Atshuar on the Copataza River. I enjoyed translating for my English friends and watching their shocked expressions. For nearly an hour we stood spellbound by the wild, swooshing water as well as by the wild and fearful tales.

When Wajare said he thought we should start moving, I shook my head. But the Indians kept trying to reassure me.

'We aren't just using pole and paddle, Panchu. We are going with your motors. The airplane propeller pulls you through the sky, doesn't it? In the same way won't the outboard motors with their propellers pull us through the water? So let's go! We can surely make it!' I almost felt like laughing at their confidence in the power of the motors.

As I kept looking up and down the river, I noticed a sandbar a little way downstream. We would have to go around that to whichever side was best. Also slightly upstream along the bank the water looked calmer.

Finally I said, 'First, let's pole the canoes upstream, then start the motors and turn toward that sandbar and into whichever channel looks the smoothest.'

Everyone liked the idea. Two men on the bank held the ropes tied to the canoes while the rest of us got on board. Mike and I took our places beside the motors. Shuunta stood in front and called back, 'When we get going, I'll signal which is the best way to go.'

We started the motors, moved cautiously upstream, and pushed the prow of the canoes into the current. Just in time, the two men moving along the bank jumped into the canoe. Doing well the first hundred yards, we picked up speed. We went to the right of a rock and gravel bar, when all of a sudden Shuunta turned toward me and made circular motions.

'Turn around quick!' he shouted. 'Rocks ahead!' So I turned around and headed upstream again. The current was so swift that we made little headway. We did inch our way past part of the sand bar. I turned again to go around it, when I heard 'clunk' on the motor in the other canoe. Then I heard another 'clunk' on my motor. We were in shallow water, had hit rocks and sheared the pins in the propellers.

'Jump out!' I yelled. Everyone splashed into the brown water and caught the canoes and towed them back to the sandbar. Quickly I opened the green box I was sitting on and took out a pair of pliers and two new shear pins. It took only a few minutes and we were ready to go again.

Indians and white men strained to push the canoes out of the muddy shallows into the brown flooded mainstream. Then with all on board we were off on what turned out to be the wildest river ride I have ever taken.

'Go here!! Go left. Now go right.' Shuunta and Wajare kept commanding. We barely managed to steer around rocks and logs.

'Close call!!' 'Wow!' we shouted, while hanging on tightly and bracing ourselves. Near misses were the common thing. Since the Indians didn't have to paddle they were pleased and quite calm. Shuunta seemed to think that the motors could make the canoes do anything we needed. He did not realize how difficult it was to steer our awkward craft in that turbulent water.

We kept going that way for several hours. Many times we saw the water go over huge rocks and shoot spray six feet in the air. Scary? Yes! Plenty! At times I wished we'd never left that little river where we had slept. 'Lord help us' was my constant prayer. There were many channels in this flooded river and I had to depend on the Indians to choose the right ones. It wasn't a smooth relaxing canoe ride that you might dream about when you go on a vacation. I was tense and ready any second to turn right or left at the command of Shuunta and Wajare. By 3:00 in the afternoon I felt like a nervous wreck. I spotted an accessible quiet place near shore and yelled to Yuu and Jimpikti.

'Grab the ropes and get ready to jump. We're going to tie up.' What a relief it was to me when my feet hit solid ground.

'Let's stop here for the night. We can get some leaves and build a shelter.' I was tired of playing with death. So we took out our rubber sacks of blankets and dry clothing and stretched them out on leaves under the shelter. I lay down completely exhausted. 'Lord, I am doing this for You and for the Indians who are slaves of fear and Satan. Thank you for protecting and providing for us. Please give us rest.'

The next morning I awoke with a song on my mind: 'Through many dangers, toil and fears, I have already come. 'Twas grace that brought me safe thus far and grace will lead me home.' My fears and tenseness had disappeared. The river had gone down and was no longer at flood stage. As we loaded the canoes, I looked downstream at what appeared to be a big lake.

'Now we'll be able to make good time,' I thought, only to be disappointed. The lake-like area turned out to be barely eight inches of water covering thick mud. We could neither run the motors nor paddle. We tried poling but finally we all got out to push and pull. We held on to the canoes to keep our feet from slipping. It took hours of patiently guiding the canoes while slogging through the mud.

Finally, we came to deeper water and again started the motors. Late in the day we arrived at the military base called Chiriboga. A dozen green-clad soldiers were stationed there. We tied up our canoes and made friends with them. Tsantiacu said Etsa lived farther downstream so we talked to the soldiers about going on.

'Only the Indians may cross into Peru. The border is another hour or more beyond us. There are no more soldiers there. This is the last checkpoint,' they said. And then they added, 'We cannot allow foreigners to go any farther.' Even when we explained our purpose they would not let us by.

We looked wistfully at the river below, where it was smooth and slow moving. It was free of rocks and rapids and would have been easier to navigate. So, feeling sad and weary, we prepared for the night. But Tsantiacu was not upset. He said that he did not want to go without us and that he had another plan. With his arm motioning and fixing his eyes upstream, he compelled me to look in that direction.

'Remember that smaller river we passed just above the military base? That is the junction of the Capaware. Let's go back there.' Tsantiacu knew that area and told us that he had friends and relatives there as well.

'They would welcome us and would want to hear God's good words of peace,' he declared confidently. As I interpreted for Mike, Ken, and Wally, I added that on a trip like this with the chief, I never knew what was going to happen next. They were agreeable, so by morning we felt cheered and ready to go.

The Capaware was sluggish and deep so we had no trouble navigating upstream. Since there were no logs or sandbars Wajare and Shuunta sat down at ease in the prow of the canoes. In the warm sun they almost went to sleep.

After six hours of uninterrupted travel, Tsantiacu pointed to a garden of banana trees and cassava plants up on the bank. 'We are almost there,' he announced. Around a few more turns we spotted several leaf-roofed houses. I throttled back and we pulled up alongside a big, fallen tree that was lodged by the shore. Indians came almost immediately from the direction of the houses. Tsantiacu began greeting them in the customary, rapid, oft-repeated staccato-sounding utterances. Then all the

Indians were exchanging greetings and talking at once, asking and answering questions about who we were and the purpose of our visit. My three friends listened and watched spellbound.

I had never even heard of this group of Atshuar before and was pleased to meet them. They took us to a new house they hadn't quite finished. All the poles of the steep roof were in place but only the lower half was covered with leaves. The opening in the roof let in more light than in any finished Atshuar house. We arranged ourselves on the bed racks they showed us.

Women began bringing bowls of freshly steamed cassava roots and pieces of wild boar meat. We relished every bite. Then, before we had quite finished eating, family members began to sit together in semicircles around the huge room. There were no stools or logs so they sat on the ground facing us. Tsantiacu stood and began to speak. Ken took several pictures of these friendly people sitting with their legs straight out in front of them. Long, black hair framed their intense faces turned toward the chief.

Tsantiacu spoke first of their complicated relationships, how his father was related to their grandfather. All Indians I knew spoke of family connections like this to overcome suspicions and prove their friendly intentions. Tsantiacu recounted some of his past war-filled life.

'But I'm different now,' he said. 'This man Panchu became my friend and tells me and my people about a man "Jesus" who was God and came down from heaven and lived on earth. He came to give His life to pay for our sins.'

As he and the people discussed all he said, I noticed they used a different word for sins. They talked it over until everyone understood what sin was. Jimpikti did his best to explain that if they would ask God to forgive their wrong thinking and doing, God would help them understand. He told them he knew how hard it was to think God's thoughts because it had taken him and the Shuar in Makuma a long time to want to change. His hearers still asked questions about why one man would die for someone else's sins. They had never heard of such a happening. When another Atshuar had wronged them they immediately planned to make the enemy pay for his evil acts. They didn't think it would be just for someone else to die in his place.

Tsantiacu motioned for me to sing some songs and explain more to them. The chief and his men knew the songs so they joined in heartedly. We sang the same words over several times until our hosts began to sing also. Then I opened The Book and told them God's words were written here on paper. He wants us to know how He had created our first ancestors. Before I finished I had covered how Adam and Eve had disobeyed God so that He had to punish them. 'Yes,' they agreed. 'Anyone who does wrong has to be punished! That is the just way.'

'But because God is also merciful,' I continued, 'He promised our forefathers that someday His Son would come to earth, live a perfect life, and take their punishment in their place. If they and their children would believe that promise and repent of their wrong doing, God would forgive them.' Again the listeners said they understood the sin part real well, but the good words about God forgiving sinful people because His Son took their punishment on Himself was still hard to understand. I longed for the day when they would be able to hear these truths many times until they believed.

After more discussion we introduced Dr. Wally and told them he knew how to help any who were sick. One by one they talked with him while I interpreted, and he used what medicines he had brought along to help them. As they responded so openly we knew they were beginning to trust us as friends. By evening the women brought more steamed roots and roasted monkey meat. We ate well and were thankful.

Early the next morning I heard the Indians who came with us chatting with the local people. Some were discussing their family relationships. Others talked of the value of the doctor and his medicine. They knew he did not treat them the same as their witch doctor who sucked out the evil spirits that some other enemy witch doctor had sent. The enemy always called on the evil spirits to curse and destroy them and diminish their numbers. This strange foreign doctor helped them feel stronger and peaceful, some said. Others wondered who these strange white men were and whether their message about being forgiven of their sins was really true.

As daylight came, some who had been too bashful the day before wanted to see the doctor. They all asked to hear more of the Creator God who sent His Son to pay for all our sins. It was worth the trip to tell these who had never before heard that they could be forgiven and live forever. I was sorry to begin preparations for leaving. These people needed to hear the gospel again and again. I had often felt this longing to help people better understand God's justice and mercy. Situations like this were increasing my desire to begin broadcasting the gospel by radio as soon as possible. Why should some people hear about the true God and our Savior over and over while others, barely once or not at all? By midday the Indians packed our dugout canoes. We said goodbye and headed toward the military base. Tsantiacu was happy to have told them of his faith in Christ.

As we tied our canoes to a dock at the military outpost, we couldn't help noticing that in another canoe alongside was a stocky Atshuar man. He glanced briefly at us and then shifted his eyes without changing his dead-pan expression. Tsantiacu and I both recognized him as Copataza Chief Tariri. I had met him a year before when I once visited the Indians far upstream on the Pastaza. He was a warrior and a respected leader. I wondered how Tsantiacu knew him and if he was alarmed.

Tariri finally met my eyes. We greeted each other briefly. Then I stepped aside to give place to the two chiefs. They both talked at once very formally and dramatically as they each repeated and added to the other's words in the typical rhythmical way. When they began to give accounts of their wars and of having killed members of each other's families, I really paid close attention.

'These two are long-time enemies,' I realized, 'but they have to act friendly and talk in a non-threatening manner because the soldiers and I are all watching them.' I knew that though they might be harboring deep distrust and even hatred toward each other, they would not attack in this public place. I listened all the more intently wondering what would come of this encounter.

Tsantiacu suddenly changed his tone and spoke more softly. 'Yes, once I did think of you as an enemy but I am a different man now. Because God has changed my heart I really want to be your friend. He has forgiven me though I had broken His laws and lived like His enemy. Now I know He wants me to stop hating and fearing and killing. So I invite you to come visit me in my house. I am a follower of Jesus Christ. I will not make war with you any more.'

Again my heart was filled with thankfulness to hear not only Tsantiacu talk like that but also to hear Tariri's warm response. 'Fine,' he said, 'the words you say are good. I'll do that. I'll visit you and then you can come to my place to stay awhile with me.'

Both men agreed amicably and walked away from each other. I watched Tariri pole upstream toward the Capaware and out of sight and wondered if he would really forget his hatred of Tsantiacu. After all, he was not a 'bowed-the-knee' one.

Leaving the soldiers we headed upstream on the Pastaza. We traveled until Tsantiacu said we should begin to look for a place to sleep.

'I know there used to be a house around here. Take me to shore so I can look for it.' As soon as we pulled the prow of the canoes up on a beach, he, with Yuu, Shuunta, Wajare, and Jimpikti, disappeared into the forest. They returned shortly, saying they had found the house. While unloading and tying up the canoes, Jimpikti motioned me to one side. The others headed down the trail but Jimpikti shook his head and said, 'I don't feel good about sleeping in that grave yard.' I didn't really know what he meant until later.

We had no choice but to follow the others. It was already becoming dark under the canopy of trees. Arriving near the clearing, I saw the stockade wall around the house and lots of tall weeds but no footprints. There were banana trees in abundance with several heads that were yellow ripe. There were cassava, sweet potatoes, and ripe papaya. Where were the people? Something terrible must have happened to them.

The door was open so we stepped inside. In the darkness several vampire bats startled us as they flittered around our heads. Otherwise this place was eerily empty and silent. Then I saw there were at least three thicknesses of walls but that they were only four feet high. I began to understand that whoever had lived here had fortified themselves against enemy attack. We found bed racks around the room, stools with wide boards planted in the earth behind them for back rests. In the kitchen there were many earthen pots and three logs with their ends together, ready to be fired for cooking.

'Where are the people who apparently had recently lived here?' I asked aloud. Tsantiacu and Wajare answered my questions.

'It is a sad story,' they told me. 'The man and his wife with two children were hiding from an enemy warrior who had threatened to kill them. They feared that the enemy was coming near, so they built the stockade wall and added the extra walls on the house so it could protect them like a fortress. They brought in extra food, barred the doors, and stayed inside. After several days they ran out of water. 'Surely no one would harm a woman,' he thought. So the man sent his wife to the spring. She was obedient and went.

'In just a few minutes he heard the shot of a gun. Though suspecting it must be the enemy, he grabbed his gun and ran out to see what had happened to his wife. By the spring he found her water gourds, fallen on the ground, and there she lay too. Terrified, he started back to the house but never reached it. With another gunshot he fell to the ground. Then the two children were killed as there was no one to protect them. No one was left alive.'

I was so stunned I could hardly tell my friends the story. This was the real world of the Atshuar. Its fear almost overwhelmed us.

But Tsantiacu continued matter-of-factly, 'Panchu you can sleep on the bed just to the left of the door. Under your bed, the man of the house is buried. The wife is under the next bed and the two children under the others.' Wally, Mike, and Ken could sleep on the beds near mine.

Later when everyone was settled, I lay in the pitch darkness unable to sleep. I kept thinking of the man in the ground underneath me. He was only a few feet away but I couldn't get to him to tell the gospel. I was too late. He was already in another world. He never knew Jesus had died to give him eternal life. I was too late, too late.

'Lord, help us to reach the living Atshuar before more are killed,' I prayed. Hours passed before I slept.

Even with the light of a new day and a good meal of garden food, our spirits did not lift. We headed for the river with heavy hearts. I started the motors and in no time we were going upstream toward home. The sun was shining and I asked Ken Gosney to guide the canoes. We had seen and felt the worst horror we could imagine. We wanted no more adventures. Now we could get home and be at peace again.

I had almost gone to sleep when all of a sudden I felt the long canoes slide up on a submerged log. Ken was alert and had seen the big pile of brush almost in the middle of the river. He swerved to avoid it. On the left was the rough water of the channel and on the right a nice quiet-looking pool between the brush pile and shore. He pointed the canoes toward the placid waters but he had not seen the log just below the surface.

Now things started to happen fast. Once the two canoes were more than half way over the top of the sunken log, the front of the canoes dipped downward. The current caught us and turned the canoes into the brush pile. I felt shocked and disoriented as we tossed and turned. The canoes almost broke apart, started to go under water but were caught by the current, and began turning downstream. I was startled to see a large bamboo log that we would have to pass under but there was too little room for me to do anything but jump over it as the canoe slipped by underneath. I came down into water and went clear under.

As I surfaced I spotted the canoes floating downstream with only four people in them. I swam as fast as I could to catch up. The canoes were full of water but at least upright. When I grabbed onto one side, I almost pulled them under. By struggling, I was able to climb aboard and yell, 'Let's bail out the water!'

'How?' they returned. 'With what?'

'We have hands, don't we?' So, cupping our hands, we worked hard and fast. By the time we finished we had floated downstream.

Jimpikti spotted our rubber bag with blankets and dry clothing inside floating on the water. So he jumped in, grabbed the bag, and swam to shore. Then the doctor's medical bag was sighted and Wajare went over the side. The last I saw of him he was nearing the shore, but farther down. A chicken we had purchased to eat was flopping in the water right ahead of us so we plucked it out and placed it at our feet. One other bag was floating too far from us, so the chief dived overboard and swam to it and on to shore.

Now there were only two of us left in the canoes. Our paddles had been lost in the spill, and we had only one pole. We couldn't even use that, as the river was too deep to reach the bottom. So, helplessly, we were carried along by the current. I detected another danger just ahead. The current was taking us to the far side of the river. The distance would be too great for us to make it back. Yuu, the chief's son, and I struggled desperately to turn the canoes toward the near shore. We got close enough to grab a tree trunk that was sticking out of the water and hung on. To my surprise the big basket with all of our food supplies appeared alongside. I grabbed the one long stick we did have in order to hook one of the rope handles of the basket. Just as I tried to reach it, a whirlpool passed by, and with a sucking sound the basket disappeared.

Jimpikti saw where we had stopped and swam to join us. He had left the rubber bag upstream on shore. He was sure we could find it again.

'Have you seen Tsantiacu?' Yuu and I asked.

'No, I haven't seen anyone.'

While scanning our surroundings I could see one of the Indians swimming downstream toward us. As he got closer I could tell it was Tsantiacu. He was straddling a log and paddling with his hands. As he climbed aboard, we shouted our delight.

'The chief is alive! He overcame the strong current!' It was so good to see him again! I asked if he had seen Wajare, Shuunta, Ken, Mike, or the doctor.

'They must be back where we tipped over on that brush pile. When I lifted my head out of the water I saw several men but I couldn't get to them or tell who they were,' he answered.

'Lord, keep them all alive and help us find each other,' I prayed.

We tried to identify where we were and how we could get back upstream in spite of the swift current. I took the spark plugs out of the motors. Water came spurting out. I put them back in and pulled the starting ropes many times but it was no use. Without the motors' help we had to separate the canoes. With two of us in each canoe we could maneuver them more easily. In order to make any headway against the current we had to pole as hard as we could.

The sun was setting behind the trees. At our slow rate of progress we knew it would be after dark before we could reach the pile of debris where we had tipped over.

'It is such a long way up there,' Tsantiacu reminded us, 'we won't make it until morning.' I thought he wanted us to stop for the night but I said, 'We have to keep going so we can see if the others need help. We don't know if they are alright or not.' I knew their dry clothes and blankets were in the bags along the shore where Jimpikti and Wajare had left them. So we kept slowly inching along. Whenever we moved away from the bank, the current would catch the canoes and turn them downstream. The force of the water was too strong for us to move far from the bank. But I wouldn't give up trying to find the rest of our party.

We pushed the canoes as hard as we could, while still keeping close to the shore. Sometimes where there were branches and brush alongside the canoes, one or two of us would jump out, walk on top, and push each canoe. In that way we got around several tight corners. We helped each other and made steady progress. I didn't think about snakes that could have been in the branches and brush. If I had, I would have been too fearful to allow any of us to clamber over them. I just knew that God was protecting us every minute of those dark night hours.

Later we were glad to see the moon come out. Its reflection on the water was a great help. We rounded another of the innumerable corners and sighted the flickering light of a fire. Even though we guessed it was a great distance upstream, we cheered and shouted and dared to hope our men were by that fire.

We had stopped once to pick up the bag Jimpikti had rescued and then a couple more times to rest. My hands were hurting from broken blisters. Should we stop again? No! We could see the fire much more clearly now. We had to keep going.

By 3:30 a.m. we pulled up in front of our men huddled around the fire. We hugged and counted everyone. No one was missing. Each one shared how the Lord had helped him through a very scary time.

'Thank You, Lord, for Your wonderful care.' Our Indian friends had made good shelters. We pulled blankets from the bags and had a great sleep.

Even the portable radio that had been wrapped with the

blankets inside a rubber sack was still dry. The next day we raised the antenna on two long poles and contacted the pilot. We recounted what had happened and that we would call him again when we arrived at Tsantiacu's. The Indians cooked the chicken we still had in the canoe. They needed strength to pole the canoes through the next two days. To lighten their loads the rest of us walked along the banks keeping the Indians in sight. Doctor Wally gave us some pills to relieve our hunger pangs. Occasionally throughout that long day we scooped a handful of soggy, wet cookies from a tin can someone had picked up after the spill.

It was nearly dark when we came to Tsantiacu's 'hunting lodge.' There was no food here but, exhausted, we slept well anyway. At dawn we left the tightly-tied canoes in the stream and the motors inside the hut. During the last hours of walking to the airstrip, I thought about my gun and remembered it was at the bottom of the Pastaza where we had tipped over. But that seemed little to have lost, compared to all we had experienced. God had helped and blessed us all the way. We had shared a great adventure with Tsantiacu and his people. We praised the Lord for leading us to another group of Atshuar whom He loved and wanted to draw close to Himself. It was worth all the struggles we had been through. We hadn't made it to Tsantiacu's relative, Etsa, but did meet and make friends with many others.

God had brought us safely through the dangers of traveling on the treacherous flooded waters, of meeting an enemy Atshuar chief, of sleeping with the dead, of being dumped out of the canoes, and of inching along through snake-infested brush. We felt it had all been worth the risks and fatigue to give the gospel to the Capaware people and to hear Tsantiacu talk honestly and fearlessly to Tariri about God.

One thing I dreaded. I didn't like saying goodbye to Tsantiacu. The thought of Tariri, his longtime enemy, troubled me. How could Tariri who was not a 'bowed-the-knee-one' keep his promise to Tsantiacu? Would he learn to trust Tsantiacu and God too? All I could do was ask God to make Himself known to the Atshuar people through Tsantiacu. Meanwhile in Makuma I would give my energies to developing the radio ministry.

# CHAPTER NINETEEN
# THE GOSPEL GOES FARTHER FASTER

Faith comes from hearing the message, and the message is heard through the word of Christ (Romans 10:17).

I remember the day when I realistically faced the seeming impossibility of evangelizing all the Shuar and Atshuar in my lifetime. Indian companions and I were standing in a dugout canoe tied along the edge of a river. We were saying final farewells to the Shuar families on the bank above us. During our three day visit, we had learned to know them by name. We had hunted wild game and fished the river together. We had talked about their relationships, their work, their fun times, and their fears. Every evening we had gathered around their fires to sing and talk. 'Yes,' one said, 'we have heard about God. When we were kids our grandmother used to warn us about Him. "Don't throw that food on the ground," she would command. "Eat it all or God will be angry at you. Then He will punish you. Did not God make us and everything else including your food? Now, eat it all!" We were afraid of God because He was always angry with us.'

I kept asking questions and learning more of their thinking. 'Where is God now?'

'Oh, who knows?' This was the same answer I had heard from many others. 'He doesn't have anything to do with us any more. He is too far away. We can't get to Him. We don't even think about Him. It's no use!' Several had pointed their fingers upwards and nodded their heads in agreement.

Their openness made it easy for me to tell them that God was really very close to us. 'He is always ready and able to help us. He wants us to know Him. He even told men to write on paper how He had made the world and all of our ancestors.'

As I had seen with previous new hearers, that last word really got their attention. All Shuar loved to tell about the first of their people who had lived in the jungle. They had endless stories about their exploits as hunters and warriors. I was always eager to hear their myth-like accounts of their history. Then they would ask to hear what God had written in His Book.

Now, even after many hours of teaching and answering questions, they were not satisfied. I knew they wanted us to stay longer and tell them more. But I couldn't stay and I couldn't promise that I would soon return. It had been such a long hard struggle to get there this time. I kept waving to them as the Indians paddled slowly downstream.

'You all keep thinking on the good words from God,' I shouted.

Within myself I prayed, 'Lord, what else can I do to help them know You? Just suppose,' I asked myself and the Lord, 'that one of these isolated tribesmen not only heard, but believed the truth and received Jesus Christ as his Savior. How could he learn to know You better and become like Christ? Who would disciple him? I can't give him a New Testament; it is not even written in his language. And even if it were he doesn't know how to read. What else can I do?'

The figures on the bank with their long, black hair and ankle-length skirts began to fade. The following long days of river and trail travel before reaching home gave me time to think. I shared my longings with God.

I knew it was hard for jungle people to understand God's ways. All their lives they had known only fear, warfare, violence, and loss of loved ones cut down by raiding parties. They lived in fear that enemy witch doctors would use the evil spirit world to curse and destroy not only strong warriors but defenseless women and children. Many listened well to our message but comprehended little. The possibility of their relating to the God of creation as the same One Who had died for them seemed very remote. My heart sank. How long would it be before they could know God well enough to stop fearing and destroying each other?

'To get new information, all these people can do is to hear, discuss, and repeat,' I said to myself. 'Yes, they can hear!' I repeated with new emphasis. 'They CAN hear! They are used to receiving information by the ear gate. And by hearing they can understand and respond in faith! Yes, Lord, that's it! They can't read but they can HEAR! Radio programs in their language would be a way they could hear over and over again! Oh Lord, do You want me to broadcast Your good words by radio?'

'As a child, I had to hear the gospel many times before I understood how I could know You. They need the same opportunity that You provided for me. I'll work with You and Your people to provide Your Word by radio for these Shuar and Atshuar Indians! Let me see this become reality!'

I never did get back to that small group, nor did we ever (even with the help of Shuar evangelists) go by foot, canoe, or plane to all the groups living and dying in the 10,000 square miles of Ecuador's jungle. But by radio we hoped to help them hear God's Word again and again.

I began by sharing my hopes with my fellow missionaries and then with electrical engineers working in Quito with Radio Station HCJB. Could they build a five-hundred-watt transmitter for use in Makuma? They set to work on the project. Some were already making small, battery-powered radios for use in remote parts of Ecuador. When we saw what they were doing, we asked if they would make several hundred for our needs, too. At the same time we applied for government permission to transmit on a certain frequency from our Makuma mission station. It would be named Radio Rio Amazonas with the call letters HCGM.

In Makuma we cleared land and then constructed the building to house the transmitter and other equipment. It took several years to get everything ready. In February 1962 we aired the first broadcast. Since the Indians were early risers we started broadcasting at dawn. They would listen before leaving their houses to hunt or clear more land. Then, later in the afternoon when they returned home, they could listen for another hour. Those closest to Makuma were the first to pay the small price for radios. Little by little, as anyone traveled farther away, receivers were placed in the outstations, in the homes of those even farther away, and eventually among the Atshuar. Radios and also batteries became favorite trading items. Soon we lost track of where the receivers were and who had them.

At that time very few jungle people had watches. This made us wonder how they would know when it was time to listen to the programs. One Atshuar woman told me how she solved the problem. Proudly showing me a stake she had placed in the dirt floor in her end of the hut, she said, 'When the sun moves past the overhead position and begins to shine through the crack in the wall, I watch until the light creeps across to this stake. Then I know it is time to listen to the singing and talking about God.' She really made my day!

The Indians thought that because we had built a separate, solid board house for Radio Station HCGM, it must be very powerful and important. One inside room held the five-hundred-watt transmitter. The entry room was often filled with curious Indians. Family groups from near and far came to see how the system worked. Then they would stay until broadcast time to listen through a loudspeaker and watch through a window in the wall to see into the broadcasting room. There I, or whoever sang or spoke, would sit at a small table before the only microphone and control panel. The watching visitors would express their wonder and ask for a radio to take home.

We began preparing taped music and messages and teaching young Shuar men who had graduated from the six grades of our schools to do the controlling, announcing, and programming. Our own son Ross, when home from boarding school in Quito, learned along with me and the Indians to run the station. For me to open my Bible, greet my Indian friends, and teach them the Word of God was a God-wrought fulfillment of the vision He had given years before.

At the same time we were beginning to broadcast from Makuma, God was doing something else to make His Word clear to jungle peoples. Together with Indian collaborators, translators Dorothy Walker of GMU and Dr. Glen and Mrs. Jean Turner of Wycliffe Bible Translators were completing the New Testament in Shuar. As they produced the first drafts of each of the twenty-seven books, we read and explained them over the radio. By 1976, the entire New Testament was printed and made available to all who could read. By radio, readers as well as non-readers could receive in their own language what God wanted them to know.

Was establishing the radio station in Makuma easier than walking the muddy trails and poling the dug-out canoes down and up the rushing rivers? No, it was not! The time, expense, and physical exertion required to set up and maintain the radio ministry was much greater. We had to saw lumber and construct the building, engineer and set up an antenna only to have it fall in a Z-shaped heap on the ground, and then weld and set it up again. When we outgrew the first radio house, we then constructed a two-story building of cement block and even installed air conditioning to keep the humidity and cockroaches from damaging the electronic equipment.

By 1972 we obtained a new five-thousand-watt transmitter. Electrical engineer Jim Hedlund with his wife Norma joined our team and began language study. They very capably took over the maintenance of everything in the new building. Later they were able to train Shuar to do well, not only at announcing, but also at creating programs.

Did the message by radio go farther than the missionary and Indian evangelists could carry it by plane or on foot? Yes, it reached across both the southern and northern borders into neighboring countries. Not only could the Shuar and Atshuar hear but also the Quichua-speaking Indians and the Spanish Ecuadorian colonists living around the edges of the jungle. Did the message of new life in Christ go faster? Oh yes, of course!

Did HCGM make the Word of God constantly available to jungle peoples? Yes! From February 1962 we daily broadcast faithfully to all we had contacted and thousands more. Though eventually jungle peoples were able to buy commercially-made transistor radios and so could listen to many other frequencies, the Shuar and Atshuar preferred Radio Rio Amazonas because it was the only station that broadcast the gospel in their language. Our programs were uniquely and personally directed to them and their life-style needs.

The Makuma church believers and I still frequently traveled either by plane or by foot to visit those at the outstations or to make new contacts. We always took batteries and radios to all who wanted them.

For a break from the constant work routine in Makuma, I knew of nothing more relaxing than fishing the Makuma River. So one day I asked three Indian friends to go with me. I offered to pay them to push the canoe while I cast my lure into the quiet pools between the many rapids. We had a great time talking and catching fish. As we worked our way up the river we came to a falls. The Indians had a hard time pushing the long dugout up the relentless flow, but they made it. We went around the corner and there was a smaller falls. Around another corner was still another waterfall. This sparked an idea in my brain that would cause me arduous work for the next thirteen years.

'There is a lot of power in that falling water. Couldn't we use it to make electricity for the radio station as well as for our clinic and missionary homes?' I even looked farther upstream and found the best possible site for such a power plant.

So many Indians were obtaining radios and asking for longer hours of programming, that every month we were giving more time, personnel, and funds to supply the demands. Our new larger diesel generator was powerful enough, but with the longer hours of broadcasting it required more fuel than we could afford. The fuel had to be flown in by plane, so the bills for flights and fuel kept increasing. I couldn't help envisioning how wonderful it would be to turn the power from all that water into electricity. Such thoughts soon developed into a plan. The next time I went to Quito I shared my ideas with Gordon Wolfram, an engineer working with Radio Station HCJB. He said he would be happy to study the situation to see if it would be feasible to install a hydroelectric plant near the area of those water falls. After evaluating the possibilities Gordon said, 'You chose an ideal site, one that should produce more electric energy than you need.'

'Praise the Lord for putting those falls right there!' I responded.

This was only the first step. What we had conceived in our minds we quickly drew up on paper. Getting the equipment, manpower, machinery, lumber, cement, stone, and gravel would take more special help from our miracle-working God. Here I was in the Amazon basin but even if I were in the States, how could I find what we needed and get it back here?

'Lord, I am not an engineer; I do not know where to find those who can help us. Lord God, You know all things. I call on You to bring to our attention the best equipment to install here and the men who can do the building and installing.'

I wrote to Murlin Hansel, a pastor friend from Bible School days. He lived in my home state of Iowa near where my family and I would be temporarily staying while on assignment in the U.S. He was also personally involved in supplying needs of third world people and knew where to find available agricultural equipment. In his answer to my letter he wrote, 'Come to see me and we'll find the machines you need.'

Once our family was settled in good home and schooling situations, I went to see Murlin. I had already learned from my engineer friends in Quito that there are two types of hydroplants and many variations of each. Some are suited for a water source with a 'high head' (meaning long drop), with a limited amount of water. Others are made to function with a greater volume of water but with a 'small head' (shorter drop). The latter type would fit our jungle situation. That was just the kind we expected to find in the flat areas of Iowa. We visited several hydroelectric plants that were no longer in use. These were too small for the current needs of Iowa's increasing population. Most were owned by Iowa Electric Light and Power Company. Of all such retired plants we saw, one in Monticello, Iowa looked the best. There were even two identical units of generators, governors, and turbines. We needed an engineer's evaluation. I thought of P. K. Myrie, whom I had known in Ecuador as one of the HCJB engineers. He now lived in Cedar Rapids, Iowa, not far from Monticello. After a thorough investigation, P. K. Myrie said that the one with the two units would be the most suitable for our use.

My next step was to write a letter to the Iowa Electric Light and Power Company. 'Would you be willing to sell the retired light plant equipment we had seen in Monticello, Iowa?' Their answer was filled with questions like: 'For what purpose do you need the two units? Where do you expect to install them?' I answered frankly, stating that I was a missionary working with the Shuar Indians in the jungles of Ecuador. I told about our schools, clinic, agriculture work, the churches, and also about the radio station and of our need for more electrical power. Since over a week passed without a reply, I feared they had turned down my request. A few days later, when their letter finally came, I hesitated at first to open it. Though I almost expected rejection, I finally tore open the envelope and began to read.

The letter said that the Board of Directors, in view of the wonderful work we were doing to help some of the world's underdeveloped people, had voted to sell both units to us for one dollar each. What joy filled my heart! This was another indication that the Lord was leading us. God had given the vision and now was supplying this equipment. 'Lord, thank You!' I took the letter to Mr. Don Shidler, then President of Gospel Missionary Union. After reading it, he smiled broadly and pulled his billfold from his pocket. 'I'll give the two dollars,' he said. We joyfully wrote our thanks to the company for their generous offer.

Murlin and I went again to see the plants. We knew that they had not been running for several years and were solidly silted in a river bed. It would require lots of work to dig, move, and ready them for shipment. Murlin talked with his friend, Mr. Vern Shield, owner and president of the Bantam Shield Company. Mr. Shield made cranes for digging ground pits. He very graciously offered his facilities where we could take these plants, have them sand-blasted, painted, and sent by rail to New Orleans.

But how could I get all that machinery dismantled and trucked to Mr. Shield's factory? I prayed, 'Lord, I come to you again with a need too big for me to handle. You are faithful to fulfill your purpose and I trust You to send men to dig out these huge pieces of machinery.'

A Christian organization called 'The Christian Farmers of South East Iowa' heard of our project. What an enthusiastic group! They were really happy to do all they could to help. Some of those big pieces of machinery could never be lifted by hand so I contacted a manager of a company that had a telescoping boom crane and asked if they would be able to help me. He said he would do it for one hundred dollars an hour. Without knowing how I could pay him, I said I would let him know when we were ready to do the job.

The Christian Farmers group quickly spread the request for men to help dig out the machines. We agreed on a Saturday. I informed the man with the crane. P. K. Myrie offered to oversee the dismantling.

Much to my surprise, on Saturday morning nearly fifty strong men came together. A machinery dealer loaned us his semi trailer to haul the equipment to Waverly, Iowa. The crane operator also arrived early. When he saw all those men, he said, 'I thought a missionary needed these machines, and missionaries don't have money to pay all these men.' I was excited to tell him that all these Christian farmers were donating their work so Indians in Ecuador could hear the gospel of Christ. He turned to one of the volunteers and asked, 'If all you men are donating your time, where does that leave me?'

Everybody worked hard. The boom was able to reach each part as it was dismantled and place it on the semi. Some of the larger parts of the generator must have weighed five to six thousand pounds. I was excited to see everything going well.

But I could work only until noon because I had to travel to another town to preach on Sunday. Before leaving, I commended the men for their wonderful help. Some time later, I heard how it all turned out. By the time all the parts of the two units were loaded on the truck, the sun was setting. A carload of men headed for the highway. The driver of the truck followed but he was so heavily loaded that he could not keep up. Before climbing the first hill he fell behind. The men in the car came to a sign that read: SCALES, ALL TRUCKS MUST WEIGH. 'Wow! What will happen to the truck when he gets here?' No one knew the weight of any of the pieces.

The driver of the truck told me, 'I never found second gear all the way.' Gradually it became dark. He kept up his slow pace. When he came to the scales, the sign read: CLOSED. He just went slowly by. In Waverly, at the Bantam Shield factory another crane unloaded everything with ease. All the men returned home, tired but pleased that they had had a part in this missions project. When the bill came from the crane operator who had helped us load the truck, it was much less than originally estimated and I had enough money to pay it.

After the equipment was sand-blasted, painted, and crated, it was placed on a train flat car, carried to New Orleans, then shipped to the port city of Guayaquil, Ecuador. Care Incorporated Project paid for the ocean freight. I knew it was God alone who was moving these light plants to where He wanted them to be used.

When the equipment arrived by ship in Guayaquil, I was on the wharf and had hired three big diesel trucks to haul the hydro turbines and generators from the coast to the mountains. We had found a safe, dry place to store them at a GMU mission station way up in the Andes. All this equipment would stay there until sometime in the future when we could find an airplane able to fly it into our jungle airstrip. When would we ever get a plane big enough to fly all those heavy pieces into our mission station? 'Lord, you gave us this equipment. Now I am trusting You to somehow, someday, get it the rest of the way.' I went back to Makuma with my head full of plans for lengthening the airstrip. I didn't know what kind of airplane the Lord would send or when it would be available but I wanted to be ready.

# CHAPTER TWENTY
# ANOTHER JUNGLE MARTYR
Jesus said ... Whoever loses his life for my sake will find it (Matthew 10:39).

*February 1964*

'Chief Tsantiacu has been killed!'

We were stunned. The news reached us on a Sunday morning in Makuma and we held up the worship service until we could learn more about the chief's death. In the jungle, news travels as fast as runners can carry it. It took only a couple days for an Indian from farther south to bring the news. We, and the Shuar, gathered for the service, bombarded the bearer with questions: 'Who killed him? When did it happen? Where was the chief? How did the killers do it? What happened after that?'

'Others told me that the Copataza River Atshuar are the ones who did it,' he answered. It was rumored that the chief's son, Yuu, and his nephew, Wajare, had also died. Could it really be true? Marie and I did not want to believe it.

I remembered that on our last trip together the chief, his men, and I had met and talked with one of the Atshuar chiefs from the Copataza River. His name was Tariri. He and Tsantiacu had been enemies for many years. But there near the Peruvian border they had talked face to face. I knew that day that, although they had each killed family members of the other in the past, they would not then revengefully harm each other. Besides our own group, there were too many Ecuadorian soldiers watching them. These two powerful chiefs had even invited each other to visit in their homes. Tsantiacu told Tariri that because God had forgiven all his bad deeds, he wanted to stop warring and forgive everyone who had harmed him and his family.

'I want to be your friend and tell you more about God who loves us both,' boldly declared my friend. Tariri had seemed to accept Tsantiacu's offer and said that he would arrive at Tsantiacu's house the following month. The two leaders had finished their conversation and peacefully turned away from each other. I was elated that Tsantiacu had not been ashamed to tell Tariri that he had 'bowed the knee' before God and would no longer hate or kill anyone. I had dared to hope that the revenge wars among these Atshuar would cease. If these two seasoned warriors would stop fighting, then others would follow. But now, with Tsantiacu's death, I was sure the killing was still going on.

I had to know more. What had happened to the rest of Tsantiacu's larger family? Were they still living in his big house at the end of their airstrip? Were there any men left? Would they welcome me there now? The next day I flew with MAF pilot Dave Osterhus to verify the rumors. As we circled the clearing and came in for landing I focused my attention on whether any Indians would be coming out to meet us. If only I could see my old friends lining up on the edge of the strip as before, I would know the rumors were untrue.

But what I saw was unlike anything I had known there before. Coming down the path were women and children but only one man. My heart sank. What had happened to the long black hair of the women? All their heads were shaven, including even the little girls'. As the plane rolled to a stop, I knew before anyone told me that the women and girls were mourning their losses. In their culture, the shaven heads were signs of having been widowed and orphaned. The terrible words we had heard the previous Sunday were all true. I grieved with them. They wailed, wiped tears from their faces, and then rubbed their hands on my shoulders. I recognized Tsantiacu's wives and daughters and also the wife of Wajare with their baby in the sling around her back. Now Wajare was gone as well as Tsantiacu and his son, Yuu, who had just entered manhood. They had been killed by Tariri and his men, by unforgiving enemies and traitors. After many minutes the wailing finally ceased but only because the one man among them started to speak.

I recognized the straight, square-shouldered Indian as Shuunta who had been with us on our wild river trip. Although he had 'bowed the knee' and professed to be a Christian we knew that under pressure he was continuing to practice witchcraft. We talked of the good times we had shared hunting and visiting and traveling together with those who had now died. I reminded him of the peaceful encounter we had witnessed between Tsantiacu and Tariri. Shuunta told me how Tariri had kept his word about coming to visit my friend. They too had hunted, fished, and eaten well together. Tariri had listened attentively to the salvation songs the family sang and to Tsantiacu's own dramatic retelling of Jesus' life and death and resurrection. When Tariri left, he solicitously invited Tsantiacu to visit him in his house along the Copataza River. At the time of the next full moon Tsantiacu, Yuu, and Wajare had gone, never to return.

Then Shuunta began to pace back and forth as he talked of revenge. His chief's death must be avenged, he declared, while lifting his gun above his head and lowering it to his shoulder, up and down, over and over. He named the relatives he would round up and said they would be courageous and take the lives of those who had wronged them.

Not wanting to hear more of such talk, I started to leave. The women followed Dave and me to the plane. All along the way they kept begging us to come again, not to forget them, but to tell them more of God and His heavenly home. I assured them that even though Tsantiacu was no longer here, I would come again. I encouraged them to keep on praying to God and trusting Him to take care of them.

'You know that we will see Wajare, Yuu, and Tsantiacu again some day in heaven,' were my final words.

More details of Tsantiacu's death reached us during the following months and years by the jungle 'grapevine'. Traveler after traveler added what he had heard until we could envision just how it all happened.

Tariri had warmly welcomed the three would-be friends into his house. They spent the day talking and eating. Tsantiacu told again how Jesus had died in his place. He had believed and received the living Savior in to his life. Now he had no desire to kill any more but wanted to forgive his former enemies and be friends.

'Why should we fight and destroy each other? God wants us to live now as well as forever with Him!' Tsantiacu had asserted. Tariri said those were good-sounding words and he liked them. But Tariri was still a deceiver and was all the while planning to kill the visitors.

Tsantiacu never used to sleep without keeping his gun in his hands as it lay across his chest. He never knew when some enemy might surprise and attack him. But that night in Tariri's house, he and his men just leaned their guns against the wall, and stepped away to the bed.

The different ones who told me all this said, 'We know Chief Tsantiacu had forgiven his enemies because he lay down without any fear or suspicions. He was at peace. Yes, Tsantiacu forgave his enemies, but his enemies did not forgive him.' Marie and I were comforted to hear that the chief had left such a clear testimony to the power of God to change a man's heart. I agreed that the victims had trusted their enemies because they had first learned to trust God.

The story continued: 'Everyone in the house was quiet but not all went to sleep. The fires flickered low until they went out. No one stirred them up again. It was very dark. Tariri and two others lifted their heads and grasped their guns. Stealthily stepping to the foot of the visitors' bed rack they pointed their muzzles at each body. The heavy breathing of the sleepers was the only sound. When the guns fired the killers were so close that later, by the light of dawn, the women saw powder burns on the shirts of the dead. As the ultimate insult, Tariri and his men threw the limp, silent bodies into the river to be eaten by fish and eventually washed downstream.'

I did fly over Tsantiacu's house several times in the following months and years. At first, I noticed weeds were growing in the gardens and airstrip. I saw just one man. Everyone else had fled. I knew he would soon leave as the garden food was diminishing. Word reached me that eighteen persons had been killed in the wars between the Copataza Atshuar and Tsantiacu's relatives. The last time I saw the place, brush and trees were growing on the airstrip and in the gardens. The roof had caved in over that big, empty house. No one was in sight.

Once again, we were without a friend among the Atshuar Indians. When would their warfare cease? Were there any among them who remembered the gospel and lived as Christians? Where were the women and children? Where could we again find them? They were lost to us. The Copataza Atshuar would not receive us either. They spread the word that since we were friends with Tariri's enemies, they never wanted to see us. Judging us by their own standards, they feared we would be as vengeful as they, and would in some way punish them.

Almost ten years had passed since Roger and I walked with Chief Tsantiacu to his group the first time. Now, it seemed like we were no closer to establishing Christian churches among the

Atshuar than when Keith Austin and I had been threatened by one named Timias in 1950.

By praying and trusting God, we knew that He would make a way for the Atshuar people to again hear and believe the gospel. We just didn't know how He would do it or when. As someone has said, 'Faith is believing God when unable to provide proof and obeying God when unsure of the outcome.'

# CHAPTER TWENTY-ONE
## 'GIVE ME THAT AIRPLANE!'
Ask and it will be given to you; seek and you will find;
knock and the door will be opened to you
(Matthew 7:7).

When the largest plane I had ever seen burned on our jungle
airstrip in Makuma, we were completely helpless to stop it. Only
God could turn this seeming disaster into good for us and our
hydroelectric project.

It happened in April 1968. Most of the parts of the hydro
equipment had been stored in the mountains for over a year and
I did not know how to move them to the jungle. The largest
plane available was a DC-3 owned by TAO, a commercial airline
based in Shell. We had lengthened our airstrip enough for TAO
to bring in the smaller hydro pieces. Then, with the use of a
tractor, we were continuing to extend the strip to at least a
kilometer. Surely this would be long enough for an even larger
plane to land. There were a few soft spots that we had yet to fill
in and pack. On good, dry days I continued improving it.

One morning as I was working, I kept hearing a loud but low-pitched motor noise. I thought it must be an airplane but the motors didn't sound like any I had heard before. As it grew louder and louder, I looked up and saw a huge four-engine Hercules plane flying from west to east.

'It must be that the oil companies are flying well-drilling equipment east of our place,' I thought. Day after day this plane would fly over in the morning and go back a couple hours later. The same flight was repeated in the afternoons.

The more I thought about it the more I hoped this was the right plane to bring in our equipment. I dared to pray, 'Lord, would You please make it possible for me to find the company that is using that plane?' Every day as I watched it fly over our strip I kept asking the Lord to give me that airplane.

August came when it was time to take the children to the capital city of Quito for school. By the time we reached the mission's home for our school children, I resolved to contact that company. Friends had told me to look up Alaska Airlines. I had no trouble finding the number in the phone book. Soon I learned their address and went to see them.

I took the elevator to the third floor and knocked on the door. I was a bit nervous, for I had never done anything like this in my life. A gentleman came to the door, invited me in, and gave me a chair. 'I am Mr. Gonzalez. How can I help you?' he asked.

'I am Frank Drown, a missionary in the jungle where I have served for many years. At present we are working on a hydroelectric project located on the Makuma River southeast of the Shell Oil Company base at the end of the road. We have some large pieces of equipment that we need to move in there and I wonder if you might be able to do it. As you know, there are no roads in that part of the jungle. Perhaps you have seen our airstrip when your plane flies over almost every day.'

'Yes, as a matter of fact, I have seen your airstrip and wondered what was going on down there. How long is your runway?' Mr. Gozalez wanted to know.

'It is one kilometer long,' I told him. 'However, it is not very wide.'

'How many pounds of equipment do you need to move?' he asked.

Now I was beginning to sense some interest on his part. I gave him an estimate of the weights and asked with increasing confidence, 'How many trips do you think it will take to do the job?'

He counted the big pieces that we had to move and began to add up the approximate weights. 'I think we could do this for you,' he returned. 'It will probably take two flights. Where is your equipment stored, sir?' he inquired.

'At our mission station in the Andes, near Latacunga,' I replied. He seemed to know where that was. I took a deep breath, tried to appear calm, and ventured another question. 'Could you give us an estimate as to the cost?'

Mr. Gonzalez figured with his pencil a few more minutes and said, 'About $2,500.'

I realized that if he had said $250 I might have come up with that amount. But I responded with a smile and said, 'Fine. We'll have to make our runway a bit wider for your plane. Someday soon, when I have that accomplished, I will communicate with you.'

'Thank you very much for stopping in, Mr. Drown. We'd like to complete those flights for you.'

I really felt elated when I left that place. I couldn't help imagining how unbelievably gigantic that C-130 would look landing on our little dirt runway.

Back home I worked on widening and packing the airfield. Rain often hindered progress. We were also very busy keeping up with broadcasts and fulfilling many requests for evangelistic trips into new places and for teaching sessions at the various outstations. Months went by.

On one outstation visit near the eastern border of Ecuador I helped the Indians ready their new airstrip for the first MAF landing. I was looking forward to flying home the next day. I got my little portable radio out of my knapsack and put the antenna up so I could contact the MAF base. I wanted to report on the condition of this new field. I heard MAF people checking on weather and flight plans with the seven other jungle stations before calling Makuma.

From Makuma Marie said the weather was fine and that she had a very urgent message for Frank. I was shocked when she told me, 'Yesterday morning we heard the loud rumble of a big plane. By the time I got to the airstrip the Alaska Airline Hercules had circled and was landing. The wheels touched down at the east end and rolled to a stop before reaching the middle of the strip. But then the right two wheels began to sink into the soft dirt until the belly of the plane was on the ground.' She went on to say that our new fellow missionary, Don Caswell, had radioed the DC-3 to bring in a wing jack and had hired Indians to dig around the wheels and fill in with rocks to form a ramp. They had worked two full days before the pilots took off from that spot to roar down the rest of the airstrip and disappear. Marie said she could hear the motors for several minutes before she saw the plane in the distance gaining altitude.

There wasn't time for me to ask many questions. I could hardly wait until MAF came to fly me home. When the pilot arrived he spent a long time making several test take-offs and landings as the new strip was still untried. Finally, he give me the signal to jump in and we took off for Makuma.

Once on the ground in Makuma, I quickly greeted everyone and walked down the wheel tracks of the Hercules toward the far end of the strip. I saw that the belly of the plane had knocked over my fence at the edge of the cow pasture. Still striding downhill through the tall pasture grass to the next fence, I noted that more fence posts were on the ground. From there the plane, by dropping into the river valley, must have gained enough air speed to safely fly away.

'How amazing and scary!' I said aloud. Shaking my head in

disbelief, I thanked the Lord that the pilots and plane had experienced all that without being harmed. I walked back to where the plane had been stuck. I had to see how much of the equipment they had brought in. There were duplicate pieces of some parts and several odd ones, two Woodward governors but none of other important items. Despairingly, I realized that not enough parts were here to complete one unit. Marie had waited for me and was watching my face.

'Oh no,' I groaned. 'Our hydro project is over! What pilot would attempt to land here again with the rest of the missing parts? After all that happened to him the last time, I don't expect he will ever come back.'

The next day we pulled the hydro equipment to the machine shed. I felt deflated all over again as I recounted the pieces. Would this be the end of the project for which I had hoped and worked so long? As many times before, my thoughts turned to God. Since He had led us to begin this enterprise, would He not continue to supply everything needed to complete it? I didn't know how or what He would do to help us but I could trust Him to fulfill the vision He had given.

When our two youngest children came home from boarding school at the end of May, we shared with them all that had happened. They enjoyed both their mountain and jungle homes and always joined with us in the activities of each day. They were eager to see the hydro site, especially when I suggested that we ride inner tubes from where the river passed near our house downstream a mile or so to where we had been grubbing out stumps and clearing brush for the hydroelectric plant.

The summer passed all too quickly and soon it was time to take our children back to school in Quito. Once they were happily settled, I went again to the office of Alaska Airlines to talk with Mr. Gonzalez. A year had passed since we first met. Would he welcome me again after having almost lost his special plane while trying to help me? I wanted to tell him I was sorry that his plane had gotten stuck on our airstrip.

From behind his desk, as I stepped into the room, Mr. Gonzalez very cordially exchanged greetings with me. Before I could speak again, he said, 'I thank you and your missionaries for helping rescue our airplane. They were all so helpful.'

'I should rather be thanking you,' I responded, 'for bringing in the pieces of our hydro equipment.'

'That's quite alright. I'm sorry there was all that trouble,' he returned.

I felt reassured enough to tell him, 'We still have a very great problem. Your men brought in two pieces of some items and none of others so we will be unable to finish the project.'

Mr. Gonzalez stood up and looked me right in the eye and said, 'Frank, I want you to know we are going to finish the job.' You could have knocked me over with a tooth-pick. I was sure that plane would never go back again. Mr. Gonzalez explained that he was not in Ecuador at the time. He said there were many things they could have done differently. They could have let some air out of the tires so they would have spread out more and not have sunk into the turf so easily.

'In the war we dropped metal mats down to roll up on and they could have done that. They could have carried less fuel and not taken the fork lift. So we will be happy to finish the job.'

I could hardly believe my ears but managed to say, 'Well, thank you, sir! I appreciate that very much. I have a few suggestions. Would you like to hear them?"

'Yes, of course,' he responded. I proceeded to tell him that the plane was flown in during one of the rainiest times of the year. Couldn't we wait until a drier month like May or August, when we often have three weeks without rain?

He then explained why they had gone in when they did. He said that the drilling operation had been suspended for a while. Since the pilot and his crew were without work they said, 'Why don't we do that job for the missionaries, instead of just sitting around?' So they went, not realizing the weather in the jungle is very different from that in the mountains.

Now we agreed that whenever we had three weeks of dry weather, I was to call him on the radio. They would send their pilot to the MAF base on the edge of the jungle and the missionary pilot would fly him to Makuma. Then we could inspect the strip together to be sure it would be okay.

Mr. Gonzalez and I shook hands and I walked out the door with new hope for the furtherance of the hydro project. Back in Makuma, I told Don Caswell and all our fellow workers of the plan. We continued working with the Indians and watching for the rains to let up.

Three weeks passed without rain, and cracks were showing in the airfield. The river was clear and low. We called the Alaska Airlines pilot and he wasted no time getting to MAF and into our station. As he walked the length of the airstrip with us he commended us for all the work we had done.

'We should have no problems landing and taking off from here,' he said. I was excited to hear that.

'We'll land from the east, but rather than stopping where we did before we'll roll on down the strip to this little rise where it should be the driest. We'll bring some heavy plywood, and while we are still rolling slowly, two crew members will jump out the doors on each side and put down the plywood for the wheels to rest on. That way the plane won't sink while we're unloading.'

'Great! It sounds good to me!' I said.

The pilot looked at me and asked, 'Are you ready to go now?' Of course I was. So we hopped into the MAF 4-place Cessna and flew back to their base at Shell. From there the pilot flew to Quito and I went to Latacunga. We were to meet each other at the Latacunga airport the next morning, he, with the Hercules, and I, with trucks loaded with the hydro machinery.

The next morning we met each other at the airfield early. We loaded all of the machinery. The pilot looked at the cargo and offered, 'Why don't you go purchase any heavy supplies like iron rod you might need? There is still plenty of room in here.'

I did buy a few shovels and several hundred-pound sacks of chicken feed but was in too much of a hurry to spend time shopping. I feared it might start raining in Makuma before this flight would be accomplished. Once we tied everything down and fastened our seat belts, there was a roar of those powerful engines and we were off the ground headed for the jungle. As we gained altitude we thrilled to see most of the snowcapped peaks of the Ecuadorian Andes. Of all my travels in Ecuador, this was the fastest and most beautiful ride I had ever had from the mountains to the jungle. In a very few minutes I could spot the MAF base. The Shell airship looked like a short, brown shoestring.

The mountains gave way to green-carpeted jungle. I pointed out the wide Pastaza River snaking south and east. We flew over the familiar Cutucu ridges where I had often spent days hiking up and down. My heart gave an extra beat as we came over the saddle-shaped hill just west of the Makuma airstrip. Now we could see our mission station and runway. As we landed, I sensed the thump of the landing gear and then the wheels easing onto the ground. Bouncing down the strip, I felt like a king. What a marvelous trip!

We slowed down to a snail's pace at the top of the rise and the two crew members jumped out with the plywood. At the same time, the plane began tipping to the left. The pilot gave a burst of power and those men with their plywood were caught in the wind blast and went sailing. As the pilot shut down the engines, I felt the plane tipping more and more. The pilot groaned, 'We're stuck again! Can you get the Indians to dig me out? I'm in a hurry and need to get back to Quito.'

With the tractor we unloaded the plane and moved the equipment to the right beyond the edge of the strip. Meanwhile, the Indians dug the earth away from the belly of the plane and made a path for the tires to get out. I suggested to the pilot that he let me go to the river with the tractor and trailer for rocks to make a solid ramp. Then he could more easily pull out of that hole.

'No,' he said. 'This plane can do anything. We'll just put two pieces of plywood under each wheel and we'll pull right up out of here and be gone.'

'Okay, sir. It's your airplane.' I moved across the strip and stood alongside the hundreds of Indians lined up to watch. They had never seen anything like this before. The pilot took his seat. He saluted me and nodded as I returned the salute and thanked him for bringing in all of our equipment. After the closing of the huge rear door, he started his four motors. Then he checked each engine. With the blast of the engines my stomach reverberated. That plane really was powerful. Once again, the captain saluted and I him. He released the brakes. The monstrous plane moved forward and up. But all of a sudden terrifying sounds like cracking of guns filled our ears. The wheels had slid back into the hole and the plane went down even lower than before. On the far left side I saw the propeller and motor hit the ground. The prop sheared off, flinging sharp pieces in every direction. One blade piece cut the fuel line on the second engine and a bright flame and thin finger of smoke began to rise. This two million dollar plane was on fire on our airstrip!

The pilot sprang out with a fire extinguisher. He shot at the engine, but the flames only increased. He picked up a second bottle, but it didn't help either. Without understanding the danger, the Indians came in closer to see what would happen next. The pilot shouted, 'Get these people out of here! The plane is going to explode! Many could get hurt or even die. Your mission buildings will very likely burn.'

At first the Indians didn't listen, but when they saw the urgent expression on my face, they knew I was serious. They began to grab each other and run in every direction. I heard later that some hid behind rocks, trees, and hills. Most headed for the river. A few crossed in the canoe but the rest swam and helped each other get across. One young boy ran so far no one found him for two days!

Now everyone had left. What a helpless feeling coursed over

me! Billows of smoke rose from the plane, blackening as it increased. Ominous hissing from the flames and occasional minor explosions held our attention. We dared not stand too close. The pilot and we ran into a little grove and stood behind the trees and watched. Any minute we expected the plane to blow up.

But when I thought of the danger to our buildings, I couldn't just stand and watch. The house closest to the fire was the most vulnerable. It had a leaf roof and the occupants were away. Wind-blown sparks could easily set it ablaze. I ran in and started to move books and correspondence to a safer place. Hours passed as I frantically packed and carried boxes and clothing out of harm's way. By the time I finished, my throat was so dry that my tongue literally stuck to the roof of my mouth.

Throughout the afternoon the plane kept slowly burning. I went over to our house to be sure that Marie was okay. About fifteen feet from my door lay one of the six-foot blades from the propeller that had sheared off. Guardian angels must have kept it from hitting anyone.

Marie gave me water and wiped my dirty face. I went back to the pilot who was standing behind a tree still watching the mushrooming cloud of smoke. We exchanged short greetings and stood silent. The whole front-end cockpit was gone. Now the flames were moving back to the wings and the fuel supply. I looked at the hydro equipment that we had unloaded, sitting right along the edge of the airstrip beneath the wing. I spotted my camera bag sitting on top of the equipment. Even though I wanted to take pictures, I dared not venture nearer that burning craft.

All at once I heard loud snapping and breaking sounds and saw those high, aluminum wings break loose from the body and collapse. The tip of the lowest wing touched the ground. Worse yet, the wing on the right (just over the hydro equipment) fell on a fence post which pierced the fuel tank. I filled with fear as I saw fuel pouring out through the hole and running right under the hydro equipment.

'That will catch on fire and it will be the final blow to our hydro project!' I thought. Then as I watched, something happened that changed my fear to admiration. God miraculously, it seemed to me, changed the direction of the wind. The smoke and heat began to move toward the nose of the plane instead of the back. The smoke curved around to the west away from the fuel tanks still in both of the wings. It blew away from our buildings and away from the hydro equipment. The fuel from the tank near our hydro equipment never did catch fire. Minute after minute the fire diminished until it looked so small that we ran for water. We poured it on by buckets until every spark was out. What a sick bird was left. It looked like a useless mess, gutted by fire, never to fly again.

The Hercules pilot learned that I was a ham radio operator and asked me to call his insurance company in the U.S. The insurance agent said he'd catch the next plane for Ecuador. When the agent arrived shortly in Makuma, he asked me to have a look at the plane with him. We made two rounds. He questioned me very little but took notes on what he saw. We were both amazed to recognize that the wing and motors on the side nearest the hydro equipment were not even blistered. Why had I feared? God is always faithful to care for everything and everyone involved with what He wants to do. If I hadn't known that before, I was sure of it now. Even the insurance agent agreed with me and said, 'Someone bigger than you is taking care of this place.'

When he talked with the pilot, the agent assured him that the insurance company would pay Alaska Airlines for the total cost of their C-130. The crew and pilot shook his hand delightedly. MAF soon came to fly them all out. They shook my hand, too, as they pointed to the charred giant and said, 'Well, Frank, there's your airplane.' Little did I imagine when I prayed, 'Lord, give me that airplane,' that God would not only use it to bring in the equipment, but would literally leave it on our airstrip!

Later I discovered that the oil company had imported the

Hercules into Ecuador. When their exploration for oil wasn't successful, they wanted to take the plane back to the U.S. However, the government officials said that since it had been imported, the Hercules had to stay in Ecuador. Now that Alaska Airlines had the insurance money, they were happy to leave the plane where it was. I was relieved it had not been a total loss for them.

A few days after everyone left, the rains came. For days water poured down. A pool formed on the airstrip around the big plane making it look bleaker than ever. When the skies cleared, I walked out to inspect the plane. A compartment door with a sign that read 'Radio Access' caught my attention. I turned the thumb screws and opened the door to find some beautiful navigation radios. They looked unharmed although water was a foot on the ground underneath them. So I carried them to the radio building where they would be kept dry. It rained again and again.

About a month after the fire, MAF brought a visitor I hadn't met before. 'My name is Bill Dugan,' he said. 'I have come from Marietta, Georgia, and am here to dismantle the airplane and salvage what might be useful. Also, I plan to clear your runway.'

'Where is your crew?' I asked.

'I have no crew. I want to hire you and your other missionary (Don Caswell). I'll hire you, your tractors, your welder, and tools. I'm sure we'll get the job done.'

I couldn't quite believe what I was hearing and so asked, 'Do you have any credentials so I'll know you are authorized to do this work?' He showed me letters that proved he was appointed by a salvage company.

Mr. Dugan was good at organizing the work. It took several weeks to take the plane apart, crate the tires, valves, and engines. Then, he said we must remove everything that remained from the airstrip, fill the hole, and restore the strip to usefulness. 'These stipulations are part of the insurance policy,' he declared.

It wasn't an easy job moving the remains of that big airplane. Our tractors did all right with the wings and auxiliary fuel tanks, but the main flight deck, cabin, and the whole tail section formed one gigantic hulk. I distinctly remember pulling one end a couple of feet, then hooking onto the other end and repeating the same see-sawing movements many times until it was finally off the runway.

Bill Dugan always knew what to do next. 'Now, please saw me some timbers to make palletts for the motors.' We did that. The runway was repaired with rocks and gravel and dirt to the satisfaction of Mr. Dugan.

'Now we are ready for the last stage,' he said. 'We are asking the TAO Transport Airline (local Ecuadorian DC-3) to make eight flights to take out all of the salvage. You can put anything you want on those eight incoming flights free of charge. Then I'll send my parts out.'

I showed Bill the radios. He hardly looked at them. 'I think they have had too much smoke,' he said. 'You can have them.' There were ten sets of rollers that could be used to move heavy machinery. 'You can have them, too,' he said. Later we used them for moving all the generators, starters, governors, and turbines into the hydroelectric power house. How would we have ever done it without those rollers!

Mr. Dugan did not take the big fuel tanks. One had been ruined in the fire, but the other was intact. We used this as a diesel storage tank for the generator which powered the HCGM Radio transmitter. We'd never have gotten that big storage tank any other way. The wings also had big tanks, one of which we would use to store water for flushing toilets in the girls' school.

There were hundreds of uses for parts that were not salvaged by Mr. Dugan's company. One example was something we used long after this incident. We thought we would make gates for the hydroplant out of the hardest wood we could find. The gates had to be in water most of the time and we knew that no wood could last very long in water. So Arlowe Becker, who had come to Makuma to engineer the installation of the hydro equipment and electric power transmission lines, used the thick aluminum skin from the wing to make gates that wouldn't rot. Rods, aluminum pipes for conduits, cables, and electrical wire (there was miles of it in all the plane's circuitry) were used for valves and lights. We gratefully accepted all these supplies as given by God.

When we added up the money paid us for wages, for renting our two tractors, and for the use of our welder and our saw mill, along with the value of the eight flights bringing supplies into Makuma, this amount more than exceeded the cost of the two flights made by the big plane. God had provided in a most unique way. How could we ever doubt His ability to meet all our needs? He had performed miracle after miracle just to get all the hydro parts from Iowa to Makuma.

There would be more to trust Him for. Work at the river site had just begun. Now we would have to believe Him for finishing the installation that would provide electricity from the river for the radio transmitter, as well as for all the mission station.

# CHAPTER TWENTY-TWO
# A GIANT STEP FORWARD

Now to him who is able to do immeasurably more than all we ask or imagine, according to his power that is at work within us, to him be glory in the church and in Christ Jesus throughout all generations, for ever and ever! Amen (Ephesians 3:20).

Our broadcasting was in trouble. A radio station from Colombia was right on our frequency and blocking our programs. Since we were not yet able to broadcast all day long, the Colombians must have thought no one was using that frequency.

'What shall we do about it?' Jim Hedlund and I asked each other.

'If they are bothering *us*, then when we are on the air we must be bothering *them*,' we agreed. So we decided to fly in more fuel and broadcast all day. 'Then maybe they will move off our frequency,' we hoped.

It took several days before they left. But when we again reduced our hours, they came back. We went through this process several times before they finally stopped using our frequency.

But we could not keep up with the cost of running the generator so many hours each day. We felt more keenly than ever the need for getting the hydroelectric plant in operation.

Not all our fellow missionaries agreed that we should go ahead with the installation of the equipment. We didn't have the trained personnel to refurbish the used machinery, or to draw the precise plans and oversee the building of a powerhouse, headgates, and canal, or to do the electrical installations. We had obtained a D-4 Caterpillar tractor and had begun clearing the site of jungle trees and undergrowth. But because we lacked the knowledge, funds, and personnel to move ahead, our field council wisely urged us to make another thorough investigation and evaluation of the entire project. It was too unusual and too big a job for ordinary missionaries like us to tackle. In Kansas City the GMU International Board of Directors chose to send an experienced civil engineer to Makuma to examine and report on the feasibility and advisability of installing the hydroelectric plant.

Mr. Junius Penny and his wife, Marylou, were our guests for several days. A civil engineer, he was also a humble Christian. We spent hours at the river site reviewing the situation and talking about our plans. He also examined the caterpillar, the statters, turbines and generators, and the shop equipment we hoped to use for welding and renewing the hydroplant parts. We showed him the radio station and explained the extent of its outreach and the kinds of programs we were broadcasting. Jim and Norma introduced him to the Ecuadorian and Shuar announcers and programmers as well as to many of the people who were local listeners. We told him about the contest with the Colombian station over the use of our frequency and of the need to reduce the fuel and flight costs of broadcasting longer hours. He was totally sympathetic and keenly interested in every part of our work. He assured me of his approval of the project.

'If I could I would stay and help put it all together!' he told me before he and Marylou left us. Back in Kansas City with our

GMU Board of Directors, he gave them a detailed report.

'The project is sound,' he declared enthusiastically, 'and to express my approval I am writing a check for ten thousand dollars to help with the installation.'

When that word reached Ecuador, our missionary group encouraged us to move ahead. I don't think anyone was more excited than I. To me, it meant that God was still supplying the needs and overcoming obstacles for completing the hydro installation.

The next step was to discover which persons God was choosing to work with us. We contacted schools and organizations about finding men who were not only trained engineers but also Christians committed to serving God anywhere in the world. A response came from Arlowe and Emma Becker from Minnesota. Arlowe was working on a Master's in Electrical Engineering. He would oversee all the electrical connections for the hydroplant operation and would create the control panel and construct the mile-long high line between the power house and the mission station. Arlowe and his family lived in Makuma for several years until the project was finished.

Another committed engineer was Mr. Ken Edgar, a missionary serving under the direction of Missionary Tech Team located in Longview, Texas. Ken had experience installing a hydro plant in Africa. We sent him all the information he needed to create sheets of plans for our situation and equipment. A few months later he arrived to begin what he called 'Phase I: The Construction of the Power House.' Later, Ken would also oversee 'Phase II' which would take place a quarter mile upstream from the power house: 'The Construction of the Headgates.' In between the power house and the headgates was to be 'Phase III: The Canal.' We did not yet know who would be in charge of that but at least we had the completed plans.

Just before Ken came, a group of single young men arrived for the summer. Some were graduates of LeTourneau College, also located in Longview, Texas, and some were still students.

They helped with work that needed to be done before the power house could be built, like clearing and rocking a mile-long road leading from the mission station to the plant site. We had an old jeep as well as a Chevy truck to haul supplies and workers back and forth. These vehicles, like the caterpillar, had been dismantled and flown to Makuma from Shell.

One of the young men named Steve Ditzler was to graduate in another year as a welding engineer. He was very creative in working with metal. He set to work preparing the hydro plant equipment for later installation. As he left after three months, he promised to return in another year or so to work until the plant was running.

These and several others who came for shorter periods of time were all prepared and sent by God to use their special skills to serve Him. We could not have asked for better friends and co-workers.

Besides arranging for these people from the States to help us, I also traveled to Ecuador's mountainous area to consult with a group of men I knew were skilled craftsmen used to working with rocks, bricks, gravel, and cement. They were very intelligent as well as strong and muscular. They spoke both Spanish and Quichua, which reflected their mixed background. I had known them and their leader, Victor, for several years and admired their work. Victor and his crew of four agreed to help us for as long as I needed them.

Victor knew how to drive a pick-up but had no experience with a caterpillar. There was still lots of brush and dirt to move so I taught him to operate the big cat. He watched as I demonstrated and explained, 'Push this lever to make the bucket go down and pull this one to make it lift into the air. Use the brakes when you need to turn.' We exchanged places and he was soon clearing an area of brush and dirt.

By the time Ken Edgar arrived, Victor and his men were ready to follow his instructions. But now I faced another problem. Ken wanted to explain his plans to our workers as well as to me. Ken knew only English, so as he presented his plans and gave instructions I had to translate into Spanish for Victor and his men and also into Shuar for local Indians who often came to help. As we walked upstream and back, Ken had to be patient with all of us as he tried to simply describe where everything would be and how it would work.

The powerhouse-canal-headgates complex was to be situated parallel to the river and between the downward-flowing water on one side and a steep, cliff-like hill on the other. River water would flow from upstream into the entry way to the canal, under and through the open headgates and downward to the power house. Once there, most of the water would be sucked into a lower room to turn the turbines while the overflow went around the hill-side wall of the power house and back to the river.

We would begin the project with the construction of the power house. He had two concerns to tell us about.

'First, we will be digging below river level so we will be needing a good pump to keep the water out of the hole while we are working. Second, because the last plant I built like this one was not built on bedrock, a flood came and washed some of the gravel from under it causing it to tip. I want this one built on solid bedrock. All right, let's get to work and dig the big hole. It won't get done in a day,' Ken told us.

We all watched as Ken took four stakes and drove them into the ground about fifty feet from the river. 'Our first job is to dig a rectangular hole with straight up and down sides. It has to be twenty-five feet deep in order to lay a cement foundation and floor for the power house. We must find bedrock before reaching that depth,' he explained.

It took a while for me to translate every detail and to answer questions. But it was not difficult to start digging. Victor operated the caterpillar removing large scoops of top soil from within those stakes. The rest of us with shovels kept digging the sides and making them straight up and down. At last we were under way.

The hard part was to continue our efforts for hours and seemingly endless days. Frequent rains made the dirt heavier and muddy. During the days there were sometimes light showers but we just kept on digging. Water also filled the hole. At the beginning of each day I would go to the site first and get the pumps running so there would be less water in the hole when the men came.

After the top soil was removed, we went through layers of gravel and rocks. Once we reached fifteen-foot depth, Ken regularly measured our progress and kept checking to see that we were doing things right. Each day his concern grew. 'Why were we not hitting bedrock?' he kept asking. We continued the same routine for weeks.

Occasionally I would be gone for several days visiting and teaching at outstations. I put Victor in charge of the water pumps. He and Ken were learning new words from each other, but still communicated mostly in sign language.

After returning from one such trip I could see the hole was much deeper. But Ken was even more puzzled.

'We are getting close to the necessary depth but are not finding bedrock,' he told me. 'I am afraid to put the footings on these rocks. I drove some rods as far down as I could but felt only rocks.'

Victor was not ready to give up. He was as involved in this project as we were and committed to getting it done. 'We'll just keep going until we find it,' he said, trying to encourage us.

Ken said, 'We only have about three feet left to dig.'

Now the rocks were bigger and progress was very slow. We were so far below the level of the river that water kept seeping into the hole. We had to keep pumps running constantly. Every little while I would ram rods into the gravel and rocks hoping to hit bedrock.

'Only two more feet to go!' Ken yelled as he looked through his transit. And again, 'Now one!'

After another hour I began to hear the shovels clanking on

rock. I stood there stunned. We had finally hit bedrock all around and with only six inches to go. We slapped each other on the shoulders and laughed with relief. It was hard to believe that the bedrock had been there all along right where we needed it. God must have done this on purpose for us.

During the night I woke up thinking about what had happened that day. Hundreds of years ago the narrow flat area we had chosen for the hydro site must have been the river bed. That is why Ken had hoped we would find bedrock there. During big floods (like I had sometimes seen) the wild powerful waters rolled huge bolders downstream, wearing the bedrock down to its present level. God knew where we were going to build this plant and prepared the way for us. What an awesome God! I began to praise Him with all my heart. 'Who am I that You would let me have this peek into the greatness of Your power and knowledge – just an Iowa farm boy like me. I'm nobody great and yet You let me see a wiggle of Your little finger to make happen what I saw today. Help us to believe You for the rest of the project.' With this I drifted back to sleep.

The next morning we were all down in that hole again. By now we had three pumps and kept two of them going constantly. We started to pour the footings while fighting off the water. Before the end of the day we faced a new problem.

A big part of my job was to keep the workers happy, well fed, and doing their part, but I was also responsible to maintain necessary supplies like cement. I had arranged with an Ecuadorian truck driver to deliver a load of cement to the MAF base in Shell. On the morning the delivery was to arrive, I received word by radio that the driver had stopped at MAF and reported that there was no cement to be had. There was a shortage in all of Ecuador so he could not fill my order.

Cement packaged in one hundred pound paper sacks did not stay usable long in our humidity. I always tried to find cement that was enclosed in additional plastic bags to keep it from hardening. But since I couldn't always get this, I hadn't ordered a lot of cement ahead of time. Now none was available and we were faced with a serious delay. Once again we took our need to God. How would He supply the needed cement?

In a few days a commercial transport plane flew into Macuma with some reinforcing rods we had ordered. As the pilot and I casually chatted, I told him about our work at the river.

'Right now we are out of cement. Would you know of any place where we might get some? Obviously, we need a lot of it!'

'Well, this is an unusual coincidence,' he answered. 'The other day I flew into the airstrip of that oil company that has been drilling east of here. They had flown in tons of cement for their oil wells. But since the wells didn't produce, they are abandoning the site. Why don't you ask them if they will sell the cement to you?'

This was good news. I didn't waste any time before asking him another question. 'If the company is agreeable, could I pay you to fly the cement here?' He was very willing.

It didn't take me long to get the MAF pilot to take me to that strip. It really wasn't a long flight. The place was almost completely abandoned. I saw one employee, but he was very busy. When I asked him about the cement he took a few minutes to show me where it was and he informed me I could have all I wanted. It was stored there in a big building.

Hoping the cement wasn't all hard and useless, I took a closer look. Much to my delight, I saw that it was all in plastic bags. 'Great! Thank You Lord, for your wonderful ways of helping us!' I felt like God was right at my side and that He was doing more than any of us to get electric power from the river.

The transport plane flew in load after load for us. We stacked the cement bags in every available space in whatever buildings we had. My faith in God kept growing stronger. I felt like telling everyone, 'How wonderful God is! If you want to see how great God is, try something bigger than you are. See Him do something you can't do. It is a thrill.'

Ken and crew poured the lower part of the cement power house. Gravel was easily available from the nearby river's edge. On stormy days, under Victor's direction we made cement blocks in a shed. These we used to make the walls above the second floor. Once the building was completed, Ken and the workers from the mountain area went home to be with their families. They all promised to return when we were ready to start the headgates. Meanwhile Arlowe and Jim continued with the electrical installations and Steve with rebuilding the equipment.

When Ken returned he brought his wife, Irene, and their two small boys. He seemed to know it would take over a year to complete Phase II. Victor, with some new team members, moved more dirt from around the area of the headgates. They also built a necessary retainer wall. There seemed to be no end to the hard physical labor. We would need nearly all the cement we had stored for the foundation and pillars between the four gates. But our former gravel hole was a fourth of a mile downstream near the power house. The road leading from there to the headgates was hardly worthy of the name. It was full of brush, rocks, and mud holes.

Ken asked me to look for gravel in the river close to where the headgates would be installed. So we cleared a fifty-foot trail to the river.

'I remember this place,' I told Ken. 'I saw it a number of times when I was fishing. See that big bend in the river and these deep pools?' As we neared the water's edge, we spotted a huge deposit of gravel in the shallow water. This was exactly what we needed.

I remembered as a boy on the farm using a three-sided box open at one end like a big scoop. My father called it a 'slip' and we moved dirt with it. I built such a scoop, and on the front, fastened a heavy bail with which to attach a cable so we could pull it with the tractor. The men maneuvered the box in the water to fill it with gravel, then we pulled it back to the road to dump it.

Soon we had a good-sized pile right where we needed it.

We built the headgate structure about thirteen feet high. The purpose of the headgates was to control the quantity of water that could enter the canal. A big flood caused the river to rise over the twelve-foot retainer wall, washing dirt out from behind it. So we had to add more height of cement to make the retainer wall as high as the headgates.

While mixing cement and filling the forms we ran out of gravel several times. We emptied the gravel bar at the water's edge repeatedly. Each time there would be a rainstorm that caused a flash flood and the river would wash down more gravel. As the water receded, the gravel collected in our big hole. Then we harvested more and hauled it out, mixed more cement and proceeded with the project. Who besides the Lord God could have continually provided gravel for us? Ken said it was like when the Lord brought food to Elijah in the bills of ravens. I answered that people wouldn't believe me if I told how the Lord refilled the hole. They might think I made it up.

In spite of many setbacks, Ken did a tremendous job. We'll always be grateful for his fine help. The structures were all done and he was pleased. He was also ready for a rest.

'Thank you!' I told Ken, 'for all you have done for us. May the Lord bless you as you move on to help some other missionary.'

Now that the cement work was done, Arlowe and Jim completed the electrical fittings and switches that would lift and lower the headgates.

It was time to dig the 1200-foot canal. The men had used the bulldozer to move all the dirt, sand, and rocks that they could. The area looked roughly like – yes, very roughly – like the length of four football fields end to end. The plans called for digging a canal about ten feet deep and twenty feet wide the whole length of the 'fields.' We could not accomplish this with only the bulldozer. Friends who came for short terms to help us kept advising me, 'We need a backhoe for this job!'

'A backhoe! A backhoe?' I responded incredulously. 'I'm not sure there is such a thing in Ecaudor! I have never seen any.' The more I thought about it the more clearly I knew they were right. I had to go to Quito to look for one.

In the capital I looked through a number of the machinery lots but found nothing. One salesman told me to go to North Quito and look at John Deere. Much to my surprise, I saw many kinds of tractors there. This looked like a big dealership. When I asked about a backhoe the salesperson motioned for me to follow him. On a cement platform lay a nice new backhoe all in pieces. 'A man came yesterday and bought a tractor with a front-end loader, but he didn't need the attached backhoe. There it is. You can buy it.' Once again I knew a heavenly engineer was supplying our every need.

We trucked the backhoe down to the airfield at Shell, and the Ecuador military graciously flew it into Macuma for us. It took several weeks for our engineer friends to get the John Deere backhoe mounted on the back of our yellow Caterpillar. I was really curious to see how it would work. What fun to finally drive it to the river and try it out! This was a great machine. It could move dirt like nothing else we had. But soon, though we had barely begun to make a small start on the canal, the short termers helping us had to leave.

Through a series of circumstances the Lord arranged for Billy Ogg, a skilled road builder from Minnesota, to join the team. Billy and Irene Ogg arrived in Makuma just when we needed his skills. Some folks had encouraged us to get a bigger bulldozer. But Billy knew how to operate huge earth-moving machines. When he had looked over our equipment, he said, 'We'll finish the job with what we have.' I knew that he was of a 'kindred spirit' and that we would work well together and become good friends.

Often when Billy was running the backhoe I would go down at noon to take his place while he ate lunch and had a cup of coffee. Then when I was just getting the hang of things, I'd feel someone hit me in the back and there was Billy wanting to get back to work again. He was used to working twelve to sixteen hours a day. Irene had a hard time getting him to quit before dark. He had long suffered from high blood pressure and I could understand why. But the change to jungle living was helping Billy. Our nurse would check his blood pressure from time to time and after a month or so in the jungle it was down to normal.

It took a whole year to dig the canal. Billy had to move much of the dirt many times to get it out of the way. In some places the dirt was easy to move, but in other parts of the canal he hit bedrock. We used dynamite to break it up. Billy and his helper drilled holes four feet down and packed them with explosives. One day we shot off over fifty sticks at once. Indians from miles away heard the explosion and some thought Ecuador was being attacked by enemy bombs.

As soon as a section of the canal was completely dug out in the proper dimensions, Victor and his men did their part. They carefully selected rocks from the river banks and arranged them by hand in tight rows on the outward-slanting walls. When they had plastered the rocks with cement, the walls looked like the cobble stone mountain roads these men had once built. It took them hours and days and months to complete this slow tedious work.

Once the canal was finished, Billy had one more job to do. The small portion in the entry-way above the head gates had to be cleared of rocks and debris. This was where the water from the river would flow into the canal. Billy maneuvered the tractor over the biggest rocks very slowly and began to dig. Shallow water surrounded him. The deepest and strongest river current was only a few feet away. I can still see him perched on the small rocky space with the backhoe reaching into the deeper stream. Before opening up the waterway he had to move the machine into deeper water, dig out the last gravel and rocks, and creep backwards out and up again onto the shore. The water filled the entry-way. Now we were ready for the big day when we would open the headgates.

A crowd of Indians, school children, and teachers gathered to see the water fill the canal. We had worked eleven years to make this happen. Our digging was done. The workers were there to receive their 'well done.' They, too, were wondering what it would look like when the water filled the canal from bank to bank. Irene, Billy's wife, Marie, and other missionaries with their children were all there to watch.

Arlowe turned the switch to start the motor that would turn the big screw to raise the first gate. (It was one of the same big screws that had been in the Hercules to wind up the landing gears.) First a spurt of white water came under the gate. As the gate lifted, the water came streaming out. Then a huge wave of water gushed into the canal. The missionary kids had it all planned. They had brought inflated inner tubes and were now riding the waves as the water rushed toward the power house. What fun for them! The canal filled a lot faster than we had thought. Arlowe was so pleased to see the canal fill as he lifted another gate or two. After watching the water flow for a little while, Billy could stand it no longer. He grabbed an inner tube and started down the canal after the kids. 'This is the great day I have been waiting to see happen. Praise the Lord!' I could hear him say as he floated along.

Of course I was excited as any child could be. With the last available inner tube I found myself traveling faster than I had expected. Before long I caught up with Billy, and we moved right into the pool just short of the trash racks at the power house. We jumped off the tubes into the water in front of the spillway. It was five feet deep, as deep as it needed to be. We clasped our hands and held them high in a celebration of praise to the Lord who had helped us so much.

It took Steve and Arlowe several more months before they could actually run the hydroplant. By this time Steve had finished overhauling the hydro equipment, making it like new. It was all painted and looked great. Arlowe had finished mounting the turbine and its generator. Since the wooden gates he had first made for the power house had rotted, he had taken the thick aluminum skin off the wings of the Hercules and made new gates out of them. These would never rot. The high line to the mission station was in place.

The day to turn on the hydroelectric plant finally came. Arlowe called on the telephone to the mission station asking to have the diesel plant turned on. Next he opened the governor and the turbine started to turn. Before long lights began to blink. Arlowe turned the governor up a tad and both lights went out. How great to see Arlowe push in the switch to put the two plants on line together. We called on the phone to tell them to shut the diesel plant off. We were now producing electrical energy from water power.

With twenty-four hour electricity at our outpost in this vast ocean of trees, a new era had begun. From now on the hydro would be making the electrical power for the radio station and our missionary homes, and in the future it would light up the homes of the Shuar people in the surrounding communities. Now the broadcast hours would be lengthened, our flight bills decreased, and our faith strengthened in our wonderful God.

# CHAPTER TWENTY-THREE
# RENEWED CONTACTS WITH ATSHUAR INDIANS

For if you forgive men when they sin against you,
your heavenly Father will also forgive you
(Matthew 6:14).

Nearly eight years had passed since Chief Tsantiacu's death. During that time we hadn't heard where any members of his family might be. In Makuma, we continued to work toward installing the hydro equipment along the river. The radio ministry was expanding. We no longer ran schools at the mission station. They were now established in surrounding community centers. New outstations opened with their own airstrips, schools, health centers, and churches. But we had had no further contacts with Atshuar groups.

But now we were beginning to hear of possible openings to recontact Atshuar. A leading Shuar from one of the newer outstations beyond Cangaimi to the south often visited our place. His name was Tsungi and his community was Putuimi. It took Tsungi three days to walk the trails to Makuma. He had heard about the schools, the church, the radio station, and the peaceful lives of Christian Shuar and came with his father and brother to see it all. Before returning he bought a radio so he and his family could hear the 'good words,' in their own place. Within three years he and several others had become Christians. In their community of fifteen homes, each family obtained a radio and listened regularly. When they agreed to build an airstrip, my son Ross and I and two Christians from Makuma flew to Cangaimi and continued by canoe and foot the rest of the way. Together with Tsungi's men, we chose a site for the strip and marked out its length and width. It took the group over a year of patient hard work to finish it.

Tsungi wanted all the side benefits as well as the gospel. He bought clothing and machetes for trading and reselling. One of the first things he had flown in for himself was a heifer calf. Though most of his people had never seen a cow, each soon wanted his own animals. They planted more pasture grass on depleted garden plots so they could bring in a bull, too. In time they would have a good herd. They often bought simple remedies for the sick. They wanted a school teacher to live with them so all the children could learn to read.

Several other outstations came into being in much the same way as Putuimi. Radios, airstrips, schools, and churches were scattered among the Shuar throughout the southern jungle.

Our missionary staff also grew until we were thirteen, living in four strategic locations. From among all the demands on our time and resources, we responded to those that would give us greater opportunities to spread the gospel and establish churches. Keeping these goals in focus, we concentrated on Bible teaching both by radio and on personal visits to the various communities. Indians in all the stations and outstations listened to 'HCGM, Radio Rio Amazonas.' Increasing numbers of Shuar children and adults were becoming 'Yus-Shuar' (God's People).

But it wasn't always easy to distinguish true followers of Christ from those who were just after material benefits. At least all were forsaking the destructive revenge killing. We kept on preaching and helping as many as possible.

I still worked at recording Bible-teaching programs. Together with Jim and Norma Hedlund we trained one of the Ecuadorian school teachers and also some Shuar Indians to do the controlling and announcing. Our tape library of messages and music filled many shelves in the cement block radio building. Others of the missionaries concentrated on creating written Bible study courses for use along with the printed New Testament. Jim, an electrical engineer, had taken over the repair of the radio sets, the care of the ten-thousand-watt transmitter and maintenance of all the electronic equipment. Eventually Jim and Norma worked more closely with the Shuar and Ecuadorian radio personnel, giving them Bible studies and on-the-job training in programming. These were challenging years for all of us and passed quickly.

Tsungi flew in occasionally and on one of his trips he told me that strange visitors sometimes came to Putuimi. They were from the even less civilized, little known southeastern frontier. By their elaborate hair styles (long ponytails in back with stiff braids in front of their ears all intertwined and fastened with red and yellow toucan feathers), we easily identified them as Atshuar warriors.

'They come peaceably,' he said, 'to trade pigskins and artifacts for white man's cloth and machetes.' Whenever they came, Tsungi also gave them something of far greater value, that is the message of forgiveness provided by their Creator God.

I was thrilled to hear about the Atshuar visitors. I asked Tsungi if they ever said anything about the lost members of Tsantiacu's people. 'Will they let us visit in their homes?' I wanted to know. 'How many days would it take to get there? Would you go with me and help tell them and their families more about God?'

We began again to plan for a trip to contact Atshuar Indians.

Our youngest son Tim had just graduated from the Alliance Academy high school in Quito and was with us for his last weeks at home. 'Dad,' he had just said, 'May I go with you on a jungle trip to some place where you have never been?' I told him of Tsungi's challenge to go to the distant homes of the Atshuar. We had certainly never been there before, nor had we known of the opportunity until now. Everything seemed to be fitting together. Tiwiaram, one of the leading Christians in the Makuma church, was also eager to go with us.

We flew all the way to Putuimi and fastened our motor to their dugout. Most of the people from surrounding houses had heard by radio that we were coming and were on hand to see what we looked like and to hear how we talked. They already knew my voice and were not afraid to spend the evening asking questions and talking about God's Word they had heard on their radios. Some prayed with us for the Atshuar we hoped to meet. After a few hours of sleep everyone was up before dawn. Tsungi and several of his men were ready to go.

Most of that first day we traveled in cold, drenching rain. Otherwise, this trip was enjoyable. The farther downstream we went, the smoother and wider the river became. We sped along swiftly, covering the same distance that would have taken us two days on foot. By mid-afternoon, Tsungi recognized a large bank almost free of trees. Pointing and shouting above the motor noise, he said we should tie up there. We were all glad to get out and stretch our stiff legs.

'This isn't much of a trail,' Tim remarked as we hacked our way through the dense undergrowth.

'Good thing Tsungi seems to know where he is going,' I encouraged both him and myself. 'He told me he hadn't been here before but had heard there were Atshuar living in this area.'

The first clearing we came to was disappointing. Brush and weeds covered the depleted gardens. The roof of the house had caved in and there was not a sign of life anywhere. The place had been abandoned. As we walked around the clearing, we noticed two little-used trails, each leading in opposite directions. The first one we tried led to another clearing. As we approached, I thought I heard music.

'Maybe people are singing,' Tim suggested. He was right. As soon as we reached the clearing, I recognized a familiar gospel song. With a shiver of delight racing up my spine, I knew it was coming from the Makuma radio station. I could hardly keep from running to the house.

Once inside, Atshuar men, women, and children received us as well-known friends. As soon as they heard my voice, they began repeating my name in astonishment. 'This is really Panchu! He's right here!' They passed the word to each other as all moved toward us. What a thrill for me to understand that God was using our radio programs to help open the way to friendship with these people! We didn't have to ask if they wanted to hear more about Him. They began asking questions and were ready and eager to listen.

After a great evening and following morning of learning to know each other and of praising God for bringing us together, we returned to the abandoned clearing and followed the other trail. The new friends had told us it would lead to another Atshuar family group.

But this was a very different situation. The people were not hostile but filled with fear and dread because one of their daughters was very sick. 'She's dying for sure,' they moaned. Some were even starting to grieve and wail. They were not unfriendly and said they did want to hear about God's love and power, but they were distracted and inattentive. Their fear of death was controlling them. In desperation, they had called for a witch doctor to perform his enchantments over the sick one. All afternoon they busied themselves in preparing and brewing the leafy mixture he would drink to enable him to see the spirits of their ancestors and even the devil himself. As I watched I prayed to our resurrected Lord who alone had power over all evil including death. He could free anyone from not only revenge wars but also from this deceitful and fearful witchcraft.

The shaman did come, briefly greeted us, and went to the bed of the sick one. No one had time for us. Though we sympathized with the family members' heartache and fear, we began to wonder why, on this day, God had led us here. It seemed a waste of time and energy. I thought we should have stayed with the first group. But it was too late in the day to go back. We would just have to endure a bad night.

The women dutifully brought us freshly-steamed garden food and indicated the bed racks in the visitors' end of the house where we could sleep. But before it grew dark, Tim and I decided to sleep outside. We cut down banana tree leaves and spread them on the ground for our bed. We did not want to be under the same roof with the witch while he tried to contact evil spirits. However, we couldn't get far enough away to keep from hearing the witch's voice, chanting and calling on the supernatural spirits he believed could overcome the curse of sickness and death. Sometimes, in between singing and repeating names of spirits he knew, he would croon and shake branches of dry leaves. I told Tim some of what I had learned about this process. While the witch was begging the spirits to come near, he was at the same time very fearful of them. His waving the leaves was meant to keep the spirits from harming his own body. The weirdest sounds came just before dawn. Sucking and drawing in deep breaths to remove the 'arrow' from the girl's body, (which he believed represented the curse), he loudly coughed and cleared his throat. Then we heard vomiting sounds as he regurgitated the supposed 'arrow.'

'That's it!' he shouted. Then, all was quiet.

Tim and I were awakened by the morning light. We rolled up our blankets and cleared away the banana leaf ground cover. We could see smoke from the fires in the house. Dim forms of people moved about as we stepped inside.

'Is the sick girl alive and well?' I asked the father.

Reluctantly he responded, 'She is alive but still very sick

and even weaker than yesterday.' Brightening a little, he lifted his head and asked Tiwiaram to find out if I had brought medicine. 'Would he not give her an injection? Surely that would help.'

I felt he regarded my treatment as another form of magic. Nevertheless, I gladly gave her the penicillin we had brought and asked the father if we could pray for her, too. He nodded dully and walked away as I prayed.

'Lord, these people need You so much. Give them a desire to know how great You are and how they need to turn from their sins and receive Your forgiveness. They are so afraid this girl will die. You can make her well if that is best for her and them. Help them to learn to trust and obey You whether she lives or dies.'

No one in this house asked us for any further teaching about God. They just seemed to ignore us and went about their daily duties. While we were preparing to walk back to the river and return upstream to Putuimi where the MAF pilot was scheduled to meet us, Tiwiaram kept talking with the men of the household. He asked if they knew any other Atshuar families in the area. One of the younger men said a relative had married into a group on another river farther east and that he would take Tiwiaram to them if he wanted to go. I listened while Tiwiaram talked excitedly about making friends with this unreached group. Turning to me he asked, 'Couldn't we all go there?' and then added, 'It is only two more days' walk from here.' When he sensed my hesitation as well as that of the Putuimi men, he offered to go without us.

'I am trusting God to take me safely,' he assured me. I saw that he was not afraid to visit among the Atshuar and quickly giving him some matches, sugar and other provisions, I said, 'God be with you and help you to make friends and teach them how to know God as you do.'

There was very little warfare between the Shuar and the Atshuar any more. For the Shuar to travel in Atshuar territory was apparently not as dangerous as it had been in earlier years. The Shuar, because many of them had become Christians, had quit warfaring. Perhaps that had influenced the Atshuar, too. I didn't know for sure. I had heard there were still strongly-believed accusations but little open warfare between various Atshuar groups. Perhaps, too, many of their own men had already been killed.

As I listened to Tiwiaram, I was not afraid to let him go with this young man. After talking and praying again, Tiwiaram stayed behind while we made the trip back to Putuimi and flew to Makuma. On the way, Tim and I talked about the different attitudes among the people in the two households. Before we met them, the first had obtained a radio and often listened to the gospel. But the other had not. What a difference that had made in their response to us and to God's Word. I was so disappointed I didn't sense the importance of the one young man's willingness to take Tiwiaram to another Atshuar group. I did not perceive that this incident would have any impact on our future ministry to the Atshuar.

For Tim, it had been a great adventure. He would never forget what it was like to live in the rain forest where peoples' minds were dominated by overpowering fears of diseases, death, and evil curses of enemy witch doctors. He had also seen how the power of the gospel could replace fear with the joy of forgiveness and with faith in God. My only regret was that we had not met anyone who knew anything about the whereabouts of Tsantiacu's people.

Eight days later, Tiwiaram came to my door. He was so happy and had so much to tell, he couldn't talk clearly. 'I met some Atshuar men who knew Chief Tsantiacu before he died,' he declared. 'Their land is a day and a half from where Tsantiacu used to live. It is by a stream called Mashumar Entsa. The leader of the group is Chumapi. He said his father was the old man named Aiju. Panchu, do you remember when you and Tsantiacu visited him years ago?' Before I could do anything but nod,

Tiwiaram went on: 'Aiju is no longer living but his son Chumapi who was there when you visited still remembers what you and Tsantiacu told about God's forgiveness.'

'Yes,' I interrupted. 'I met Chumapi then. That was the time Tsantiacu went across the border to visit relatives in Peru. We stayed with Aiju and Chumapi while the chief was gone. I think Chumapi was a witch doctor. Is he still practicing witchcraft?'

'Yes,' admitted Tiwiaram, 'but he and his people are interested in hearing more about God and heaven. They already had a radio that they had gotten through trading and said they listened to the messages every day. I believe Chumapi is sincere and I promised to talk to him every Saturday morning on the greetings program.'

'Hey, Man! That's great! He will want to listen to everything you say.' I hugged Tiwiaram while he took a deep breath.

'That's not all, Panchu. Some of the women said they knew you, too. They were living with Tsantiacu's group when you used to teach them. They remember how Tsantiacu changed from being a fierce warrior to making friends with his enemies. They said they knew that God had forgiven the chief because he had then learned to forgive his enemies. "Yes," they said, "we know he forgave his enemies because in Tariri's house he set his gun down and went peacefully asleep. He really forgave them but they did not forgive him!" Those women have told everyone at Mashumar that they know God is real because He changed Tsantiacu into a peaceful man.'

'Oh Panchu, that is not all, either. Then the men there agreed that they will clear land for an airstrip like Chief Tsantiacu had done. I even helped pick out the site and staked it out for them. They want to make it easy for you to visit them often. All the people want to hear more of God's wonderful way of living without fear. What do you say about that, Panchu? Now I am telling you everything they told me. When do you think you can go?'

I couldn't have been more excited and told him I believed

that God had used him to renew the friendly contact that we had been praying for. 'Someday you and I will fly down there together.'

Every Saturday morning Tiwiaram showed up to talk by radio to his new friends at Mashumar. He told them to keep trusting in God to help them. I smiled to hear him say, 'Don't give up working on MY airstrip!' I felt that Tiwiaram really loved those people and had gained their respect and trust.

Months later, word reached us by traveling Indians, who had heard it from others who passed it on, that Chumapi says, 'The airstrip is finished. I want Panchu to land here.' It was still amazing to me how efficiently and quickly the 'jungle grapevine' worked. I certainly wanted to accept that invitation but faced the obstacle of 'civilized bureaucracy.' We discovered that MAF pilot Dave Osterhus couldn't leave Shell without declaring his destination as Mashumar Entsa. Government permission to have an airstrip there hadn't been granted as yet because neither he nor I knew exactly where on the map it was. Military leaders at the Shell base would not give Dave permission to land there because they thought it was too close to the Peruvian border.

We kept trying to find a way to legally open and use the new airstrip. Dave came up with the best suggestion. 'Let's fly over the area to mark the spot on my map. Then we can describe it clearly and request permission.' We also learned that there was a military base with an airstrip a day's walk northeast of the new airstrip. Tiwiaram said he had heard it was a long walk from there through swampy land to Mashumar.

Eventually, Dave did get permission to land at the base. He brought an Ecuadorian soldier to Makuma, then flew the two of us to their military base. Indian guides from Mashumar were to meet us there. But before landing we wanted to spot the Mashumar airstrip from the air. We headed east to where we hoped to sight Mashumar and the new airstrip. During many minutes of flying, all we could see was the blanket of trees dotted with dark shadows made by clouds. We knew we would have to be right over the house and strip in order to see them. We went back part way, turned, and continued searching through the solid forest canopy until we finally spotted the tiny strip straight under us. It looked like another little brown shoestring, though it was even shorter than we expected. Dave marked it on his map. He turned back to the base and dropped off the soldier and me.

The soldier and I were to walk to Mashumar where I was to follow Dave's instructions for checking on the readiness of the landing strip. The Indian guides met us. I was eager to find the foot trail and be on our way. But those who knew the area urged me to stay overnight. The trail was too long and difficult to make our destination before dark.

So at daybreak we started the long hike. Marie had packed some goodies for everyone along with my dry clothes to change into once we got there. I missed her but was certainly glad she hadn't come along. The trail took much longer than I had hoped. 'Once the airstrip is operable,' I kept thinking, 'she can come to see the women she knew before and help with Bible teaching.' Thoughts of her made me forget how tired my legs were from slogging through the mud. In this flat, low area there were no hills to climb, but the many swamps with black, stagnant water that slopped over our knees exhausted us even more. Or was my problem related to the fact that I was twenty years older than when Keith and I had first hiked to Atshuar homes?

By late afternoon we came to the airstrip. Tiwiaram had done a good job marking it out for them. It was as straight as an arrow even though the length barely reached Dave's minimum requirement. I felt it would have to do. It did seem necessary that during our stay we would have to cut down more trees to make longer approaches.

Tired as we were, we thought the house was a long way from the strip. Once there Chumapi and I recognized each other and exchanged friendly greetings. His house was filled with family members who crowded around us. Chumapi talked most of the evening about his father, Aiju, and Chief Tsantiacu. He asked many questions, especially about heaven. 'When he died, did our relative, Tsantiacu, really go there? Is he with the Creator God now? Is he happy and not suffering like the rest of our ancestors?' I hoped he kept on thinking about the wonder of God's forgiveness as I knew he still harbored hatred for his many traditional enemies.

Early the next morning, the Atshuar men chopped down enough trees on the approaches to make it easier for Dave to land. On the regular radio contact with MAF, I was able to tell them the strip was ready. Dave had received legal permission for the landing, so that afternoon, we were all happy to welcome Dave on his first landing in Mashumar Entsa.

Chumapi did not long remain the leader at Mashumar. The more powerful and skilled he became at manipulating evil spirits, the more enemies he made among other Atshuar groups along the border. To protect himself and his household, he constructed a thick stockade wall around his home. This made it less likely that someone would shoot him in his sleep. Sometimes, the sick ones he treated did not get well. When anyone died, the bereaved and mourning ones would come to Chumapi for further help. 'If only we knew who it was who cursed our loved one and caused his death, then we would avenge his death by killing him. Whoever sent the curse must pay with his own life. Then the departed spirit will be able to rest from suffering and we also will feel less grief. You, Chumapi, must find out who is to blame!'

Feeling great pressure from his own people to conform, Chumapi then contacted the evil spirits to learn the name of some enemy witch doctor. Once discovering the culprit's name, the aggrieved warrior relatives would go to kill him. In this way, Chumapi was not only respected by his own family, but hated by increasing numbers of other Atshuar.

Although he had many opportunities to learn more about God, Chumapi grew less responsive. During the times that

Tiwiaram and I visited, he was usually gone or would leave to hunt or visit relatives.

Other Atshuar families, who had known Chief Tsantiacu in Peru, moved to Mashumar in order to be closer to the airstrip, school, and church that eventually developed.

Later, when we returned from a short visit in the United States, we heard that Chumapi had been killed. But by this time many of the men had become bowed-the-knee ones. The new leader, Wasum, together with the Christians, influenced the group strongly enough so that no war party was formed to avenge this death. Chumapi's death by revengeful enemy warriors was the last among the Atshuar as far as we know.

Wasum was one who had first heard the gospel in Peru from Chief Tsantiacu. Because Tsantiacu had been enabled by the Lord Jesus Christ to forgive his enemies, Wasum found grace to do the same. We tried to comfort Chumapi's sad, desolate widows but it took a long time for them to find relief. Most of the rest were at peace with God and each other.

God was using the memory of the forgiving heart of the former killer Chief Tsantiacu to slowly end the revenge wars among the Atshuar. What better could we do than to praise God for letting us be there to see this victory?

# CHAPTER TWENTY-FOUR
# CELEBRATING
# MAKUMA'S FIFTIETH

Be on your guard so that you will not be carried away
by the error of lawless men... But grow in the grace
and knowledge of our Lord and Savior Jesus Christ.
To Him be glory both now and forever. Amen
(2 Peter 3:17, 18).

I had never seen so many Shuar Indians in one place. It was 9
November, 1995 and they had come together to celebrate the
most important day in their history: the fiftieth anniversary of
the coming of the gospel to Makuma. Marie and I had left
Makuma in 1982 but had been invited back for this special
occasion.

Groups of people were everywhere: near the missionary
houses, on the airstrip, beyond the airstrip, and in the community
center. Anywhere Marie and I looked we saw congenial, happy
Shuar. None were shouldering guns. None were cringing in the
brush for fear of enemies. I needed someone to pinch me. Were
these really the same people that we had begun to work with so
many years before? Yes, they were the same people. It wasn't a
dream. We were still alive to get a fresh view of how much they

had changed since those early years. Despite the changes, they had retained their cultural family values and their desire to develop and live on their own land. The coming of the gospel of Christ had brought unity and hope to this tribe of jungle people.

I walked to the center where festivities would begin. Here were new buildings I had never seen before: a grade school, a high school, and a large cement block structure which provided an auditorium for community gatherings and offices for appointed leaders.

Many of the Shuar I knew greeted me and recounted their family growth and experiences since I had last seen them. Innumerable curious young ones stood near enough to listen. One little boy came even closer. I greeted him in his own language. He told me his name and that of his father and then, with a twinkle in his eye and a broad grin, he said, 'Panchu, you talk like my grandfather.' He laughed and so did the rest of us. To him my speaking style was amusing and I understood why. I had learned his language years before when his grandparents were young. Not only had the Shuar culture changed through the years but even the language.

Marie and I had lived in Makuma for most of our thirty-seven years in Ecuador. After Gospel Missionary Union leaders asked us to serve as Midwestern Representatives, we had moved back to the United States. We were to encourage young people and churches to become more involved in the missionary enterprise.

We built our home near Edgerton, Missouri, and every fall and spring we were traveling to churches and schools, helping with missions conferences, and speaking in various settings. During the summers we conducted ten weeks of Family Camps for Missions at beautiful Dog Lake in Ontario, Canada. Campers enjoyed good fishing during the daylight hours and in the evenings we presented films and teaching about missions. We knew God was still calling Christians to follow Him wherever He would lead. There were still many people groups who had yet to hear the gospel. The mandate of Christ to take His truth to all the world was a continuing challenge to every generation.

On two different occasions we had returned to Makuma to help with teaching sessions and to maintain contact with the Indians. Five years had passed since we had last been to the jungles.

In 1994 Jim and Norma Hedlund had written us of the community's plan for a fiftieth anniversary celebration. Could we return to Makuma for this important event? They had also invited Jean Johnson because she and her husband and children were the first missionary family to live with the Shuar in the Makuma area. Ernest Johnson had died several months before this invitation came. But Jean arrived in Makuma for this special time along with her grown daughter, Karen.

This was Sunday, the first day of the festivities. To gather everyone together, one of the young men blew a loud blast on a cow horn. Church and community leaders requested that Jean, Karen, the Hedlunds, Glen and Jean Turner, Nettie Buhler, new missionaries Jim and Debbie Shoberg, Marie, and I lead the parade from the airstrip to the community center. The procession was very long. Just behind us were several older respected men, some of whom were present when Ernest and Jean had arrived fifty years before. When we reached the center, we were directed to seats on a second story balcony. Some church and community leaders were seated with us. Those who followed marched forward to take their places in the yard below. There were ranks of school children in crisply starched blue and white uniforms. Those in the first row carried the Ecuadorian flag.

I couldn't believe my eyes. 'How many schools are represented today?' I asked one of the community leaders. He listed four or five communities. All were in the immediate vicinity. The whole crowd was so large I couldn't imagine they were just from nearby. None were from as far away as Cumai or Cangaimi, though these were the first and nearest outstations Roger and I had opened years before. I knew that now they had their own expanding populations and schools.

The program leaders asked us to greet everyone and recount some of what it was like when we first came. Jean began by telling of the seven-day trip on foot from Sucua in the Upano River Valley to Makuma. Everyone paid close attention as she told of their exhausting trip. The Johnsons had brought only clothing, sparse food supplies, their two children, and a burro. Jean named the few families who then lived on either side of the Makuma River, and which ones had helped them secure land, plant garden food, and build a small house of bamboo walls and leaf roof. She named some she had helped with medicines and the few boys (now older men) who had come to their first school. There were many dreaded diseases, snake bite victims, revenge killings, and unhappy, fear-filled people during the years she and Ernest were here.

'What helped us the most was to remember that God had sent us here,' she stated confidently, 'not to exploit the Shuar or take their land, but to show them how much the God Who had created them still loved them.' When she finished everyone clapped loudly.

Others on the balcony added greetings, anecdotes from Shuar history, testimonies to the wonderful changes God had brought about in their lives and communities, and expressions of thankfulness that God had helped many to accept His forgiveness and stop killing their enemies. A Shuar pastor invited everyone to the meeting hall for singing and hearing God's Word.

On the way the pastor asked me to give the sermon. No doubt he thought the people would like to hear from me. He didn't realize that I hadn't heard or spoken the Shuar language for a number of years and I wasn't sure how well I could do it. I was like a computer. I had lots of memory but I lacked 'RAM' to bring up the words as fast as I needed them. I began slowly but little by little I found it easier to express myself. By the close of my message I was doing better. I was surprised when the pastor stood beside me and challenged any who wanted to become a

Yus-Shuar to stay for prayer. My eyes filled with tears as I saw five Shuar pray for forgiveness and eternal salvation.

When we walked out into the sunny yard again, we were surrounded by many friends we had known years before, and spent hours talking with them and their families. When I finished with one group there was a long line of others waiting. By mid-afternoon my voice gave out. I began taking pictures with my video camera and promised to show them in the evening. Everyone, it seemed, wanted me to include them and their many children. I asked several what they thought the current population might be.

'Oh, Panchu,' they said. 'We are many more than when you first came. There are nearly four thousand in this area alone. Our men don't die in revenge wars any more. Unlike past generations, our people don't go hungry for lack of food. Our children are more healthy and are growing taller than their parents. There are trained Shuar health promoters in each of our communities and Ecuadorian doctors or nurses are often here at the Makuma clinic. And of course, if someone needs more help than is available here, we can call the airplane to come take him or her to the hospital in Shell. We are not so afraid of sickness and death as our people used to be. God has blessed us with His true words as well as with good health care.'

One of the married couples I recognized as having grown up in our early school sessions, and who later worked with us at some of the outstations, approached with their children. Juwa and his wife Carmen wanted me to take a picture of their family, too. I admired the neatly dressed children and began to talk with them and learn their names. But Juwa kept calling others to join them. Minutes went by as I unbelievingly watched the group increase. When they were all lined up I understood why it took him so long to get them together. There were fifteen children. What a beautiful family! Not one of their babies had died. I met many other families like them with ten or more young ones. No wonder the population had soared!

The next day hundreds of Shuar came again for more festivities. This time as people were gathering in the public square, the Shuar community leaders seated all the speakers and missionaries on the porch of the largest school building. Both the high school youth and grade school children marched toward us. We all stood to sing Ecuador's stirring national anthem. But these young people were not the only ones to participate in the program. Their parents and grandparents acted out the typical dramatic Shuar greetings and 'Call to War' demonstrations they had learned from their predecessors. Others sang the ancient chants their forefathers and mothers had used to make the garden food grow, ballads about the creation and naming of the rivers, and songs to express their hopelessness when a loved one died. One of the women we had known since her childhood sang to a haunting chant-like melody. The words she had composed were about the coming of missionaries with God's Word, the beginning of churches and schools, and the cessation of old destructive customs replaced by new life-giving ones.

The smallest grade school girls skipped in circles and sang both in Shuar and Spanish. They were dressed in typical old Shuar style with dark cloth wrapped around their bodies held in place with vine belts and fastened at the top over one shoulder. The older children and young people in modern dress, using Spanish language and style, presented patriotic poems, songs, gymnastic exercises, and relay-type dances. Their teachers and community-elected officers also spoke in both Spanish and Shuar about historical events in their development and hopes for future improvements. They praised God and honored the missionaries for all the help they had received. 'If you had not come,' one said, 'most of us would not be alive today. We would have died of sickness and revenge killings.'

We were given opportunity to thank them for welcoming us so graciously and for having let us live with them and learn so much from them. As I spoke, I commended them for their hard work in caring for their families and for their commitment to serve God and their country. I reminded them that it was God who had sent them His Word. It was because God had changed their hearts that the wars had ceased and they were able to live in peace. I warned them not to forget Him but to continue loving and honoring Him with their obedience. Living for the pleasures of drunkenness and immorality would result in divided families and communities. They should not think that if they gained education and money that they wouldn't need God. I encouraged them to continue to learn more of God and His Word, to worship Him in their homes and churches, and to train their children to pray and serve God all their lives. I led in a prayer of praise to the Lord for all His goodness to the Shuar. I asked God to also free them from the ever-present threat of sorcery and witchcraft. I prayed they would be increasingly concerned for the widely scattered groups of their people who still did not know the life-giving power of God.

Jim and Norma Hedlund then presented specially-engraved plaques to two families. Ramon and his family had walked with the Johnsons in November 1945 from Sucúa, guiding them through the tangled jungle and carrying their children and bundles all that long journey. Later, in April 1948, Yangura and his family had done the same for Marie, our first two children, and me. These families had stayed in the Makuma area even though some longtime residents regarded them as 'outsiders.' Ramon and Yangura were among the first to send their children to school and to help build the earliest church.

We thought the program was over but then one of the older men rose from the crowd and stepped up to the porch. Facing us, he recounted in Shuar the details of his own conversion and change from being afraid of God to trusting and loving Him. As he spoke he placed a beautiful bead necklace he had made for the occasion around Jean's neck. A younger man followed with bright feather earrings for Karen. Then, spontaneously it seemed to us, more than a dozen came up with other similar gifts and artifacts for them and for us. They had made these especially for this occasion. One man gave me a newly-made spear like the ones used for hunting wild boars. We hugged and cried tears of love and joy on each other's shoulders. This was the first time we missionaries had received such expressions of gratitude from the Indians. Both the Indians and we were deeply moved.

'Now that you are here,' some asked wistfully, 'why don't you just stay on living with us?'

'We are old now and not strong enough,' I explained. 'If we were young again like when we first came, we would stay right here. But now you must help the new missionaries learn your language and how to live with you. We will tell our people about you so they can pray for you.'

Soon, others of the men began setting up tables and covering them with clean banana leaves. They invited us to eat with them around the tables. Women brought plates of hot garden foods, savory meats, and steamed rice. Hundreds more families were served wherever they were standing or sitting around the open square. The sun began to set as people ate and visited, said their farewells, and began to leave. It had been a wonderful two days.

With some feelings of sadness Marie and I knew that the whole culture would continue to change as the people adopted more values of Ecuadorian life. We felt sorry that these young people were no longer learning the individual names and uses of every bird, insect, plant, tree, and animal in the jungle environment. Nor were their parents teaching them how to make the blowguns, tightly woven cloth, split-vine baskets, or clay pottery. On the other hand, parents still spoke their own language in their homes and they had stopped instilling hatred into their children for their traditional enemies. They would not grow up to be revenge killers.

Yes, some good things were being lost along with the destructive ones. Young people were learning to become school teachers, government-appointed officials, nurses, writers, doctors, engineers, agriculturalists, and trained military leaders as well as good parents, Bible teachers, and preachers.

They were not forming a nation of their own as some outsiders were trying to influence them to do. They would not become a warring tribe, but peaceful and productive citizens of Ecuador. Marie and I were so thankful God had allowed us to be with the Shuar through many of the fifty years of transition.

The process of adapting to both a new culture and a new language too quickly could cause the loss of personal identity and values. Because of this, many tribes in the Amazon basin had vanished, but this one was surviving and multiplying. We were thankful that not many young people had left the area to live in the towns and cities outside the jungle. We had learned that it is better for a tribe to make cultural changes while living in their own environment. Here, they could learn about the major culture and adapt gradually. The Shuar school children and many of the adults could read and speak very fluently in Spanish about superficial things. But it would take most of their lives to learn to express spiritual and good character values in any but their own language. In their mother tongue new concepts were clothed with their own culture. Thus it is easier for any people to understand the gospel in their own language and cultural setting than in a foreign one.

While Marie and I were in Makuma, we had the opportunity to meet with the Shuar translators. Dorothy Walker, the Turners, and the Hedlunds had been training and working with them to translate major portions of the Old Testament. Dorothy had been unable to return for these special days but we met with the rest in one of the large rooms of the concrete radio building. Some of the Indians were from different communities far from Makuma. Three of the same men that Dorothy had started teaching in 1980 were still involved. New ones had joined the team from time to time as others had needed to drop out. The day we were there, about seven came together. What a thrill for us to hear them discuss the problems they encountered and the insights gained. For them it was like attending a Bible seminary as they learned the depths of meaning and applications to their own lives in each passage.

In the fifties and sixties, long before their retirement, both the Turners and Dorothy had worked together to translate the New Testament. Only one or two Shuar had helped somewhat erratically at that time. Now the men we were sitting with were doing most of the work and the missionaries were their helpers. Jim and Norma Hedlund, though not formally trained linguist-translators, had learned right along with the Shuar team. They helped them to understand difficult Old Testament passages and also instructed some of the group on how to use the computer and the special programs that modern translators find so helpful.

One of the translators with sparkling eyes and a radiant smile was paraplegic. We remembered hearing of the accident that had damaged his spinal cord long before we left Makuma. After we had moved to Missouri, one day something Marie heard on Christian radio caught her attention. It was Joni Eareckson Tada talking about meeting a badly crippled jungle Indian in Ecuador. Marie stopped what she was doing to listen more carefully. Joni's voice continued, 'Missionaries had arranged for him to be flown to the capital city while I was there so he could receive a new wheel chair. His name was Humberto and he told me how God had cared for him,' she said.

Marie spoke aloud as though Joni could hear her, 'I know Humberto. He lived at a jungle community far from Makuma and more than once stopped at our station as he was being flown to or from the hospital.' She recalled details of the accident that had crippled him. While Humberto was felling trees to clear land for an airstrip, he had been knocked to the ground by one of the falling timbers. When his people discovered that he couldn't walk, they carried him on a home-made stretcher to an airstrip a day or more away. From there we learned that he was flown to the HCJB hospital on the edge of the jungle. Missionaries helped provide him with a wheelchair. When he returned to his jungle home, he was no longer able to work. His brothers would regularly carry him to the nearby river and lower him into the water. He loved to swim for the good exercise and refreshment it gave him. Since he had considerably improved his use of Spanish during the many months he had spent under treatment in the Shell hospital, one of our missionaries interested him in translating the book of Proverbs. Later, as a member of the translation team, he had learned so much about translation principles that he laughed with embarrassment at his earlier attempts with Proverbs. We could see that translating had become his chief work and delight.

The translators would take the passages they were working on back to their communities to discuss with their people. 'Do you clearly understand what you are hearing? How would you say this in your own words?' they asked those who were considering these Scriptures for the first time. We could easily understand how the translators, while reading and explaining the Scriptures to their people, were also teaching them to take in truth for themselves. During their monthly team sessions the men compared notes and checked their work with the missionaries working with them. Some Old Testament books and portions were printed and made available to believers in Makuma and other communities.

Before we left Makuma we enjoyed visiting with another missionary couple. Dwain and Lois Holmes had lived in our Makuma house since shortly after we left in the early eighties. They had started life in Makuma by studying the Atshuar language. God had given them the deep desire to work with the Atshuar people and develop churches among them. They would spend weeks at a time at Mashumar Entsa and walk to other groups in the area in order to more directly learn the language from these Indians. By now there were many airstrips among them where groups of new believers needed Bible teaching, schools, cattle, and medical help. A Wycliffe Bible translator in Peru had produced a translation of parts of the Old Testament and the entire New Testament in the Atshuar language. We were thrilled to hear that various Atshuar believers we knew were increasing their Bible knowledge and ability to help teach their own people. God had wonderfully provided salvation from their destructive lifestyle as He had for the Shuar.

Work on producing the Scriptures for both groups was progressing rapidly. God had given us the privilege of seeing the cessation of the revenge wars and the beginnings of churches and schools and community living. Now the missionaries currently involved with the Shuar and Atshuar would see the Bible completed in both languages, resulting in better trained Indian preachers and teachers in their churches.

Marie and I returned to Missouri wishing we could have a greater part in all that God was doing now in the jungle. Even so we went rejoicing because of all we had seen and heard during this special celebration.

# EPILOGUE
## SHUAR + ATSHUAR
## IN THE NEW MILLENNIUM
The seed is the word of God (Matthew 13:23).

Like the 'sower of good seed' that Jesus talked about, Shuar and Atshuar believers are scattering the Word of God throughout the southeastern jungle of Ecuador as far as the Peruvian border. Their favorite way of spreading any news is still by walking and talking. They are few in number compared to the rapidly increasing population, like flickering candles in their dark world.

Missionary and Indian translators keep producing new editions of Christian literature including the New Testament, hymnbooks, Bible study courses, and Sunday School materials all in the Shuar language and some of the same in Atshuar.

The number of missionaries involved in serving the Indians is decreasing. At present, only two missionary couples are living among the Indians, Jim and Norma Hedlund and Dwain and Lois Holmes. In addition, Bob and Janice Stuck have lived in

Shell near the MAF base for many years and fly from there for Bible teaching sessions among the Shuar. Jim and Debbie Shoberg are joining them there. Besides these, Dorothy Walker and Glen and Jean Turner make regular extended visits to Makuma to teach and work with the Shuar translation team. All are devoted to training church leaders to teach their own people. By working together, they make the Word of God available to speakers of Shuar and Atshuar who in turn are establishing their own Christian churches.

In Makuma most of the land Ernest Johnson originally bought from local Indians is now owned by the community organization or neighboring communities. No longer is there a school, a church, or a medical dispensary at the mission. All such buildings and services have been moved to the village center across the airstrip. There local Indians and some government personnel are in charge. Our goal that the Indians be responsible for their own needs is being fulfilled.

In sixty Indian centers the people have built their own community buildings. In most of these communities the people cleared their own airstrips and all are maintained by them. In five communities around Makuma the people benefit from electricity provided by the hydroelectric plant.

Churches are developing in many of the communities. Of what does a Christian church among jungle tribal people consist? By definition and practice, it is a group of Christians who meet to worship God and to hear what God is saying to them through the Bible (or whatever portions of the Bible they may have).

The goal of the Shuar translation team working in Makuma with the Hedlunds, Dorothy Walker, and the Turners is to prepare for publication much of the Old Testament. When this is finished they will apply their skills to improving the New Testament that was first printed in 1976. Not only are the translators growing in ability to express God's Word in their own language but also in Christian character. Since paraplegic Humberto regularly needs hospital care, they give from their limited means to help cover his expenses. This is just one of the ways they are lovingly caring for each other.

Dwain and Lois Holmes are committed to teaching Atshuar church leaders. With the help of Atshuar Christians they are translating from Spanish and adapting a comprehensive series of Bible study courses. They are away from Makuma for months at a time visiting the twelve main Atshuar centers located within a 50 x 70 mile area. Dwain has walked with the Indians on tangled, swampy jungle trails leading from the centers to groups of new believers needing encouragement and teaching. As a result, many more smaller groups are involved in Bible study. As these students grow more motivated to continue learning, they walk to the main centers to receive training. By February 2001, from 150 to 200 Atshuar students were enrolled. These represent over 30 different communities.

We asked Dwain how many churches he knows of among the Atshuar. 'It is hard to say how many groups meet on their own,' he wrote. 'When we are with them, they always have services. When we aren't there, I would think, of all the centers in which we regularly work, about twenty-five hold worship services.' These meetings are led by lay leaders. There are no paid pastors, no appointed deacon or elder boards. They make decisions by consensus among those in each individual congregation.

Bob Stuck travels regularly from Shell to the numerous communities among the Shuar. He is teaching the same comprehensive Bible courses used by the Atshuar but translated into Shuar. He is helping the developing churches in over forty centers.

In each community Christians are in the minority but they do have a good influence on their people. They are helpful to those in need. Polygamous households are much fewer than when we first lived among the Shuar, and are continuing to decrease. Some of the young women resist becoming second or third wives. Nearly all children attend school. A few young literate adults are creating Bible lessons for use in Sunday School and required public school religious training. In many communities, schools and churches are presenting Bible-related Christmas programs.

Both government and non-governmental agencies offer more help to developing jungle communities. They provide school teachers and visiting doctors. Ecuadorian law requires that religion be taught in all public schools. Another department is offering personnel and funds to help with maintenance of some airstrips. There are non-government organizations offering to help the Shuar in securing ownership of their ancestral lands. In one Shuar village located between Makuma and the Upano Valley, several Indians sold their land to Ecuadorian colonists. Most others feel very threatened by this incident. Village leaders around Makuma have worked to secure their land under a "global" plan meaning that land ownership is registered in the name of the entire community. This prevents any individual from being pressured, either by others or his own needs, into selling his land.

The Shuar church association has appointed two mature families to serve as Bible teachers where there is a lack of consistent teaching. In recent years the church association has also been sending teams to witness in an area where there are as yet no Shuar churches. Maturing believers in churches around Makuma are struggling to help support them.

In all of the Ecuadorian jungle, the Shuar and Atshuar population numbers over 200,000. An estimated 1000 believers live in the southeastern jungle influenced by missionaries of the Gospel Missionary Union and the Shuar Indian Church Association. These comparatively few believers, though no longer threatened by enemy warriors, are continuing to face evil forces of witchcraft and modern materialism. There are still many Indians who have not heard the gospel. This is an ongoing challenge to the present generation of followers of Christ. If Marie and I were in our twenties again, we would gladly respond to this need.

We are moved to note that wherever in the jungle the Bible is read, believed, and obeyed, the people are more content and more accepting of each other. They also form more stable families and tend to remain more committed to God, to each other and to their country. It is their reverence for God and His Word that has made these good changes in the daily lives of the Shuar and Atshuar Indians of Ecuador, South America. Present-day believers are living as brothers and sisters in God's family, and the tribe as a whole is no longer known for being revengeful headhunters.

# GLOSSARY

Aiju (AHE-hew) neutral Atshuar; trader of pigskins

Ambato (ahm-BAH-toh) mountain town in central Ecuador

Antri (AHN-dree) a young Atshuar widow protected by Tsantiacu

Atshuar (aht-SHWAHR) Indian tribe living in southeastern Ecuador, speaking a dialect of Shuar; enemies of the Shuar

Auca (OW-cah) tribe of savage Indians living in north Ecuador's jungle that killed the five missionaries at 'Palm Beach'

Big Saantu (SAHN-doo) witch doctor living across the river from Makuma mission; brother of Capitu

Cajecai (cah-HE-cae) former Makuma schoolboy, who, lured by easy money, ran away to the coast and disappeared

Cangaimi (cahng-GUY-me) mission station about fifteen miles south of Makuma on Cangaimi River

Canusa (cah-NOO-sah) Shuar from Makuma, wavering between witchcraft and Christianity

Capaware (ca-pa-WAR-ee) a community of Atshuar

Capitu (cah-PEE-tyu) Shuar chief living across river from Makuma; brother of Big Saantu

Cashpa (CASH-pa) small river in Atshuar territory

Casent (cah-SEND) son of Uyungara; survivor of freakish accident

Cashijintu (cah-SHEE-heen-diu) Atshuar killer; brother of Timas

Catani (cah-TAH-nee) Shuar chief and witch doctor; principal enemy of Tsantiacu

Chiip (cheep) Atshuar living near Tsantiacu

chicha (CHEE-chah) Spanish word for a Shuar household drink, made from fermented cassava

Chingasu (cheeng-YAH-soo) effective teacher of gospel to women; wife of Chumpi; mother of Wampiu

Chiriapa (chee-ree-AH-pah) Atshuara whose head was taken and shrunk by Shuar on a killing raid

Chumpi (chuum-BEE) Chingasu's young husband

Copataza (co-pah-TAH-sah) river north and east of Makuma flowing into the Pastaza

Cumai (cuu-MAE) first of the mission outstations; ten miles north of Makuma

Curaray (coo-rah-RAY) river on whose banks the five missionaries were killed by Auca Indians

Cusutca (coo-SOOT-cah) church built by Indians of Cusutca River area

cutanga (coo-TAHNG-ah) carved, two-legged stool, used by Shuar and Atshuar men; most important piece of household furniture

Cutucú (coo-too-COO) range of mountains east of the Andes; clearly seen from Makuma

ekenta (e-KEN-dah) women's section of the Shuar house

Etsa (ET-sa) Atshuar man

Icam (EE-kyam) Shuar who became a Christian; son of Big Saantu

Itipi (ee-TEE-pee) wrap-around skirt worn by Shuar men

Jeencham (HEEN-jahm) Shuar for 'bat'; name of Indian who explained witchcraft; went along on first trip to Atshuar; father of Tsapacu

Jimpikti (heem-BEEK-tee) one of the first five Shuar converts; son of Washicta

Jintachi (HEEN-dyah-chee) Cangaimi Shuara who opposed building the airstrip

Jisma (HEES-mah) Cangaimi Shuar injured by falling tree

Jivaro (HEE-vah-roh) Spanish name for the Shuar

Juwa (hoo-WAH) schoolboy who married Tsapacu; Jeencham's daughter

Juani (hwah-NEE) young Shuar girl whose baby was delivered in Makuma dispensary

Juang (jwang) brother-in-law of Nawich; killed by Uyungara

Huasaga (wah-SAH-gah) river running through Atshuar territory

Little Saantu (SAHN-doo) Shuar who went on first trip to Atshuar; no relation to Big Saantu

Macas (MAH-cahs) provincial capital in Ecuador's jungle

Makuma (mah-COO-mah) jungle mission station on banks of Makuma river; later base for other mission outstations

maicua (MAE-kyoo-ah) drug drunk by witch doctors to induce visions; similar to belladonna

Mamatu (mah-MAH-too) first Atshuar believer

Mangash (MAHNG-gahsh) Makuma Shuar; wounded by Tsantiacu

Mashumar Entsa (MAHSH-u-mar END-sa) an Atshuar community

Masuinga (mah-SWEENG-ah) sick wife of Uyungara who became a Christian before dying

Mayacu (MAY-ya-coo) Christian Shuar from Cangaimi

Mayapruwa (may-YA-proo-wah) young son of Tucupe

Mura Shuara (MOO-rah SHWAH-rah) literally, the hill people; Shuar from around the Cutucus

Naicta (NAEK-tah) Makuma Shuar who related story of the last killing raid and head-shrinking in the Makuma area

nantar (NAHN-dar) good-luck stone placed in Shuar gardens to make crops grow

natema (nah-TE-mah) narcotic drink used by witch doctors to induce visions

Nawich (NAH-weech) Shuar who plotted and executed the death of his own son-in-law

Oriente (oh-ree-EN-te) jungles of eastern Ecuador

paani (PAH-nee) piranha fish; sometimes called the man-eating fish

Pakesh (pah-KESH) one of the first Shuar girls to be baptized; daughter of Puanshira

Panchu (PAHN-choo) name given Frank Drown by the Shuar

pangu (PAHN-goo) small jungle bird which makes a peculiar sound disagreeable to the Shuar

Pastaza (pah-STAH-sah) large river flowing from Shell Mera southeast past Cumai

pinta (PEEN-tah) disease that causes discoloration of the skin

Pitur (PEE-tyoor) Shuar who took missionaries on first trip to the Atshuar

Puanshira (poo-AHN-chee-rah) father of Pakesh

Quichua (KEE-choo-ah) large tribe of Indians living in the high Andes and northern jungles of Ecuador

Ramon (rah-MOHN) head elder of the church at Makuma

Shuara (SHWAH-rah) Indians; people; Shuar name for themselves

shuartica (SHWAR-tee-kyah) ancient Shuar customs and traditions

shuni (SHOO-nee) bug that eats wood

Shuunta (SHOON-dah) nephew of Tsantiacu; young warrior and witch doctor

sua (SOO-ah) jungle tree whose fruit gives a stain used as a black body paint; camouflage for hunting or war parties

Sucúa (soo-COO-ah) jungle town south of Macas where first mission to the Shuar was established in the early 1920s

Tatsemai (tah-TSE-may) young daughter of Catani; in school at Makuma

Tucupe (too-COO-pe) father of Mayapruwa; member of Tsantiacu's household

Taisha (TAY-shah) Shuar chief living on border of 'no-man's-land'

Tangamash (TANG-gah-mahsh) men's section of the Shuar house; also name of Shuar who went on first trip to the Atshuar tribe

Tariri (Tah-REE-ree) Atshuar chief who pretended forgiveness and friendship with Chief Tsantiacu

Tayujinta (tah-yoo-HEEN-dya) Atshuar living with Tsantiacu

tikishmamtaicawaru (tee-KEESH-mahm-day-kyah-wah-roo) literally 'bowed-the-knee-one'; Atshuar expression for one who has become a Christian

Timas (TEEM-yas) hostile Atshuar chief who planned to kill missionaries

Tirisa (tee-REE-sah) young schoolgirl among the first to be baptized

Tiwi (TEE-vee) schoolboy who deceived Ernest Johnson and helped kill Nawich's son-in-law

tsaangu (TSAHNG-goo) a brew of tobacco leaves drunk by witch doctors to induce visions

Tsamaraing (tsah-mah-RAYNG) young Shuar preacher who was bitten by a snake and recovered; son of Chief Washicta

Tsantiacu (tsahn-DYAH-coo) Atshuar chief; longtime enemy of Catani; reached by Christianity, but wavering

tsantsa (TSAHN-tsah) shrunken head of an enemy that becomes a talisman of power and strength to the possessor

Tsapacu (TSAH-pah-coo) Makuma schoolgirl and bride of Jua; daughter of Jeencham

Tserempu (TSE-rem-boo) Makuma schoolboy who became a Christian

Tsetsempu (tse-TSEM-boo) mother of 'Big Eyes'

Tsungi (TSOONG-guee) young Shuar who became a Christian; husband of Juani

Tuitsa (TWEE-tsah) Shuar host on first visit of missionaries to Cangaimi

Tungi (TOON-guee) Atshuar man

Turuti (Tu-ru-TEE) missionary Dorothy Walker

Upano (oo-PAH-noh) large river starting in eastern Andes and flowing past Macas and Sucúa

Uyungara (oo-YOON-gah-rah) Shuar killer from the upper Makuma, who cared faithfully for his wife until her death; husband of Masuinga; father of Casent and Wachapa

Wachapa (wah-chah-PAH) young son of Uyungara who attended mission school

Wampiu (wahm-BYOO) brightest boy at the first Makuma school who became a preacher; son of Chingasu

Washicta (wah-SHEEK-ta) patriarchal chief who had nine sons, among them Tsamaraing and Jimpicti

Wasum (Wah-SUUM) Atshuar chief who became a Christian

Wichur (vee-CHOOR) Shuar from Cumai who became a preacher there

Yangura (Yang-GOO-rah) Christian father of a family of many children

Yus Shuara (YOOS SHWAH-rah) a Christian; one who had become God's Indian; used by both Shuar and Atshuar

Yus shuartica (YOOS shwar-TEE-kyah) Christian customs

Yuu (YOU) teenage son of Chief Tsantiacu

Yuwientsa (yoo-vee-EN-tsah) church between Makuma and Cangaimi on the Yuwientsa River

For more information about GMU, you can write, phone, e-mail or visit there website

Gospel Missionary Union
10000 N. Oak Trafficway
Kansas City, MO 64155
tel: 1-800-GMU-1892
fax: 816-734-4601
e-mail kreimer@gmu.org


GMU Canada
2121 Henderson Hwy.
Winnipeg, MB R2G 1P8
tel: 204-338-7831
fax: 204-339-3321
e-mail dpickel@gmu.org


www.gmu.org

Christian Focus Publications publishes biblically accurate books for adults and children. The books in the adult range are published in three imprints.

*Christian Heritage* contains classic writings from the past.

*Christian Focus* contains popular works including biographies, commentaries, doctrine, and Christian living.

*Mentor* focuses on books written at a level suitable for Bible College and seminary students, pastors, and others; the imprint includes commentaries, doctrinal studies, examination of current issues, and church history.

For a free catalogue of all our titles, please write to

Christian Focus Publications, Ltd
Geanies House, Fearn,
Ross-shire, IV20 1TW, Great Britain

For details of our titles visit us on our website

http://www.christianfocus.com